FOUNDATION MATHEMATICS
FOR TECHNICIANS

LEVEL 1

Foundation Mathematics for Technicians

LEVEL 1

R. J. BESANKO

F. I. Plant E.
Lecturer in the Department of Engineering, Brooklyn Technical College, Birmingham.
Chief Examiner in Engineering Science and Mathematics (Mechanical Engineering Technicians Course: Second Year) to the Union of Educational Institutions.

AND

T. H. JENKINS

B.Sc., A.M.B.I.M., A.F.I.M.A.
Vice-Principal, Foley College of Further Education, Stourbridge.
Chief Examiner in Engineering Mathematics (General Course in Engineering: Second Year) to the Yorkshire and Humberside Council for Further Education.

1978

OXFORD UNIVERSITY PRESS

Oxford University Press, Walton Street, Oxford OX2 6DP

OXFORD LONDON GLASGOW NEW YORK

TORONTO MELBOURNE WELLINGTON CAPE TOWN

IBADAN NAIROBI DAR ES SALAAM LUSAKA ADDIS ABABA

KUALA LUMPUR SINGAPORE JAKARTA HONG KONG TOKYO

DELHI BOMBAY CALCUTTA MADRAS KARACHI

ISBN 0 19 859609 X

© Oxford University Press 1978

*Typeset by The Universities Press (Belfast) Ltd.
Printed in Great Britain
by Fletcher Son & Co. Ltd., Norwich*

PREFACE

The Technician Education Council (TEC) was established in March 1973 in fulfilment of a recommendation of the Haslegrave Committee on Technician Courses and Examinations, which reported in 1969.

This book is written especially for students taking TEC Certificate and Diploma Courses.

Particular attention has been paid to the correct use of units, symbols and abbreviations. The system of units used is the Système International d'Unités (SI)—International System of Units—adopted by the General Conference of Weights and Measures and endorsed by the International Organization for Standardization. Certain non-SI units have been included where their use is permitted. Each chapter contains sufficient theory, description, and explanation to provide the readers with enough material to satisfy their requirements at this early stage, and to lay a firm *foundation* for further studies.

Numerous worked examples are included at frequent intervals throughout the book. Each of these examples has been carefully chosen, and the solutions presented in a detailed and easy-to-follow manner. At the end of each chapter there is a wide selection of graded problems many of which have been taken from past examination papers of the main examining bodies.

R. J. B.
T. H. J.

Birmingham
August 1977

ACKNOWLEDGEMENTS

We gratefully acknowledge the co-operation given by the following Examining Bodies in granting permission to include a selection of questions from past examination papers and for allowing us to modify some of these questions in order that the terms and units may be in agreement with the International System of Units (SI).

City and Guilds of London Institute (C.G.L.I.)
East Midland Educational Union (E.M.E.U.)
Northern Counties Technical Examinations Council (N.C.T.E.C.)
Union of Educational Institutions (U.E.I.)
Union of Lancashire and Cheshire Institutes (U.L.C.I.)
Welsh Joint Education Committee (W.J.E.C.)
Yorkshire and Humberside Council for Further Education (Y.H.C.F.E.)

Our special thanks are also due to Commodore Business Machines (U.K.) Limited and British Thornton Limited for kindly allowing us to include diagrams and details of their products.

Finally we express sincere appreciation to the staff of the Oxford University Press for their guidance and advice during the preparation of the book, and to our wives for their encouragement and for typing and checking the manuscript.

R. J. B.
T. H. J.

CONTENTS

SIGNS, SYMBOLS, AND ABBREVIATIONS DENOTING MATHEMATICAL OPERATIONS AND CONSTANTS

$+$	plus
$-$	minus
$\pm$	plus or minus
$\times$ or $\cdot$	multiplied by
$\div$ or $/$	divided by
$=$	is equal to
$\neq$	is not equal to
$\equiv$	is identical with
$\approx$	is approximately equal to
$\propto$	is proportional to, varies directly as
$>$	is greater than
$<$	is less than
$\parallel$	parallel to
$\perp$	perpendicular to
∞	infinity
$\sqrt{x}$, $x^{1/2}$	square root of x
$x^{1/3}$	cube root of x
$\log_a x$	logarithm of x to base a
$\lg x$, $\log_{10} x$, $\log x$	common logarithm of x
antilog	antilogarithm
π (Greek pi)	ratio of circumference to diameter of a circle
$\sin y$ $\cos y$ $\tan y$ $\operatorname{cosec} y$ $\sec y$ $\cot y$	trigonometric (circular) functions of y
$\arcsin y$ $\arccos y$ $\arctan y$ $\operatorname{arccosec} y$ $\operatorname{arcsec} y$ $\operatorname{arccot} y$	inverse trigonometric functions of y

SYMBOLS FOR PHYSICAL QUANTITIES

A area: area of surface
a linear acceleration
B magnetic flux density
b breadth
c specific heat capacity
d diameter: relative density
E Young's modulus of elasticity: electromotive force
F force
f frequency
G shear modulus of rigidity: conductance
g local gravitational acceleration
h height or depth
I electrical current
l length
M moment of force
m mass
N number of turns
n rotational speed: number in a sample
P power
p pressure
Q quantity of heat: quantity (or charge) of electricity
R resistance: resisting force
r radius
s distance travelled
T torque: thermodynamic temperature value
t time
u velocity
V volume: capacity: voltage: potential difference

v velocity
W work or energy (all forms): weight
x rectangular coordinate
y rectangular coordinate
z rectangular coordinate

Note: The following letter symbols are taken from the Greek alphabet.

α (alpha)	plane angle: angular acceleration: thermal coefficient of linear expansion: temperature coefficient of resistance
β (beta)	plane angle: thermal coefficient of cubical expansion
γ (gamma)	shear strain
δ (delta)	deflection
ε (epsilon)	direct strain
η (eta)	efficiency
θ (theta)	plane angle: temperature value (other than thermodynamic)
λ (lambda)	wavelength
μ (mu)	coefficient of friction
ρ (rho)	density: resistivity
σ (sigma)	direct stress
τ (tau)	shear stress: periodic time
Φ (capital phi)	magnetic flux
ϕ (small phi)	plane angle
ψ (psi)	plane angle
ω (omega)	angular velocity

1 | Measurements, units, and calculations

1.1. MEASUREMENT—INTEGERS

In science and technology one often wants to measure *physical quantities*, such as the diameter of a shaft, the speed of a train, or the pressure of air in a tyre. The first step is to select an appropriate defined *unit*. One then measures the *number* of units required to equal the physical quantity. The measured value of a physical quantity, such as length, speed, or pressure, is then equal to a numerical value multiplied by a unit; for example, a length of 3 metres, a speed of 40 metres per second, or a pressure of 200 kilopascals.

In some cases it may be convenient to use *negative* numbers.

Take the example of a locomotive on a length of track running east–west. During shunting operations it moves first 3 kilometres west, then 4 kilometres east, and finally 5 kilometres west. What is its final position relative to its starting point? Call the easterly direction positive and the westerly negative. Then the locomotive's movements can be expressed as successively -3, $+4$, and -5 kilometres. Adding these together gives the total net movement.

$$(-3)+(+4)+(-5) = -8+4$$
$$= -4 \text{ kilometres.}$$

The final position is therefore 4 kilometres west of the starting point. The negative sign indicates the westerly direction.

The concept used here is that of *directed* numbers, positive and negative. These are quite distinct from the mathematical operations of addition and subtraction. These operations, as well as multiplication and division, may be performed on negative numbers with equal validity as on positive numbers. Positive and negative whole numbers, and the number zero, are termed *integers*, as opposed to fractions (see Chapter 2). All integers may be multiplied and divided, although in the case of division the answer may be a fraction. Only division by 0 is not permitted, as this gives no definite answer.

To add two directed numbers, if the signs are alike add the numbers and give them that sign. To add if the signs are unlike, subtract the smaller number from the larger and give the result the sign of the larger number.

For multiplication of directed numbers the rules to be followed are:

$$(+1)\times(+1) = +1$$
$$(+1)\times(-1) = -1$$
$$(-1)\times(+1) = -1$$
$$(-1)\times(-1) = +1$$

When two signs occur together, separated by brackets, the rules for multiplication are also followed. Thus:

$$2-(-4) = 2+4 = 6.$$

Two integers may be added in any order, and they may be multiplied in any order. For example,

$$-6+2 = -4$$
$$\text{or} \qquad +2-6 = -4;$$
$$-6\times2 = -12$$
$$\text{or} \qquad 2\times(-6) = -12.$$

When the addition or multiplication involves three integers, any pair may be taken first, without changing the result. For example,

$$(-6+2)+3 = -4+3 = -1$$
$$\text{or} \qquad -6+(2+3) = -6+5 = -1;$$
$$(-6\times4)\div2 = -24\div2 = -12$$
$$\text{or} \qquad -6(4\div2) = -6\times2 = -12.$$

If both addition or subtraction and multiplication or division occur in a calculation, the multiplication or division is carried out first unless there are brackets. If there are brackets, which imply multiplication, as in $5(1-3)$, we can either carry out the addition or subtraction first, as $5(1-3)=5(-2)=-10$, or multiply each term in the brackets by the number outside, as $5(1-3)=5-15=-10$. Thus $5(1-3)=5\times1-5\times3$.

1.2. INTERNATIONAL SYSTEM OF UNITS

The system of units of measurement used in this book is the Système International d'Unités (SI)—International System of Units. SI units are of three kinds: base, supplementary, and derived. The SI is based upon seven fundamental units, namely,

Quantity	Unit
length	metre (m)
mass	kilogram (kg)
time	second (s)
electric current	ampere (A)
thermodynamic temperature	kelvin (K)
luminous intensity	candela (cd)
amount of substance	mole (mol)

The two SI supplementary units are

Quantity	Unit
plane angle	radian (rad)
solid angle	steradian (sr)

The seven physical quantities, length, mass, time, electric current, thermodynamic temperature, luminous intensity, and amount of substance, are by convention regarded as being dimensionally independent. For any other quantity, the SI unit is derived by a dimensionally appropriate combination of the base units and supplementary units. For example, angular velocity equals angle turned through divided by time, so that the SI derived unit of angular velocity is the SI supplementary unit of plane angle divided by the SI base unit of time, i.e. radians per second (rad/s). Similarly, quantity of electricity (or electric charge) equals electric current multiplied by time, so that the SI derived unit of quantity of electricity is the SI base unit of electric current multiplied by the SI base unit of time, i.e. ampere-second (A s), which is given the special name of coulomb (C).

1.2.1. Multiples and submultiples of basic units. For large and small quantities it is convenient to use multiples and submultiples of the basic units. Only one prefix is applied at a time to a given unit. For example, one thousandth of a milligram is referred to as 1 microgram (1 μg), not as 1 millimilligram (1 mmg). [See Table 1.1.]

TABLE 1.1 *The following table shows the prefixes denoting decimal multiples or submultiples.*

Multiple or Submultiple	Prefix	Symbol
1 000 000 000 000 = 10^{12}	tera	T
1 000 000 000 = 10^9	giga	G
1 000 000 = 10^6	mega	M
1000 = 10^3	kilo	k
100 = 10^2	hecto	h
10 = 10^1	deca	da
0.1 = 10^{-1}	deci	d
0.01 = 10^{-2}	centi	c
0.001 = 10^{-3}	milli	m
0.000 001 = 10^{-6}	micro	μ
0.000 000 001 = 10^{-9}	nano	n
0.000 000 000 001 = 10^{-12}	pico	p

1.3. SOME QUANTITIES AND THEIR UNITS

1.3.1. Length. The measurement from end to end of a body or from point to point in space is called length or distance.

Distance is measured in units such as the metre (m) and the kilometre (km).

1.3.2. Mass. The mass of a body is the quantity of matter in it. Matter occupies space and can be solid, liquid, or gaseous.

The mass of a body never varies; it is constant under all conditions.

The kilogram (kg) and tonne (t) are two units of mass. 1 tonne = 1000 kg.

1.3.3. Time. The measurement of duration from one event to another is called time.

The second (s) is the basic unit of time, but certain non-SI units such as the minute (min) and the hour (h) will be used in many practical cases.

1.3.4. Area. Area is defined as extent of surface, and is measured in square units of length—e.g. square metres (m^2) or square millimetres (mm^2).

1.3.5. Volume. The amount of space occupied by a body is known as its volume.

Volume is measured in cubic units of length such as cubic metres (m^3) or cubic centimetres (cm^3).

1.3.6. Capacity. Capacity may be defined as cubic content. It is generally considered as the amount of space available within a container, and is measured in litres (l).

The word 'litre' is used as a special name for the cubic decimetre. Thus 1.0 l (litre) = 1.0 dm^3 (= 0.001 m^3).

1.3.7. Density. The density of a body is defined as the *mass per unit volume*, e.g. the number of kilograms per cubic metre (kg/m^3) or grams per cubic centimetre (g/cm^3).

$$\text{Density}\,(\rho) = \frac{\text{mass}\,(m)}{\text{volume}\,(V)}$$

1.3.8. Relative density. The relative density of a substance may be defined as the ratio:

$$\frac{\text{density of the substance}}{\text{density of pure water at 4 °C (277 K)}}$$

or

$$\frac{\text{mass of the substance}}{\text{mass of an equal volume of water}}.$$

It should be remembered that the density of pure water is a maximum at 4 °C, and at that temperature 1 gram occupies 1 cubic centimetre, so that the density of water is 1 g/cm^3. It follows that the density of water is also 1000 kg/m^3.

1.3.9. Force. Force may be defined as *that which changes, or tends to change, the state of rest of a body or its uniform motion in a straight line.*

The unit of force is the newton (N) and is that force which, when acting on a mass of one kilogram (1 kg) gives it an acceleration of one metre per second per second (1 m/s^2). Note that, expressed in terms of base units, 1 N equals 1 m kg/s^2.

1.3.10. Pressure. When a compressive force is distributed over a surface area a pressure is set up. Pressure is a measure of concentration of force and may be expressed as *normal force per unit area*, where normal means at right-angles to the surface,

$$\text{pressure } p = \frac{\text{normal force } F}{\text{area } A}.$$

The SI unit of pressure is given the special name of pascal (Pa). In terms of other SI units, $1 \text{ Pa} = 1 \text{ N/m}^2$. Expressed in terms of base units, $1 \text{ Pa} = 1 \text{ kg/(m s}^2)$. It should be noted that

$$1 \text{ MPa} = 1 \text{ MN/m}^2 = 1 \text{ N/mm}^2.$$

1.3.11. Weight. The force of gravity acting on a body is called the weight of the body. This force may vary depending on the position of the body. Weight, due to the force of gravity, is measured in units of force such as the newton (N) and kilonewton (kN).

The force of gravity acting on a body of mass m (kilograms) is equal to mg (newtons), where g is the acceleration due to gravity in metres per second squared (m/s^2).

1.3.12. Plane angle. The amount of rotation or the inclination of two meeting lines or planes to each other is known as plane angle. The SI unit of plane angle is the radian (rad).

The degree (°), minute ('), and second (") are units outside the SI which, because of their practical importance, are in general use.

$$360° = 2\pi \text{ rad}; \quad 1' = (1/60)°; \quad 1'' = (1/60)'$$

The unit degree, with its decimal subdivisions, is recommended for use when the unit radian is not suitable.

1.4. TEMPERATURE AND MEASUREMENT

1.4.1. Temperature. The degree of hotness of a body compared with some standard hotness is known as its temperature.

The SI unit of thermodynamic temperature is the kelvin (K). In 1962 the Celsius scale (°C) was adopted as the standard practical temperature scale in the U.K. The freezing point of water, measured at standard atmospheric pressure (101 325 Pa), is 0 °C and is exactly equal to 273.15 K, which for most practical purposes is taken as 273 K. Temperature differences may be expressed in terms of either degrees Celsius (°C) or kelvins (K) because the Celsius degree and kelvin intervals are identical.

$$0 °C = 273 \text{ K}; \quad 100 °C = 373 \text{ K}.$$

1.4.2. Measurement. In general, changes in temperature and pressure affect the properties of a substance. It is necessary, therefore, to make scientific measurements

under standard temperature and pressure (s.t.p.) conditions. Standard temperature is taken as 0 °C (273 K) and standard pressure of the atmosphere as 101 325 Pa, say 0.1 MPa, except where the most accurate work is required.

The standard temperature for engineering measurement is 20 °C and all accurate measurements should be made at, or very close to, this temperature.

Whenever a measurement or calculation is made it is essential to state the unit of measurement as well as the numerical value. The worked examples which follow show how, throughout the calculations, the units are easily obtained, together with the numerical answer.

EXAMPLE 1.1. A piece of chromium, of mass 448 grams, is immersed in water in a measuring jar and found to have a volume of 64 cm³. Calculate the density of the chromium.

SOLUTION

$$\text{Density} = \frac{\text{mass}}{\text{volume}}.$$

$$\therefore \text{ density of chromium} = \frac{448 \text{ g}}{64 \text{ cm}^3},$$

$$= 7.0 \text{ g/cm}^3.$$

$$\left[\text{Note: } \begin{aligned} & 1 \text{ kg} = 1000 \text{ g} \\ & 1 \text{ m}^3 = 1\,000\,000 \text{ cm}^3 \end{aligned} \right]$$

It will, therefore, be seen that the density of chromium is also 7000 kg/m³.

EXAMPLE 1.2. The piston of a diesel engine has an effective area of 200 cm². What is the mean pressure of the gas in the cylinder when the total force exerted on the piston is 15 kN?

SOLUTION

$$\text{Pressure} = \frac{\text{normal force}}{\text{area}},$$

$$= \frac{15 \text{ kN}}{200 \text{ cm}^2},$$

[Note: $1 \text{ m}^2 = 10\,000 \text{ cm}^2$.]

$$\therefore \text{ pressure} = \frac{15 \text{ kN}}{0.02 \text{ m}^2}$$

$$= 750 \text{ kN/m}^2.$$

Since $1 \text{ kN/m}^2 = 1 \text{ kPa}$ and $1000 \text{ kPa} = 1 \text{ MPa}$, the gas pressure is 750 kPa or 0.75 MPa.

EXAMPLE 1.3. A car is travelling at a speed of 108 km/h. What is its speed expressed in metres per second?

SOLUTION

$$\left[\text{Note: } \begin{array}{l} 1 \text{ km} = 1000 \text{ m} \\ 1 \text{h} = 3600 \text{ s} \end{array}\right]$$

Speed $= 108$ km/h,

$$= \frac{108 \times 1000 \text{ m}}{3600 \text{ s}},$$

$$= 30 \text{ m/s}.$$

The car is travelling at a speed of 30 m/s.

1.5. DEGREE OF ACCURACY— SIGNIFICANT FIGURES

In practical calculations, only so many figures are used as are necessary to express the quantity to the degree of accuracy required. The quantity is then said to be correct to a given number of significant figures (sig. fig.).

In reducing the number of significant figures the following rules should be adopted:

(i) if the rejected digit (i.e. numeral from 0 to 9) is 5 or greater, add 1 to the preceding digit;
(ii) if the rejected digit is 4 or less, leave the preceding digit unaltered.

Consider, for example, the integer (i.e. whole number) 50 726 and suppose that a bin contains exactly that number of screws. It is often only necessary to know approximately the number of screws in the bin at any particular time, and the degree of accuracy required can be expressed as follows.

(i) The number of screws in the bin is 50 726 exactly.
(ii) The number of screws in the bin is 50 730 to 4 sig. fig., which means that the exact number lies between 50 725 and 50 735 (i.e. between 50 730 ± 5).
(iii) The number of screws in the bin is 50 700 to 3 sig. fig., which means that the exact number lies between 50 650 and 50 750 (i.e. between 50 700 ± 50).
(iv) The number of screws in the bin is 51 000 to 2 sig. fig., which means that the exact number lies between 50 500 and 51 500 (i.e. between 51 000 ± 500).
(v) The number of screws in the bin is 50 000 to 1 sig. fig., which means that the exact number lies between 45 000 and 55 000 (i.e. between 50 000 ± 5 000).

From the above it can be seen that the accuracy is increased by increasing the number of significant figures.

1.6. USE OF ROUGH CHECKS

In making calculations, especially when using a slide rule, it is desirable to have some idea of the magnitude of the answer. This often prevents a serious error from being carried forward into later work. The use of a 'rough check' will be found very useful, and often the check is not as 'rough' as may be supposed. By 'rounding-off' the given values (i.e. reducing the number of significant figures) to some convenient amount, an approximate answer can be obtained which will remove any doubts about whether the answer is, for instance, nearer 10, 100, or 1000.

EXAMPLE 1.4. Evaluate $\dfrac{578 \times 192 \times 710}{643 \times 27}$.

SOLUTION

By calculation it is found that $\dfrac{578 \times 192 \times 710}{643 \times 27}$ equals 4538. By 'rounding-off' the given values a rough check can be made as follows:

$$\frac{600 \times 200 \times 700}{600 \times 30} = \frac{140\,000}{30},$$

$$\text{say } \frac{150\,000}{30}, \text{ which is 5000.}$$

This agrees approximately with the calculated answer of 4538 and shows that the answer is not, for example, 45 380.

1.7. FACTORS AND MULTIPLES

If a number is contained an exact number of times in another it is said to be a factor of that other number. Thus each of the numbers 2, 3, 6, and 9 is a factor of 18, while 18 is a multiple of 2, 3, 6, and 9. A prime number is a number which is exactly divisible only by itself and unity (1), for example, 2, 3, 5, 7, 11.

1.7.1. Factors. The factors of a number are often found by inspection, but when this is not possible several tests may be applied as given below.

(a) All even numbers are divisible by 2.
(b) A number is divisible by 4 if its last two digits are also divisible by 4. Thus, 1128 is divisible by 4 because $28 \div 4 = 7$. Then $1128 \div 4 = 282$.
(c) All numbers ending in 0 or in 5 are divisible by 5.
(d) A number is divisible by 8 if its last three digits are also divisible by 8. For example, 7736 is divisible by 8 because $736 \div 8 = 92$. Then $7736 \div 8 = 967$.
(e) A number is divisible by 9 if the sum of its digits is also divisible by 9. Take, for example, the number 804 816. It can be seen that the sum of the digits is $8 + 0 + 4 + 8 + 1 + 6 = 27$. Now 27 is divisible by 9 ($= 3$) so that 804 816 is thus known to be divisible by 9. Then $804\,816 \div 9 = 89\,424$.
(f) A number is divisible by 11 if the difference between the sum of the 1st, 3rd, etc. digits and the

sum of the 2nd, 4th, etc. digits is 11 or zero. Thus, 80 674 is divisible by 11 because the difference between $8+6+4$ and $0+7$ is 11. Then $80\,674 \div 11 = 7334$. Also, 16 247 352 is divisible by 11 because $1+2+7+5$ minus $6+4+3+2$ is zero. Then, $16\,247\,352 \div 11 = 1\,477\,032$.

1.7.2. Highest common factor. The highest common factor (H.C.F.) of two or more numbers is the greatest number which divides into each of them exactly.

EXAMPLE 1.5. Find the H.C.F. of 210 and 252.

SOLUTION

Resolve both numbers into their prime factors as shown below.

$$210 = 2 \times 3 \times 5 \times 7.$$
$$252 = 2 \times 2 \times 3 \times 3 \times 7.$$

By inspection, common factors are 2, 3, and 7.

$$\therefore \text{H.C.F. is } 2 \times 3 \times 7 = 42.$$

The H.C.F. of 210 and 252 is 42.

1.7.3. Lowest common multiple. The lowest common multiple (L.C.M.) of two or more numbers is the smallest number which is a multiple of each of them.

EXAMPLE 1.6. Find the L.C.M. of 6, 10, 15, and 16.

SOLUTION

Resolve each number into its prime factors as shown below.

$$6 = 2 \times 3.$$
$$10 = 2 \times 5.$$
$$15 = 3 \times 5.$$
$$16 = 2 \times 2 \times 2 \times 2.$$

By inspection, prime factors are 2, 3, and 5. One of the numbers has the factor 2 four times, while the factors 3 and 5 are not contained in any of the numbers more often than once.

$$\therefore \text{L.C.M. is } 2 \times 2 \times 2 \times 2 \times 3 \times 5 = 240.$$

The L.C.M. of 6, 10, 15, and 16 is 240.

1.8. ORDER OF PROCEDURE

Quantities are often arranged in a series of operations and a definite order of procedure must be followed. It can be seen that $2+3 \times 4$ may be interpreted as $2+12$ which is 14 (correct), or as 5×4 which is 20 (incorrect). Multiplication (and division) must be done before addition (and subtraction).

Where an expression may appear to be ambiguous, brackets are used for convenience to group terms together and the quantities within a pair of brackets are then treated as one quantity. Thus, when a quantity in brackets is multiplied by a factor, each term in the brackets is multiplied by that factor. For example, $5(6+4)$ means 5 times the sum of 6 and 4, i.e. $5 \times 10 = 50$. Alternatively, $5(6+4)$ could be written as $5 \times 6 + 5 \times 4 = 30 + 20 = 50$. Thus $5(6+4) = 5 \times 6 + 5 \times 4 = 50$. Similarly, when a quantity in brackets is divided by a factor, each term in the brackets is divided by that factor. It can be seen from $5 \times 6 + 5 \times 4 = 5(6+4)$ that the use of brackets also serves to simplify an expression. Where brackets occur within other brackets, the innermost brackets must be evaluated first.

The order of procedure to be followed when dealing with any calculation is:
1. evaluate the contents of brackets,
2. carry out any multiplication and division, and
3. perform any addition and subtraction.

A useful memory aid is the acronym BODMAS which, as shown below, sets out a convenient order of procedure:

1. Brackets (evaluate the contents)
2. $\begin{cases} \text{Of (which means multiply—see Ex. 2.3.)} \\ \text{Divide} \\ \text{Multiply} \end{cases}$
3. $\begin{cases} \text{Add} \\ \text{Subtract} \end{cases}$

EXERCISES 1

1. State which of the following are prime numbers and express the others as the product of prime factors:
   (a) 179, (b) 447, (c) 533, (d) 873, (e) 919.

2. Find the H.C.F. of:
   (a) 208 and 819, (b) 247 and 570,
   (c) 1815 and 4158.

3. Find the L.C.M. of:
   (a) 25, 60, and 84, (b) 63, 420, and 560.

4. An exact number of small articles of the same size are to be made from each of three quantities of metal having masses of 3.328 kg, 4.563 kg, and 5.005 kg respectively.
   Assuming that all the material is used in the manufacturing process, what is the mass of each article?

5. Three wheels measure 750 mm, 800 mm, and 880 mm in circumference. Calculate the shortest distance, in metres, in which they will all turn an exact number of times when moving along a straight track. How many revolutions will be made by each wheel?

6. Find the value of each of the following.
   (a) $5 \times 7 - 2 + 6 \times 4$
   (b) $10 \times 9 - 8 \div 4 + 3$.
   (c) $18 - 12 \div 3 + 4(5-2)$.
   (d) $114 - 2[9 + 8(10-4)]$.
   (e) $14 - 14 \div 2 - 4(7-5)$.

7. Without the aid of a calculator, slide rule, or tables, find the value of

$$\frac{11 \times 156 \times 19}{4 \times 39}.$$

Obtain an approximate answer by means of a 'rough check'.

8. Determine, by any method, the exact value of

$$\frac{121 \times 405 \times 1053}{297 \times 39}.$$

Also state the answer correct to (i) 3 and (ii) 2 significant figures.

9. If seven pieces of wire, each 135 mm long, are cut from a single piece 1 metre long, what length is left over?

10. Five steel rods have the following lengths:
2 m, 220 mm, 73 cm, 650 mm, and 40 cm.
Find their total length in metres.

11. The density of paraffin is 800 kg/m³. What mass of paraffin will fill a tank of capacity 400 litres?

12. A slab of tin, of mass 437 kg, is lowered into a tank full of water and 60 litres of the water overflows. Find the density of the tin.

13. A railway engine is travelling at a speed of 144 km/h. Convert this speed to metres per second.

14. A tonne of water is to be pumped into a tank. How long will it take at a rate of 20 litres per second?

15. The piston of a reciprocating pump has an effective area of 800 cm². What pressure is exerted on the fluid in the cylinder when the force in the piston rod is 30 kN?

ANSWERS TO EXERCISES 1

1. (a) Prime   (b) 3×149 (c) 13×41
   (d) $3 \times 3 \times 97$ (e) Prime.

2. (a) 13   (b) 19   (c) 33.

3. (a) 2100   (b) 5040.

4. 13 grams.

5. 132 metres, 176, 165, 150.

6. (a) 57   (b) 91   (c) 26   (d) 0   (e) -1.

7. 209.

8. 4455, 4460, 4500.

9. 55 mm.

10. 4 metres.

11. 320 kg.

12. 7283 kg/m³.

13. 40 m/s.

14. 50 seconds.

15. 375 kPa.

2 | Fractions

2.1. VULGAR FRACTIONS

When a quantity is divided into a number of parts, each of the parts is said to be a fraction of the whole. For example, if a metre is divided into ten equal parts each is one-tenth of the whole. One such part can be represented as 1/10, two parts as 2/10, three parts as 3/10, and so on. Fractions of this type are known as vulgar fractions. The two numbers in a vulgar fraction are known as:

the *Numerator*, i.e. the number of equal parts in the fraction

the *Denominator*, i.e. the number of equal parts into which the quantity is divided

A proper fraction is a vulgar fraction in which the denominator is greater than the numerator, for example, 2/5, 3/10.

An improper fraction is a vulgar fraction in which the numerator is greater than the denominator, for example 7/5, 21/20.

A mixed number is partly integer (whole number) and partly proper fraction, for example, $5\frac{1}{2}$, $8\frac{3}{4}$.

2.1.1. Addition and subtraction.
The addition and subtraction of vulgar fractions having different denominators is carried out by first expressing them with a common denominator. The numerators are then added or subtracted as required. For convenience, the common denominator should be the lowest possible, namely, the lowest common multiple (L.C.M.) of the different denominators.

EXAMPLE 2.1. Simplify $3\frac{5}{6} - 2\frac{1}{12} + 4\frac{3}{20} - 2\frac{4}{15}$.

SOLUTION

Although the whole numbers involved are small, the calculation is simplified by dealing with them separately first. Thus $3\frac{5}{6} - 2\frac{1}{12} + 4\frac{3}{20} - 2\frac{4}{15}$ becomes

$$(3 - 2 + 4 - 2) + (\frac{5}{6} - \frac{1}{12} + \frac{3}{20} - \frac{4}{15})$$

$$= 3 + (\frac{5}{6} - \frac{1}{12} + \frac{3}{20} - \frac{4}{15})$$

The L.C.M. of the denominators is 60 so that the expression can now be written as

$$3 + \frac{10 \times 5 - 5 \times 1 + 3 \times 3 - 4 \times 4}{60}$$

$$= 3 + \frac{50 - 5 + 9 - 16}{60} = 3\frac{38}{60} = 3\frac{19}{30}.$$

2.1.2. Multiplication.
The multiplication of vulgar fractions is achieved by first multiplying the numerators together to obtain the new numerator, and then multiplying the denominators together to obtain the new denominator. Mixed numbers must be expressed as improper fractions before multiplication is carried out. Calculations may be simplified by cancelling factors common to the numerator and denominator.

EXAMPLE 2.2. Simplify $3\frac{1}{7} \times 4\frac{2}{3} \times 2\frac{5}{8}$.

SOLUTION

Convert each mixed number in the expression $3\frac{1}{7} \times 4\frac{2}{3} \times 2\frac{5}{8}$ to an improper fraction, giving $\frac{22}{7} \times \frac{14}{3} \times \frac{21}{8}$. Simplify wherever possible by cancelling factors common to numerators and denominators, so that

$$\frac{\overset{11}{\cancel{22}}}{\cancel{7}} \times \frac{\overset{7}{\cancel{14}}}{\cancel{3}} \times \frac{\cancel{21}}{\underset{2}{\cancel{8}}} = \frac{77}{2}$$

$$= 38\frac{1}{2}.$$

EXAMPLE 2.3. Evaluate $\frac{2}{5}$ of $6\frac{3}{10} - \frac{1}{2}$ of $3\frac{2}{5}$.

SOLUTION

The meaning of the fraction '2/5' is '2/5 of 1', which will be seen to be $2/5 \times 1$. Likewise, '$\frac{1}{2}$ of 1' means $\frac{1}{2} \times 1$. The word 'of', therefore, has the same meaning as the sign '$\times$', i.e. multiply. Thus,

$$\frac{2}{5} \text{ of } 6\frac{3}{10} - \frac{1}{2} \text{ of } 3\frac{2}{5} = \frac{2}{5} \times 6\frac{3}{10} - \frac{1}{2} \times 3\frac{2}{5}$$

$$= \frac{2}{5} \times \frac{63}{10} - \frac{1}{2} \times \frac{17}{5}$$

$$= \frac{126}{50} - \frac{17}{10}$$

$$= \frac{126 - 5 \times 17}{50}$$

$$= \frac{126 - 85}{50}$$

$$= \frac{41}{50}.$$

2.1.3. Division.
The division of vulgar fractions is carried out by inverting the divisor (i.e. placing the denominator over the numerator) and then proceeding as for multiplication. As in the case of multiplication of vulgar fractions, mixed numbers must be converted to improper fractions and, for simplification, factors common to the numerator and denominator cancelled. It should be noted that division by zero is not permissible.

EXAMPLE 2.4. Calculate the value of

$$\frac{7\frac{3}{13} \times 3\frac{1}{4}}{4\frac{2}{3} \times 5\frac{2}{9}}.$$

SOLUTION

In the given expression convert the mixed numbers to improper fractions as follows.

$$\frac{\frac{94}{13} \times \frac{13}{4}}{\frac{14}{3} \times \frac{47}{9}}.$$

Invert each fraction in the divisor and follow the normal procedure of multiplication cancelling common factors wherever possible.

$$\therefore \frac{94}{13} \times \frac{13}{4} \times \frac{3}{14} \times \frac{9}{47}$$

$$= \frac{27}{28}.$$

EXAMPLE 2.5. Simplify: (i) $\frac{1}{\frac{2}{3}}$; (ii) $\frac{\frac{3}{4}}{5}$.

SOLUTION (i)

Invert the fraction $\frac{2}{3}$ and multiply.

$$\therefore \frac{1}{\frac{2}{3}} = 1 \times \frac{3}{2}$$

$$= \frac{3}{2}$$

$$= 1\frac{1}{2}.$$

In this example it should be noted that 1 is being divided by a number less than 1, i.e. $\frac{2}{3}$. Therefore the answer must be greater than 1.

SOLUTION (ii)

In this case $\frac{3}{4}$ is being divided by 5 and therefore the answer must be less than $\frac{3}{4}$.

Write the expression $\frac{\frac{3}{4}}{5}$ as $\frac{\frac{3}{4}}{\frac{5}{1}}$. Invert the divisor $(\frac{5}{1})$ and multiply.

$$\therefore \frac{\frac{3}{4}}{\frac{5}{1}} = \frac{3}{4} \times \frac{1}{5}$$

$$= \frac{3}{20}.$$

EXAMPLE 2.6. Simplify $\dfrac{(1\frac{2}{5} + 2\frac{1}{3}) \times (4\frac{3}{4} - 3\frac{1}{2})}{(2\frac{2}{5} - \frac{3}{4}) \times (3\frac{2}{3} + 4\frac{1}{2})}$

SOLUTION

The value of the quantity within each pair of brackets must first be obtained in the form of a single fraction.

The procedure is as follows.

$$(1\tfrac{2}{5} + 2\tfrac{1}{3}) = \frac{7}{5} + \frac{7}{3} = \frac{21+35}{15} = \frac{56}{15}.$$

$$(4\tfrac{3}{4} - 3\tfrac{1}{2}) = \frac{19}{4} - \frac{7}{2} = \frac{19-14}{4} = \frac{5}{4}.$$

$$(2\tfrac{2}{5} - \tfrac{3}{4}) = \frac{12}{5} - \frac{3}{4} = \frac{48-15}{20} = \frac{33}{20}.$$

$$(3\tfrac{2}{3} + 4\tfrac{1}{2}) = \frac{11}{3} + \frac{9}{2} = \frac{22+27}{6} = \frac{49}{6}.$$

The problem is now reduced to a calculation involving division and multiplication only, i.e.

$$\frac{\frac{56}{15} \times \frac{5}{4}}{\frac{33}{20} \times \frac{49}{6}}.$$

The fractions in the divisor are now inverted giving

$$\frac{56}{15} \times \frac{5}{4} \times \frac{20}{33} \times \frac{6}{49}$$

$$= \frac{80}{231}.$$

EXAMPLE 2.7. Find the value of

$$\tfrac{3}{5}\{5\tfrac{1}{4} + 3\tfrac{1}{2}(\tfrac{1}{4} \text{ of } 5\tfrac{2}{5} - \tfrac{17}{20})\} + \tfrac{3}{4} \div \tfrac{1}{2}.$$

SOLUTION

When calculating the value of compound fractions it is essential that the different processes are carried out in the correct sequence (see section 1.7) as follows.
1. Find the value contained by each pair of brackets present. Where brackets occur within other brackets, the innermost brackets must be evaluated first.
2. Work any multiplication or division.
3. Carry out any addition or subtaction.
Thus,

$$\tfrac{3}{5}\{5\tfrac{1}{4} + 3\tfrac{1}{2}(\tfrac{1}{4} \text{ of } 5\tfrac{2}{5} - \tfrac{17}{20})\} + \tfrac{3}{4} \div \tfrac{1}{2}$$

$$= \tfrac{3}{5}\{5\tfrac{1}{4} + 3\tfrac{1}{2}(\tfrac{1}{4} \times \tfrac{27}{5} - \tfrac{17}{20})\} + \tfrac{3}{4} \times \tfrac{2}{1}$$

$$= \tfrac{3}{5}\left\{5\tfrac{1}{4} + 3\tfrac{1}{2}\left(\frac{27-17}{20}\right)\right\} + \frac{3}{2}$$

$$= \tfrac{3}{5}\{5\tfrac{1}{4} + 3\tfrac{1}{2} \times \tfrac{1}{2}\} + \tfrac{3}{2}$$

$$= \tfrac{3}{5}\{5\tfrac{1}{4} + 1\tfrac{3}{4}\} + \tfrac{3}{2}$$

$$= \tfrac{3}{5} \times 7 + \tfrac{3}{2}$$

$$= \tfrac{21}{5} + \tfrac{3}{2}$$

$$= \frac{42+15}{10}$$

$$= \frac{57}{10}$$

$$= 5\tfrac{7}{10}.$$

2.2. DECIMAL FRACTIONS

In decimals a decimal point separates the integer from the fractions. Each digit of the integer as well as of the fraction has one-tenth of the value it would have if its position were one place to the left. Thus 45.67 represents 4 tens + 5 units + 6 tenths + 7 hundredths, which is $40 + 5 + \frac{6}{10} + \frac{7}{100}$ or $45\frac{67}{100}$.

2.2.1. Addition and subtraction. The addition and subtraction of decimals is carried out by arranging the numbers so that the decimal points are placed one under the other, and then proceeding as with whole numbers.

EXAMPLE 2.8. Find the (i) sum of and (ii) difference between 967.201 and 75.7334.

SOLUTION

Proceed as described in section 2.2.1 above.

967.201	967.2010
75.7334	75.7334
Sum = 1042.9344	Difference = 891.4676

2.2.2. Multiplication. The multiplication of decimals can be achieved by proceeding in the same way as for whole numbers. The number of decimal places in the product is found from the sum of the decimal places in the numbers being multiplied together.

EXAMPLE 2.9. Find the product of 27.58 and 4.369

SOLUTION

Proceed as described in section 2.2.2 above. Multiply 27.58 successively by 9, 6, 3, and 4 and place the product at each multiplication one place to the left in successive lines. Then add the products of each separate multiplication to give the total product.

```
        27.58    (Note the total of
         4.369    5 decimal places)
       _____
       24 822
      165 48
      827 4
    11032
```

Total product = 120.49702   (Note the 5 decimal places in the answer)

Rough check: say $30 \times 4 = 120$. This confirms that the decimal point is in the correct place.

2.2.3. Division. The division of decimals can be carried out in the same manner as that used for whole numbers. The process is continued until the quotient terminates or until the required number of figures is obtained. It is often found convenient to convert the divisor into a whole number by shifting the decimal point to the right, not forgetting to shift the decimal point in the dividend by the same number of places.

EXAMPLE 2.10. Divide 45.47 by 12.5

SOLUTION

The divisor (12.5) is converted into a whole number (125) by shifting the decimal point one place to the right (i.e. by multiplying 12.5 by 10). The decimal point in the dividend (45.47) is also moved one place to the right giving 454.7 (i.e. by multiplying 45.47 by 10).

```
              3.6 3 7 6 = Quotient
    125 | 454.7 0 0 0
          375 ↓
          _____
          79 7
          75 0 ↓
          _____
            4 7 0
            3 7 5 ↓
            _____
              9 5 0
              8 7 5 ↓
              _____
                7 5 0
                7 5 0
                _____
                    0
```

Rough check: say $48 \div 12 = 4$. This confirms that the decimal point is correctly positioned.

2.3. DEGREE OF ACCURACY—DECIMAL PLACES

In practical calculations in which decimals occur, only so many figures are used as are required to express the quantity to the degree of accuracy needed. The quantity is then said to be correct to a given number of decimal places (dec. pl.).

Significant figures (section 1.4) do not have anything to do with the decimal point and must not be confused with the number of decimal places. Using 276 as an illustration of three significant figures, then 27 600; 276; 27.6; 0.276; 0.00276 are all examples of these three significant figures. Thus the number of zeros to the left of the first significant figure or to the right of the third significant figure does not affect the significant figures themselves.

In reducing the number of decimal places the following rules should be applied:

(i) if the rejected digit is 5 or greater, add 1 to the preceding digit;
(ii) if the rejected digit is 4 or less, leave the preceding digit unaltered.

EXAMPLE 2.11. Express 3.6376 to (i) 1, (ii) 2, and (iii) 3 decimal places.

SOLUTION

Apply the rules given in section 2.3 above. The number 3.6376 is

(i) 3.6 to 1 dec. pl.
(ii) 3.64 to 2 dec. pl.
(iii) 3.638 to 3 dec. pl.

From the above it can be seen that the accuracy is increased by increasing the number of decimal places.

2.4. CONVERSION OF VULGAR AND DECIMAL FRACTIONS

It was shown in section 2.2 that 45.67 could be written as $45\frac{67}{100}$. Any decimal fraction can similarly be converted into a vulgar fraction. The digits following the decimal point in the quantity to be converted are written as the numerator, and the denominator is formed by '1' followed by as many 0's as there are digits after the decimal point. Where possible, the resulting vulgar fraction should be simplified by cancelling, for example $0.225 = \frac{225}{1000} = \frac{9}{40}$.

To reduce vulgar fractions to decimals, the numerator is divided by the denominator. It is, however, often found that the division does not end. For example $2/3 = 0.6666\ldots$, $3/11 = 0.2727\ldots$, and $1/7 = 0.142857142857\ldots$.

At a certain stage the same figures are repeated in the same order. Such decimals are termed recurring decimals, and a dot is placed over the first and last of the repeating digits to indicate the period. Then only one period need be written. For example, $2/3 = 0.\dot{6}$, $3/11 = 0.\dot{2}\dot{7}$, and $1/7 = 0.\dot{1}4285\dot{7}$.

2.5. TOLERANCES

As it is impossible to produce components to precise dimensions, it is necessary to introduce extreme values of size known as 'limits'.

Upper limit—the greatest size permitted.

Lower limit—the smallest size permitted.

The difference between the upper and lower limits is called the 'tolerance'. The amount of tolerance chosen varies considerably according to circumstances. For example, in a precision machining operation the tolerance will be much less than that allowed in making a heavy casting. For various reasons, such as cutting production time and cost, tolerances are as large as satisfactory operating will allow.

Two methods of expressing limits of size are given below.

(1) By specifying plainly both limits of size, for example

45.11
44.89

The larger limit of size is given first, and both dimensions are expressed to the same number of decimal places.

(2) By specifying a size with limits of tolerance above and below that size, and preferably of equal amount, for example

45 ± 0.11

Where the limits of tolerance are not equally disposed they are expressed to the same number of decimal places, for example

$\begin{matrix} +0.12 \\ 45 - 0.10 \end{matrix}$

When one of the limits of tolerance is 'nil' it is represented by the cipher '0', for example

$\begin{matrix} 0 \\ 45 - 0.1 \end{matrix}$

EXAMPLE 2.12. Two holes, H_1 and H_2, are to be drilled in a steel component as shown in Fig. 2.1. All

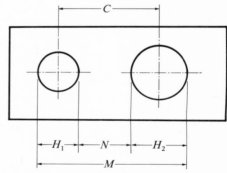

Fig. 2.1

dimensions are in millimetres (mm). The distance, C, between the centres is to be 45 ± 0.02. The diameter of H_1 is to be 7.5 ± 0.01 and of H_2 is to be 12.5 ± 0.01. Determine, in each case, the maximum and minimum distance of M and N.

SOLUTION

The distance M will be a maximum when C is a maximum and the hole diameters are also a maximum.

$$\therefore M_{max} = (45 + 0.02) + \left(\frac{7.5 + 0.01}{2}\right) + \left(\frac{12.5 + 0.01}{2}\right)$$

$$= 45.02 + \frac{20.02}{2}$$

$$= 45.02 + 10.01$$

$$= 55.03 \text{ mm.}$$

The distance M will be a minimum when C is a minimum and the hole diameters are also a minimum.

$$\therefore\ M_{min} = (45 - 0.02) + \left(\frac{7.5 - 0.01}{2}\right) + \left(\frac{12.5 - 0.01}{2}\right)$$

$$= 44.98 + \frac{19.98}{2}$$

$$= 44.98 + 9.99$$

$$= 54.97\ \text{mm}.$$

The distance N will be a maximum when C is a maximum and the hole diameters are a minimum.

$$\therefore\ N_{max} = 45.02 - 9.99 \quad \text{(see working above)}$$

$$= 35.03\ \text{mm}.$$

The distance N will be a minimum when C is a minimum and the hole diameters are a maximum.

$$\therefore\ N_{min} = 44.98 - 10.01 \quad \text{(see working above)}$$

$$= 34.97\ \text{mm}.$$

EXERCISES 2

1. Simplify: (a) $\dfrac{\frac{2}{3}}{\frac{3}{5}}$, (b) $\dfrac{\frac{3}{5}}{12}$, (c) $\dfrac{\frac{1}{2}}{\frac{2}{3}} - \dfrac{\frac{3}{4}}{5}$.

2. Simplify: (a) $3\frac{7}{16} + 2\frac{3}{4}$, (b) $6\frac{1}{4} - 2\frac{5}{8}$.

3. Find the value of:
   (a) $6\frac{3}{8} - 3\frac{1}{2} + 1\frac{1}{4}$, (b) $3\frac{3}{4} \times 3\frac{1}{5}$.

4. Evaluate: (a) $6\frac{3}{4} \div \frac{3}{8}$, (b) $(2\frac{1}{4} \times \frac{2}{3}) - \frac{13}{16}$.

5. Simplify: (a) $\dfrac{\frac{5}{8}}{\frac{1}{3} \times \frac{5}{16}}$, (b) $\frac{2}{3}$ of $(\frac{1}{7} + \frac{1}{8})$.

6. Simplify: $\dfrac{9\frac{1}{7}(1\frac{2}{5} + 3\frac{2}{3})}{18\frac{2}{7}(4\frac{2}{15} + 6\frac{2}{5})}$.

7. Simplify: $\dfrac{\frac{1}{2} + \frac{2}{3} \text{ of } (5\frac{5}{8} - 3\frac{7}{12})}{7\frac{3}{4} - 7\frac{1}{18} + 1\frac{1}{9}}$.

8. Simplify: $\frac{3}{4}[2\frac{1}{2} + 7\frac{1}{2}(\frac{1}{3} \text{ of } 6\frac{1}{4} - \frac{3}{4})]$.

9. Evaluate:
   (a) $2.8 + 0.07 + 10.4$, (b) $12.1 - 4.73$.

10. Find the value of:
    (a) 0.3×0.4, (b) 1.02×0.03.

11. Evaluate:
    (a) $0.0072 \div 0.09$, (b) $\dfrac{0.3 \times 0.6}{0.5}$.

12. Simplify: (a) $\dfrac{0.024 \times 56.8975}{0.00012}$,

    (b) $\dfrac{0.23 \times 0.518 + 0.375 \times 0.518}{0.259}$.

13. Express as vulgar fractions:
    (a) 0.1625, (b) 0.53125, (c) 10.2225.

14. Express as decimal fractions correct to 3 places:
    (a) $\frac{5}{32}$, (b) $\frac{9}{22}$, (c) $\frac{13}{16}$.

15. A water tank can be filled from one pipe in 20 minutes and from a second pipe in 30 minutes. The tank can be emptied through a drain pipe in 15 minutes. How long would it take to fill the tank if all three pipes were opened? The tank was empty at the start.

16. The products of a certain firm are subjected to two inspections. At the first inspection of one batch, $\frac{1}{8}$ were rejected, and finally $\frac{5}{6}$ of that batch were placed on the market. What fraction of the total product was rejected at the second inspection?

17. A cooling water tank is full at the beginning of a certain process, containing 7500 litres. After completing $\frac{3}{4}$ of the process, the tank contains 1200 litres. The tank then receives 2500 litres and the process is continued. Find what fraction of the tank contains water at the end of the process, assuming that the rate of water consumption is constant.

18. An engineering company employs $\frac{4}{5}$ of its staff on production, $\frac{2}{15}$ on plant maintenance and works services, and the rest in the various offices. Ten of the staff retire from the offices and thus reduce the office staff to $\frac{5}{6}$ of its former number. What was the original number of employees of the company?

19. On a drawing, a shaft is dimensioned as $63.37\overset{0}{-}0.04$ mm diameter and the bearing into which it is to fit as $63.5\overset{0}{+}0.04$ mm diameter. Calculate the maximum and minimum diametral clearance between the bearing and shaft.

20. A bar of steel is to be turned to a diameter of $44.45\overset{0}{-}0.05$ mm and then ground to a diameter of $44.32\overset{0}{-}0.04$ mm. Determine the greatest and least possible amounts of steel to be removed by grinding calculated on the diameter.

ANSWERS TO EXERCISES 2

1. (a) $3\frac{1}{3}$ (b) $\frac{1}{20}$ (c) $1\frac{7}{20}$.
2. (a) $6\frac{3}{16}$ (b) $3\frac{5}{8}$.
3. (a) $4\frac{1}{8}$ (b) 12.
4. (a) 18 (b) $\frac{11}{16}$.
5. (a) 6 (b) $\frac{5}{28}$.
6. $\frac{19}{79}$.
7. $1\frac{2}{65}$.
8. $4\frac{11}{16}$.
9. (a) 13.27 (b) 7.37.
10. (a) 0.12 (b) 0.0306.
11. (a) 0.08 (b) 0.36.
12. (a) $11\ 379.5$ (b) 1.21.
13. (a) $\frac{13}{80}$ (b) $\frac{17}{32}$ (c) $10\frac{89}{400}$.
14. (a) 0.156 (b) 0.409 (c) 0.813.
15. 1 hour.
16. $\frac{1}{24}$.
17. $\frac{16}{75}$.
18. 900.
19. 0.21 mm, 0.13 mm.
20. 0.17 mm, 0.08 mm.

3 | Average, ratio, and percentage

3.1. AVERAGES

The average, or mean, value of a set of quantities is their sum divided by the number of quantities in the set.

Because no measurement is exact, it is usual to assume that a given dimension is an average dimension, obtained by making several measurements and dividing their sum by the number of measurements taken.

EXAMPLE 3.1. In an experiment on friction, the following values were obtained for the coefficient of friction between rubber and asphalt: find the average value.

$$0.653, 0.667, 0.648, 0.656, 0.642, 0.664$$

SOLUTION

Average value

$$= \frac{\text{sum of values}}{\text{number of values}}$$

$$= \frac{0.653 + 0.667 + 0.648 + 0.656 + 0.642 + 0.664}{6}$$

$$= \frac{3.930}{6}$$

$$= 0.655,$$

The average value of the coefficient of friction between rubber and asphalt is found to be 0.655.

EXAMPLE 3.2. The average mass of five castings is 14 kg, and four of them have masses of 13.83, 14.37, 14.12, and 14.26 kg respectively. Find the mass of the fifth casting.

SOLUTION

$$\text{Total mass} = 14 \text{ kg} \times 5 = 70 \text{ kg.}$$

$$\text{Mass of four castings} = 13.83 + 14.37 + 14.12 + 14.26$$
$$= 56.58 \text{ kg.}$$

$$\text{Mass of fifth casting} = 70 \text{ kg} - 56.58 \text{ kg}$$
$$= 13.42 \text{ kg.}$$

3.2. RATIO

When comparing the magnitudes of two quantities of the same kind it is usual to state the ratio which one bears to the other. One of the quantities is said to be so many times greater or smaller than the other quantity. The ratio of two numbers is the quotient obtained when one of the numbers is divided by the other. A ratio, such as 1/2 may be written as 1:2 (and is read as 1 to

2). It should be observed that the sign : is giving the instruction 'divide 1 by 2'.

EXAMPLE 3.3. The perimeter of a triangle is 12 metres, and the sides are in the ratio of 2:3:4. Determine the lengths of the sides.

SOLUTION

The sum of the three sides of the triangle is 12 metres, and they are in the ratio 2:3:4. This means that the second is $1\frac{1}{2}$ times the first, and the third is twice the first. Consider the perimeter as being divided into $2+3+4=9$ equal sections. The first side is, therefore, 2/9, the second 3/9, and the third 4/9 of the perimeter. Then,

1st side = 2/9 of 12 metres = $2/9 \times 12 = 2\frac{2}{3}$ metres.
2nd side = 3/9 of 12 metres = $\frac{1}{3} \times 12 = 4$ metres.
3rd side = 4/9 of 12 metres = $4/9 \times 12 = 5\frac{1}{3}$ metres.
check: $2\frac{2}{3} + 4 + 5\frac{1}{3} = 12$ metres.

EXAMPLE 3.4. Two gear wheels have their pitch circle diameters (P.C.D.s) in the ratio 2:3. The wheels form a simple gear train, the distance between their centres being 240 mm. Calculate the pitch circle diameters of the two wheels.

SOLUTION

Fig. 3.1. shows the simple gear train.

Radius R_1 + Radius R_2 = 240 mm.
∴ P.C.D. of wheel 1 + P.C.D. of wheel 2 = 480 mm.
Ratio of pitch circle diameters is 2:3, and $2+3=5$.
∴ P.C.D. of wheel 1 = 2/5 of 480
$$= 2/5 \times 480 = 192 \text{ mm.}$$
P.C.D. of wheel 2 = 3/5 of 480
$$= 3/5 \times 480 = 288 \text{ mm.}$$
check: $192 + 288 = 480$ mm.

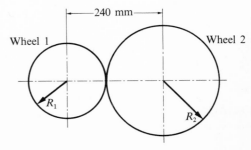

Fig. 3.1

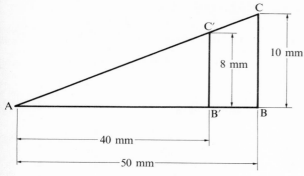

Fig. 3.2

3.3. PROPORTION

3.3.1. Direct proportion. Consider the triangles ABC and $AB'C'$ in Fig. 3.2. It will be seen that the ratio of $B'C'$ to AB' (i.e. 8:40, or 1/5) is equal to the ratio BC to AB (i.e. 10:50, or 1/5). When two ratios are equal the four terms form a proportion. The above proportion can be written

$$B'C':AB' :: BC:AB \text{ (i.e. } 8:40 :: 10:50)$$

or $\qquad B'C':AB' = BC:AB \text{(i.e. } 8:40 = 10:50)$

or $\qquad \dfrac{B'C'}{AB'} = \dfrac{BC}{AB} \left(\text{i.e. } \dfrac{8}{40} = \dfrac{10}{50} \right).$

If one quantity, P, depends on another quantity, Q, in such a way that if Q is increased or decreased in a given ratio, P increases or decreases in the same ratio, then P is said to be directly proportional to Q.

$$P \propto Q.$$

EXAMPLE 3.5. An important gas law (Charles's law) states that the volume, V, of a gas is directly proportional to the thermodynamic temperature, T, provided that the pressure remains constant.

A quantity of gas has a volume of 120 cm³ at 288 K. What will be its volume at 360 K if the pressure is maintained constant?

SOLUTION

The volume is directly proportional to the thermodynamic temperature, $V \propto T$,

$$\therefore \frac{V_1}{T_1} = \frac{V_2}{T_2}.$$

Multiplying both sides of the equation by T_2, the new volume

$$V_2 = \frac{V_1 T_2}{T_1}$$

$$= \frac{120 \times 360}{288}$$

$$= 150 \text{ cm}^3.$$

3.3.2. Inverse proportion. When a quantity, P, depends on another quantity, Q, in such a way that if Q is increased or decreased in a given ratio, P respectively decreases or increases in the same ratio then P is said to be inversely proportional to Q.

$$P \propto 1/Q.$$

EXAMPLE 3.6. Boyle's law, another important gas law, states that the absolute pressure, p, of a given mass of any gas is inversely proportional to the volume, V, provided that the temperature remains constant.

If the absolute pressure of 2 m³ of gas is increased from 0.24 MPa to 0.275 MPa at constant temperature, find the new volume.

SOLUTION

The absolute pressure is inversely proportional to the volume, $p \propto 1/V$,

$$\therefore p_1 V_1 = p_2 V_2.$$

Dividing both sides of the equation by p_2, the new volume

$$V_2 = \frac{p_1 V_1}{p_2}$$

$$= \frac{0.24 \times 2}{0.275}$$

$$= 1.75 \text{ m}^3.$$

3.4. PERCENTAGE

A percentage is a fraction in which the denominator is 100 and, like a ratio, is a comparison between two quantities of the same kind.

The ratio 1:100, equal to 1/100, may be termed 'one per cent' and denoted by 1 %. Similarly, $1/4 = 25/100 = 25 \%$; $1/2 = 50/100 = 50 \%$; $3/2 = 150/100 = 150 \%$; etc.

It will be seen that one number may be expressed as a percentage of another by multiplying the first number by 100 and dividing the product by the second number. Also, it will be noted that a percentage can be greater than 100 %.

EXAMPLE 3.7. A rough casting has a mass of 8.5 kg. After machining, the finished component has a mass of 5.95 kg. What percentage of the original mass has been removed?

SOLUTION

$$\text{Mass removed} = 8.5 - 5.95 = 2.55 \text{ kg.}$$

$$\text{Fraction of original mass removed} = \frac{2.55}{8.5}.$$

$$\text{Percentage of original mass removed} = \frac{2.55}{8.5} \times 100 \%$$

$$= 30 \%.$$

3.5. PERCENTAGE ERROR

The temperature coefficient of resistance of nickel at 0 °C is known to be 0.0056/ °C. Suppose that in an experiment to determine the temperature coefficient of resistance of nickel a value of 0.005/ °C was obtained. This represents an absolute error of $0.0056 - 0.005 = 0.0006$ which appears to be an insignificant amount. However, the true and experimental values are better compared by calculating the percentage error.

$$\text{Percentage error} = \frac{\text{absolute error}}{\text{true value}} \times 100\ \%$$

Thus in the above experiment the percentage error is $(0.0006/0.0056) \times 100\ \% = 10.72\ \%$.

EXAMPLE 3.8. A shaft is erroneously machined to 124.2 mm diameter when it should have been 125.0 mm diameter. Calculate the percentage error.

SOLUTION

$$\text{Absolute error} = 125.0 - 124.2 = 0.8\ \text{mm}.$$
$$\text{Percentage error} = \frac{\text{absolute error}}{\text{true diameter}} \times 100\ \%$$
$$= \frac{0.8}{125} \times 100\%$$
$$= 0.64\ \%.$$

EXERCISES 3

1. Five pins are carburized for case hardening. The depth of case in each is found to be 0.304 mm, 0.330 mm, 0.355 mm, 0.355 mm, and 0.406 mm. Calculate the average depth of case. If the pins were in the furnace for 1.75 h, find the average rate of penetration.

2. During a laboratory experiment the readings of a thermometer immersed in a liquid were 50.4 °C, 50.6 °C, 51.2 °C, 52.35 °C, 54.25 °C, and 56 °C. Find the mean temperature of the liquid correct to two decimal places.

3. Three similar components are manufactured on three different machines and the manufacturing costs are 35p, 30p, and 55p respectively. Find the average cost. Taking this as 100 %, what is the percentage cost of component per machine?

4. (a) If in a certain period of time the daily circulation of a newspaper is increased by 15 % and this increase represents 63 000 copies, what is the new daily circulation of the paper?
   (b) In a batch of steel pegs three are measured for length and their average length is found to be 30.2 mm. If two of the lengths are 29.9 mm and 30.1 mm respectively, what will be the length of the third peg?
   (U.L.C.I.)

5. A tank contained 7800 litres of oil. If $16\frac{2}{3}$ % of the oil was drawn off, how many litres remained in the tank?

6. An alloy contains 25 % of an element A. How much of this alloy must be added to 10 kg of element A in order to form another alloy containing 40 % of A? Assume no loss on mixing.
   (G.G.L.I.)

7. Complete the following table:

Vulgar fraction	Decimal fraction	Percentage
$\frac{1}{2}$	0.5	50 %
$\frac{1}{4}$	—	—
—	0.25	—
—	—	$12\frac{1}{2}$ %
$\frac{3}{8}$	—	—

8. The nominal value of a resistor is given as $150\ \Omega \pm 15\ \%$. What are the possible limits of the value of this resistor?

9. A bronze used for bearings consists of 74 % copper (Cu), 20 % lead (Pb), and 6 % tin (Sn). Find the mass of each element in a bearing of mass 15 kg.

10. The temperature coefficient of resistance of nickel, at and from 0 °C, is 0.0056/°C. From the results of an experiment it was found to be 0.005/°C. What is the percentage error in the experimental value?

11. A cutting-oil mixture is made up of water and oil in the ratio 18 : 1. How many litres of oil must be added to 72 litres of water?

12. How much copper (Cu) and zinc (Zn) will be required to make a 39 kg brass casting if the elements are to be in the ratio of 7 : 3 by mass?

13. If $(3R - r)/(2R + 3r) = 4/5$, find the ratio of $r : R$.

14. In a certain brass, the ratio of the mass of copper (Cu) to the mass of zinc (Zn) is 13 : 7.
    (a) How much copper should be mixed with 50 kg of zinc?
    (b) What mass of each element is contained in 60 kg of brass?
    (c) What is the percentage composition of brass by mass?

15. How long should seven pumps take to empty a large storage tank if it is known that three pumps can empty it in 19.25 hours? Assume that all the pumps are identical.

16. The quantity S is directly proportional to the square of d. If $S = 12\frac{1}{2}$ when $d = \frac{1}{2}$, calculate the value of S when $d = \frac{3}{4}$.

17. Hooke's law states that within the elastic range of a material the deformation is directly proportional to the applied force producing it. A helical spring shortens by 25 mm when a compressive force of 150 N is applied. Calculate the total shortening if an additional 90 N were applied.

18. The strength of a beam is inversely proportional to its span. If a certain beam will carry a uniformly distributed dead load of 2 tonnes over a span of 4 metres, what load would it carry over a span of (i) 3 m and (ii) 5 m?

19. An electrical immersion heater will raise the temperature of 10 litres of water by 60 °C in 20 minutes. Assuming that heat losses occur at a constant rate, how long will it take to heat (i) 10 litres through 45 °C and (ii) 15 litres through 30 °C?

20. When two pulleys, diameters d_1 and d_2, are connected by a belt, the rotational speeds n_1 and n_2 are given by $n_1 : n_2 = d_2 : d_1$. Assuming that no slip or creep occurs between the belt and the pulleys, find the rotational speed of the larger one if their diameters are 140 mm and 350 mm and the smaller pulley makes 130 rev/min.

ANSWERS TO EXERCISES 3

1. 0.35 mm, 0.2 mm/h.

2. 52.47 °C.

3. 40p, 87.5 %, 75 %, 137.5 %.

4. (a) 483 000,   (b) 30.6 mm,

5. 6500 litres.

6. 40 kg.

7. 0.75, 75 %, $\frac{1}{4}$, 25 %, $\frac{1}{8}$, 0.125, 0.375, $37\frac{1}{2}$ %.

8. 172.5 Ω, 127.5 Ω.

9. Cu 11.1 kg, Pb 3 kg, Sn 0.9 kg.

10. 10.71 %.

11. 4 litres.

12. Cu 27.3 kg, Zn 11.7 kg.

13. 2.429:1.

14. (a) 92.86 kg,   (b) Cu 39 kg, Zn 21 kg,
(c) Cu 65 %, Zn 35 %.

15. 8.25 h.

16. 28.1.

17. 40 mm.

18. (i) 2.67 t,   (ii) 1.6 t.

19. (i) 15 min,   (ii) 15 min.

20. 52 rev/min.

4 | Indices, standard form, and binary notation

4.1. INDICES

In mathematics it is often convenient, particularly for ease of calculation, to use a shortened method of writing long and sometimes repetitive statements. Consider, for example, the simple conversion of 1 cubic metre into cubic centimetres. The method of conversion is as follows:

$$1 \text{ cubic metre} = 100 \times 100 \times 100$$
$$= 10 \times 10 \times 10 \times 10 \times 10$$
$$\times 10 \text{ cubic centimetres.}$$

If, therefore, in a problem it was necessary to repeat this statement a number of times, the process would undoubtedly become extremely laborious. To overcome this repetition the quantity $10 \times 10 \times 10 \times 10 \times 10 \times 10$ is written as 10^6; the 6, written to the right and slightly higher than the 10, is called the *index or power* and indicates the number of times the 10 is written down and multiplied together. The 10 is termed the *base*. Further examples showing the use of *indices* (plural of *index*) are given below:

$$3 \times 3 \times 3 \times 3 = 3^4 \quad index = 4, \; base = 3$$
$$6 \times 6 \times 6 \times 6 \times 6 = 6^5 \quad index = 5, \; base = 6$$
$$a \times a = a^2 \quad index = 2, \; base = a$$
$$l \times l \times l = l^3 \quad index = 3, \; base = l$$

Numbers having an *index* are said to be 'raised to a *power*'. In the preceding examples,

3^4 is expressed as '3 *raised to the power* 4'.
6^5 is expressed as '6 *raised to the power* 5'.
a^2 is expressed as '*a raised to the power* 2', or '*a squared*'.
l^3 is expressed as '*l raised to the power* 3', or '*l cubed*'.

Note. 1 cubic metre may be written as $1\,\text{m}^3$, since $1\,\text{m} \times 1\,\text{m} \times 1\,\text{m} = 1\,\text{m}^3$. Similarly $1\,\text{cm} \times 1\,\text{cm} \times 1\,\text{cm} = 1\,\text{cm}^3$ or 1 cubic centimetre.

4.1.1. Laws of indices.
LAW 1. When multiplying quantities together containing powers, having the same base, *add the powers*.

EXAMPLE 4.1. Simplify $3^2 \times 3^5$.

SOLUTION

Method 1 $3^2 = 3 \times 3$
$$3^5 = 3 \times 3 \times 3 \times 3 \times 3$$
$$\therefore \; 3^2 \times 3^5 = 3 \times 3 \times 3 \times 3 \times 3 \times 3 \times 3$$
$$= 3^7$$

Method 2 $3^2 \times 3^5 = 3^{2+5} = 3^7$

The second method is obviously the one used in normal calculations.

EXAMPLE 4.2. Simplify $2^2 \times 2 \times 2^3$.

SOLUTION
$$2^2 \times 2 \times 2^3 = 2^{2+1+3} = 2^6$$

A number written without an index, such as the 2 in this question, indicates 2^1. The power 1 is normally omitted. Summary of Law 1: $a^m \times a^n = a^{m+n}$, where a, m and n are any numbers.

LAW 2. When dividing quantities containing powers, having the same base, *subtract the powers*.

EXAMPLE 4.3. Simplify $\dfrac{5^4}{5^2}$.

SOLUTION

Method 1 $5^4 = 5 \times 5 \times 5 \times 5$
$$5^2 = 5 \times 5$$
$$\therefore \; \frac{5^4}{5^2} = \frac{5 \times 5 \times 5 \times 5}{5 \times 5} = 5 \times 5 = 5^2$$

Method 2 $\dfrac{5^4}{5^2} = 5^{4-2} = 5^2$

As in example 4.1, the second method is obviously preferred in any calculation.

EXAMPLE 4.4. Evaluate $\dfrac{7^3}{7^5}$.

SOLUTION
$$\frac{7^3}{7^5} = \frac{1}{7^{5-3}} = \frac{1}{7^2}$$

Summary of Law 2: $\dfrac{a^m}{a^n} = a^{m-n}$ where a, m, and n are any numbers.

LAW 3. When a quantity containing a power is raised to a further power *multiply the powers together*.

EXAMPLE 4.5. Simplify $(6^4)^3$.

SOLUTION
$$(6^4)^3 = 6^4 \times 6^4 \times 6^4 = 6^{12}$$
$$\text{or} \quad (6^4)^3 = 6^{4 \times 3} = 6^{12}$$

EXAMPLE 4.6. Simplify $\left(\dfrac{1}{5^3}\right)^2$.

SOLUTION

$$\left(\frac{1}{5^3}\right)^2 = \frac{1}{5^{3\times2}} = \frac{1}{5^6}$$

Summary of Law 3: $(a^m)^n = a^{mn}$ and $\left(\frac{1}{a^m}\right)^n = \frac{1}{a^{mn}}$ where a, m, and n are any numbers.

4.1.2. Negative indices. It is sometimes more convenient and often necessary to express an index as a negative quantity. The significance of the negative index can be seen by comparing the following two statements:

$$\frac{1}{3^4} \times 3^6 = \frac{3^6}{3^4} = 3^{6-4} = 3^2 \quad \text{(see Law 2)}$$

$$3^{-4} \times 3^6 = 3^{6-4} = 3^2 \quad \quad \text{(see Law 1)}$$

Since the multiplication of $\frac{1}{3^4}$ and 3^{-4} by 3^6 gives the same result, i.e. 3^2, then it must be concluded that

$$\frac{1}{3^4} \equiv 3^{-4}.$$

The above example shows, therefore, that a number raised to a negative power is equal to the inverse of the number raised to the same (numerically equal) positive power.

Expressed in another way, $a^{-m} = \frac{1}{a^m}$ and $\frac{1}{a^{-m}} = a^m$ where a and m are any numbers.

EXAMPLE 4.7. Express the following quantities with negative indices:

(a) 2^4 (b) 10^6 (c) $\frac{1}{8^3}$ (d) $\frac{1}{9^2}$.

SOLUTION

(a) $2^4 = \frac{1}{2^{-4}}$

(b) $10^6 = \frac{1}{10^{-6}}$

(c) $\frac{1}{8^3} = 8^{-3}$

(d) $\frac{1}{9^2} = 9^{-2}$

EXAMPLE 4.8. Express the following as positive powers:

(a) 5^{-3} (b) 10^{-1} (c) $\frac{1}{6^{-2}}$ (d) $\frac{1}{7^{-4}}$

SOLUTION

(a) $5^{-3} = \frac{1}{5^3}$

(b) $10^{-1} = \frac{1}{10^1} = \frac{1}{10}$

(c) $\frac{1}{6^{-2}} = 6^2$

(d) $\frac{1}{7^{-4}} = 7^4$

4.1.3. Fractional indices—roots of a number. Again it is often more convenient to express the root of a quantity in the form of a fractional power. Compare the following two statements:

$$\sqrt{4} \times \sqrt{4} = 4$$

$$4^{\frac{1}{2}} \times 4^{\frac{1}{2}} = 4^{\frac{1}{2}+\frac{1}{2}} = 4 \quad \text{(see Law 1)}$$

$$\therefore \sqrt{4} = 4^{\frac{1}{2}}$$

Hence any number raised to the power $\frac{1}{2}$ is the same as the square root of that number. In the same way, any root of a number can be represented by means of a fractional index. In general, $\sqrt[n]{a} = a^{\frac{1}{n}}$.

EXAMPLE 4.9. Express the following roots in fractional index form:

(a) $\sqrt{10}$ (b) $\sqrt[3]{6}$ (c) $\sqrt[7]{98}$

SOLUTION

(a) $\sqrt{10} = 10^{\frac{1}{2}}$.
(b) $\sqrt[3]{6} = 6^{\frac{1}{3}}$.
Check: $6^{\frac{1}{3}} \times 6^{\frac{1}{3}} \times 6^{\frac{1}{3}} = 6^{\frac{1}{3}+\frac{1}{3}+\frac{1}{3}} = 6$,
or $\sqrt[3]{6} \times \sqrt[3]{6} \times \sqrt[3]{6} = 6$.
(c) $\sqrt[7]{98} = 98^{\frac{1}{7}}$.

EXAMPLE 4.10. Express the following with fractional indices:
(a) $\sqrt[3]{9^2}$ (b) $\sqrt[3]{8^4}$ (c) $\sqrt[4]{625^3}$

SOLUTION

(a) $\sqrt[3]{9^2} = 9^{\frac{2}{3}}$. (In words this means 'square the cube root of nine').
(b) $\sqrt[3]{8^4} = 8^{\frac{4}{3}}$. (In words 'raise the cube root of eight to the power of four').
(c) $\sqrt[4]{625^3} = 625^{\frac{3}{4}}$. (This indicates 'cube the fourth root of 625').
Note 1. In every case the denominator of the fraction represents the required root of the number and the numerator is the power to which that root must be raised.

EXAMPLE 4.11. Evaluate $25^{\frac{3}{2}}$.

SOLUTION

$$25^{\frac{3}{2}} = (25^{\frac{1}{2}})^3 = 5^3 = 125.$$

Note 2. The arithmetic involved in the questions is simplified if the root of the number is first calculated and then raised to the required power.

EXAMPLE 4.12. Evaluate $8^{-\frac{2}{3}}$.

SOLUTION

$$8^{-\frac{2}{3}} = \frac{1}{8^{\frac{2}{3}}} \quad \text{(Invert to make the index positive).}$$

$$\frac{1}{8^{\frac{2}{3}}} = \frac{1}{\sqrt[3]{8^2}} = \frac{1}{(\sqrt[3]{8})^2} = \frac{1}{2^2} = \frac{1}{4}$$

EXAMPLE 4.13. Evaluate $\sqrt[4]{16^3} \times \sqrt[4]{16^5}$.

SOLUTION

$$\sqrt[4]{16^3} \times \sqrt[4]{16^5} = 16^{\frac{3}{4}} \times 16^{\frac{5}{4}}$$
$$= 16^{\frac{3}{4}+\frac{5}{4}}$$
$$= 16^{\frac{8}{4}} = 16^2$$
$$16^2 = 256.$$

4.1.4. Quantities to power zero. Consider the following statements:

$$\frac{1}{5^2} \times 5^2 = 5^{2-2} = 5^0. \quad \text{(see Law 2)}$$

$$\text{or} \quad \frac{1}{5^2} \times 5^2 = \frac{1}{5^{2-2}} = \frac{1}{5^0}.$$

$$\text{But} \quad \frac{1}{5^2} \times 5^2 = 1 \quad \text{(by inspection)}$$

$$\therefore \ 5^0 = 1.$$

Similarly, any quantity raised to the power 0 equals 1.

EXAMPLE 4.14. Simplify without using any tables:

(i) $\dfrac{\sqrt{63}}{\sqrt{7}}$ (ii) $16^{\frac{3}{4}}$ (iii) $(6\frac{1}{4})^{\frac{1}{2}}$ (E.M.E.U.)

SOLUTION (i)

Method 1: $\dfrac{\sqrt{63}}{\sqrt{7}} = \sqrt{9} = 3.$

Method 2: $\dfrac{\sqrt{63}}{\sqrt{7}} = \dfrac{\sqrt{(9 \times 7)}}{\sqrt{7}} = \dfrac{9^{\frac{1}{2}} \times 7^{\frac{1}{2}}}{7^{\frac{1}{2}}}$ since power $\frac{1}{2}$ means 'square root of' this simplifies to $9^{\frac{1}{2}} = 3.$

SOLUTION (ii)

$$16^{\frac{3}{4}} = (16^{\frac{1}{4}})^3.$$

The fourth root of $16 = 2$

$$\therefore \ 2^3 = 8.$$

In this problem had the 16 been raised to the power 3 before the fourth root was found, then the arithmetic would have been much more involved.

SOLUTION (iii)

$$(6\tfrac{1}{4})^{-\frac{1}{2}}$$

The mixed number $6\frac{1}{4}$ must first be written as an improper fraction,

i.e. $6\frac{1}{4}$ becomes $\dfrac{25}{4}$.

$$\left(\frac{25}{4}\right)^{-\frac{1}{2}} = \frac{1}{\left(\dfrac{25}{4}\right)^{\frac{1}{2}}} \quad \text{(The power } -\tfrac{1}{2} \text{ becomes } \tfrac{1}{2} \text{ after inversion)}$$

$$\frac{1}{\left(\dfrac{25}{4}\right)^{\frac{1}{2}}} = \left(\frac{4}{25}\right)^{\frac{1}{2}} = \frac{2}{5}$$

since $\left(\dfrac{4}{25}\right)^{\frac{1}{2}} = \sqrt{\dfrac{4}{25}}.$

Note. The square root sign applies to both the numerator and denominator of the fraction.

EXAMPLE 4.15. Express the following as powers of 2:
(a) 16
(b) 1
(c) $\frac{1}{8}$.

SOLUTION

(a) $16 = 2^4$
(b) $1 = 2^0$ (Any quantity to the power of 0 equals 1).
(c) $\dfrac{1}{8} = \dfrac{1}{2^3} = 2^{-3}$

EXAMPLE 4.16. Evaluate $\dfrac{10^2 \times 10^{-3} \times 10^7}{10 \times 10^4 \times 10^{-1}}$.

SOLUTION

$$\frac{10^2 \times 10^{-3} \times 10^7}{10 \times 10^4 \times 10^{-1}} = \frac{10^{2-3+7}}{10^{1+4-1}}$$
$$= \frac{10^6}{10^4}$$
$$= 10^{6-4}$$
$$= 10^2 = 100$$

4.2. STANDARD FORM

Calculations involving very large or very small numbers can often be simplified by writing them in standard form and then applying the laws of indices.

A number is said to be expressed in standard form when it is written in the following manner,

$N \times 10^m$ where N is a number lying between 1 and 10 and m is a positive or negative power.

EXAMPLE 4.17. Express the following in standard form:
(a) 1 000 000 (b) 610 000 (c) 0.000 0016
(d) 0.00053

SOLUTION

(a) $1\,000\,000 = 1.0 \times 10^6$ (or simply 10^6).

(b) $610\,000 = 6.1 \times 10^5$

(c) In this case, for simplicity, the decimal 0.000 001 6 may be written as $\dfrac{1.6}{1\,000\,000} = \dfrac{1.6}{10^6}$.

Then $\dfrac{1.6}{10^6} = 1.6 \times 10^{-6}$ (see section 4.1.2).

(d) $0.000\,53 = \dfrac{5.3}{10\,000}$

$\qquad = \dfrac{5.3}{10^4} = 5.3 \times 10^{-4}$

EXAMPLE 4.18. Express the following thermal coefficients of linear expansion in standard form:

(a) Aluminium 0.000 024 per °C
(b) Copper 0.000 017 per °C
(c) Brass 0.000 019 per °C
(d) Iron 0.000 011 per °C.

SOLUTION

(a) Aluminium:
   0.000 024 per °C $= 2.4 \times 10^{-5}$ per °C.
(b) Copper:
   0.000 017 per °C $= 1.7 \times 10^{-5}$ per °C.
(c) Brass:
   0.000 019 per °C $= 1.9 \times 10^{-5}$ per °C.
(d) Iron:
   0.000 011 per °C $= 1.1 \times 10^{-5}$ per °C.

Note. It can be seen that it is much easier to make a comparison between these values when they are written in standard form, as one doesn't get confused by the number of zeros.

EXAMPLE 4.19. Evaluate:

(a) $0.000\,25 \times 4\,000\,000$.

(b) $\dfrac{39\,000\,000}{0.000\,013}$.

SOLUTION

(a) Expressed in standard form

$$0.000\,25 = 2.5 \times 10^{-4}$$

$$\text{and } 4\,000\,000 = 4 \times 10^6$$

$$0.000\,25 \times 4\,000\,000 = 2.5 \times 10^{-4} \times 4 \times 10^6$$

$$= 2.5 \times 4 \times 10^{-4+6}$$

$$= 10 \times 10^2 = 10^3 = 1000.$$

(b) Again expressing the two quantities in standard form

$$\frac{39\,000\,000}{0.000\,013} = \frac{3.9 \times 10^7}{1.3 \times 10^{-5}}$$

$$= 3 \times 10^{7+5}$$

$$= 3 \times 10^{12}$$

$$= 3000\,000\,000\,000.$$

EXAMPLE 4.20. Evaluate: $1.27 \times 10^6 + 6 \times 10^7$.

SOLUTION

$$1.27 \times 10^6 + 6 \times 10^7 = 1.27 \times 10^6 + 6 \times 10 \times 10^6$$

$$= (1.27 + 60) \times 10^6$$

$$= 61.27 \times 10^6.$$

EXAMPLE 4.21. Convert the following to standard form and hence find their sum: 0.000 17, 0.000 86, and 0.000 188.

SOLUTION

$$0.000\,17 = 1.7 \times 10^{-4}$$

$$0.000\,86 = 8.6 \times 10^{-4}$$

$$0.000\,188 = 1.88 \times 10^{-4}$$

$$1.7 \times 10^{-4} + 8.6 \times 10^{-4} + 1.88 \times 10^{-4}$$

$$= (1.7 + 8.6 + 1.88) \times 10^{-4}$$

$$= 12.18 \times 10^{-4}.$$

In standard form, $12.18 \times 10^{-4} = 1.218 \times 10^{-3}$.

EXAMPLE 4.22. Express 1/250 000 in standard form.

SOLUTION

Written in index form

$$\frac{1}{250\,000} = \frac{1}{25 \times 10^4}$$

$$= \frac{1}{25} \times \frac{1}{10^4}.$$

Written as a decimal $\dfrac{1}{25} = \dfrac{4}{100} = 0.04$.

$$\therefore \frac{1}{25} \times \frac{1}{10^4} = 0.04 \times 10^{-4} \quad \text{(see section 4.1.2)}$$

Written in standard form $0.04 = 4 \times 10^{-2}$

$$\therefore \ 0.04 \times 10^{-4} = 4 \times 10^{-2} \times 10^{-4}$$

$$= 4 \times 10^{-6} \text{ (see section 4.1.1)}$$

$$\therefore \frac{1}{250\,000} = 4.0 \times 10^{-6}.$$

4.3. BINARY NOTATION

The binary system of numbers may be better understood if our normal number system, i.e. the denary or decimal system, is more closely examined.

4.3.1. Denary or decimal system.
All numbers of the denary or decimal system are formed by multiplying powers of 10, i.e. base 10, by a selection of integers chosen from 0 to 9. Consider the following table.

TABLE 4.1. *Denary (decimal) system.*

	10^6	10^5	10^4	10^3	10^2	10^1	10^0 $(10^0 = 1)$	10^{-1}	10^{-2}	10^{-3}
Example (a)				1	5	9	2			
Example (b)						8	9	(.)1		
Example (c)		2	3	0	6	1	8			
Example (d)					2	0	1	(.)4	6	

Example (a)
$$1592 = 1 \times 10^3 + 5 \times 10^2 + 9 \times 10^1 + 2 \times 10^0$$
$$= 1000 + 500 + 90 + 2$$
$$= 1592.$$

Example (b)
$$89.1 = 8 \times 10^1 + 9 \times 10^0 + 1 \times 10^{-1} \quad \text{(See section 4.1.2)}$$
$$= 80 + 9 + 0.1$$
$$= 89.1$$

Example (c)
$$230\,618 = 2 \times 10^5 + 3 \times 10^4 + 0 \times 10^3 + 6 \times 10^2 + 1 \times 10^1 + 8 \times 10^0$$
$$= 200\,000 + 30\,000 + 0 + 600 + 10 + 8$$
$$= 230\,618$$

Example (d)
$$201.46 = 2 \times 10^2 + 0 \times 10^1 + 1 \times 10^0 + 4 \times 10^{-1} + 6 \times 10^{-2}$$
$$= 200 + 0 + 1 + 0.4 + 0.06$$
$$= 201.46$$

The table, together with the examples (a) to (d), is intended to illustrate the following points.
1. The base of the denary (decimal) system is 10.
2. All numbers in this system are obtained by multiplying a power of 10 by an integer chosen from 0 to 9. Note that the highest integer used, i.e. 9, is one less than the base 10.
3. The powers of 10 increase by one with each step from right to left.
4. Where a certain power of 10 does not occur in a number this is indicated by a zero.

5. Negative powers of 10 give rise to decimal fractions (see section 4.1.2).
6. The final number is arrived at by adding together the various powers of 10.

4.3.2. Binary system.
The binary system (bi meaning two) has a base of 2. All numbers in this system are therefore obtained by multiplying a power of 2 by 0 or 1. Note that the highest integer used, i.e. 1, is one less than the base 2. Compare the following table and examples with examples (a) to (d) given under the decimal system (section 4.3.1)

TABLE 4.2. *Binary system.*

	2^6	2^5	2^4	2^3	2^2	2^1	2^0 $(2^0 = 1)$	2^{-1}	2^{-2}	2^{-3}
Example (a)			1	0	1	1	0			
Example (b)					1	1	1			
Example (c)			1	0	1	1	(.)1	0	1	
Example (d)							1	(.)0	1	

Example (a) Binary number $10110 = 1 \times 2^4 + 0 \times 2^3 + 1 \times 2^2 + 1 \times 2^1 + 0 \times 2^0$. Written in the denary or decimal system this becomes
$$16 + 0 + 4 + 2 = 22.$$
$\therefore$ binary number $10110 = 22$ on the denary system.

Example (b) Binary number $111 = 1 \times 2^2 + 1 \times 2^1 + 1 \times 2^0$. Written in denary this becomes
$$4 + 2 + 1 = 7$$
$\therefore$ binary number $111 = 7$ denary.

Example (c) Binary number $1011.101 = 1 \times 2^3 + 0 \times 2^2 + 1 \times 2^1 + 1 \times 2^0 + 1 \times 2^{-1} + 0 \times 2^{-2} + 1 \times 2^{-3}$. Written in the denary system this becomes
$$8 + 4 + 2 + 1 + \frac{1}{2^1} + 0 + \frac{1}{2^3}$$
$$= 15 + \tfrac{1}{2} + \tfrac{1}{8}$$
$$= 15\tfrac{5}{8}$$
$\therefore$ binary number $1011.101 = 15.625$ $(\tfrac{5}{8} = 0.625)$

Example (d) Binary number $1.01 = 1 \times 2^0 + 0 \times 2^{-1} + 1 \times 2^{-2}$. Written in the denary system
$$1 + 0 + \frac{1}{2^2} = 1\tfrac{1}{4}$$
$\therefore$ binary number $1.01 = 1.25$ denary.

Note. To prevent continued repetition of the terms denary, binary, etc. it is usual to indicate the base of a number in the following manner. Referring to examples (a) to (d):

(a) $10110_2 = 22_{10}$
(b) $111_2 = 7_{10}$
(c) $1011.101_2 = 15.625_{10}$
(d) $1.01_2 = 1.25_{10}$.

4.3.3. Applications of the binary system. The great importance of the binary system is in its ability to express all numbers in terms of 0 and 1. This feature is particularly significant since it allows numbers to be represented very easily both mechanically and electrically. One example of this is the use of the binary notation in computer work.

Paper tape containing certain patterns of holes is used to feed information to the computer. The patterns of punched holes can be read by an input device which consists of a source of light above the tape and photoelectric cells below the tape. The holes in the tape allow light to reach the photocells, which in consequence generate electrical pulses. The blanks in the tape give rise to no pulses. This results in a full pattern of pulses and no pulses being sent to the computer. Referring to the binary system, a pulse represents 1 and the absence of a pulse represents 0.

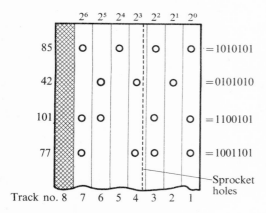

Fig. 4.1

Fig. 4.1 is a diagrammatic representation of an eight-track computer paper tape. Track eight is hatched out as this is normally used for checking purposes. The other seven tracks provide the means of denoting a power of two.

A one is represented by a hole in the tape which allows a signal to pass; a zero is represented by a blank which prevents a signal passing. Hence Fig. 4.1 shows how the numbers 85, 42, 101, and 77 may be represented on a computer tape. For example $85_{10} = 1010101_2$.

On the tape this is arrived at in the following manner:

Track No.	7	6	5	4	3	2	1
Power of 2	2^6	2^5	2^4	2^3	2^2	2^1	2^0
Tape state	hole	blank	hole	blank	hole	blank	hole
Binary equivalent	1	0	1	0	1	0	1

$\therefore$ Number recorded $= 1 \times 2^6 + 0 \times 2^5 + 1 \times 2^4 + 0 \times 2^3 + 1 \times 2^2 + 0 \times 2^1 + 1 \times 2^0$

$$= 85_{10}.$$

Fig. 4.2 shows the numbers 85, 42, 101, and 77 expressed diagrammatically as electrical pulses.

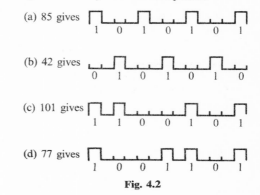

Fig. 4.2

4.3.4. Conversion of binary numbers to denary form. Although the method of conversion was explained earlier in the chapter a further number of worked examples are now given.

EXAMPLE 4.23. Express the following numbers in denary (decimal) form.
(a) 1101_2 (b) 1001_2

SOLUTION

Note. In the binary system the 1 or 0 indicate the presence or absence of a power of 2. Moving from right to left the powers of 2 increase by one, the starting point being 2^0. Note particularly that $2^0 = 1$.

(a) $1101_2 = 1 \times 2^3 + 1 \times 2^2 + 0 \times 2^1 + 1 \times 2^0$

$$= 8 + 4 + 0 + 1$$

$$= 13_{10}$$

$\therefore 1101_2 = 13$

(b) $1001_2 = 1 \times 2^3 + 0 \times 2^2 + 0 \times 2^1 + 1 \times 2^0$

$$= 8 + 0 + 0 + 1$$

$$= 9_{10}$$

$\therefore 1001_2 = 9$

4.3.5. Conversion of denary form to binary. The conversion of a number from the denary (decimal) form to the binary form is illustrated in the following examples. It is achieved by repeatedly dividing the number given by 2 and recording the remainders.

The remainders written in the correct sequence provide the answer.

EXAMPLE 4.24. Convert 47_{10} to binary form.

SOLUTION

Divide 47 repeatedly by 2 and record the remainders as follows.

Expressed in words:

2 into 47 goes 23 remainder 1.

2 into 23 goes 11 remainder 1.

2 into 11 goes 5 remainder 1.

2 into 5 goes 2 remainder 1.

2 into 2 goes 1 remainder 0.

2 into 1 goes 0 remainder 1.

Or, briefly,

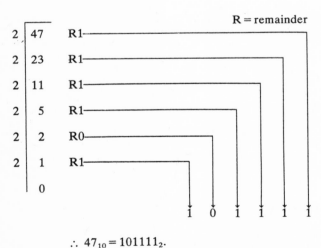

$$\therefore 47_{10} = 101111_2.$$

EXAMPLE 4.25. Convert 26_{10} to base 2 (binary).

SOLUTION

The method of solution is as described in Example 4.24 above.

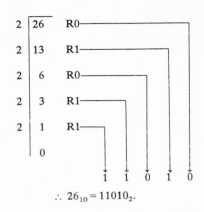

$$\therefore 26_{10} = 11010_2.$$

4.3.6. Addition of binary numbers. The method of addition in the binary system is very similar to that applied in the decimal system and can be achieved by applying three simple rules, which are as follows:

$$\text{Rule 1. } 0 + 0 = 0$$

$$\text{Rule 2. } 0 + 1 = 1$$

$$\text{Rule 3. } 1 + 1 = 0 \text{ carry } 1$$

EXAMPLE 4.26. Add the numbers 1101_2 and 1001_2.

SOLUTION

$$
\begin{array}{r}
1101_2 \\
1001_2 \\
\hline
10110_2 \\
\hline
\end{array}
$$

Check. Convert all quantities back to the decimal system.

$$
\begin{array}{r}
1101_2 = 13_{10} \\
1001_2 = 9_{10} \\
\hline
10110_2 = 22_{10} \\
\hline
\end{array}
$$

EXAMPLE 4.27. Find the value of

(a) $1111_2 + 1011_2$ (b) $11011_2 + 111_2$

(c) $11_2 + 1100_2$

SOLUTION

(a)
$$
\begin{array}{r}
1111_2 + \\
1011_2 \\
\hline
11010_2 \\
\hline
\end{array}
$$

Check.
$$
\begin{array}{r}
1111_2 = 15_{10} + \\
1011_2 = 11_{10} \\
\hline
11010_2 = 26_{10} \\
\hline
\end{array}
$$

(b)
$$
\begin{array}{r}
11011_2 + \\
111_2 \\
\hline
100010_2 \\
\hline
\end{array}
$$

Check.
$$11011_2 = 27_{10} +$$
$$111_2 = 7_{10}$$
$$\overline{100010_2 = 34_{10}}$$

(c)
$$11_2 +$$
$$1100_2$$
$$\overline{1111_2}$$

Check.
$$11_2 = 3_{10} +$$
$$1100_2 = 12_{10}$$
$$\overline{1111_2 = 15_{10}}$$

A fuller explanation of the three rules for the addition of binary numbers is given below.

Rule 1. $0 + 0 = 0$ (self explanatory).

Rule 2. $0 + 1 = 1$ (self explanatory).

Rule 3. $1 + 1 = 0$ carry 1 to the next column.

Consider the following examples:
$$2^0 + 2^0 = 2 \times 2^0 = 2^{1+0} = 2^1$$
$$2^1 + 2^1 = 2 \times 2^1 = 2^{1+1} = 2^2$$
$$2^2 + 2^2 = 2 \times 2^2 = 2^{1+2} = 2^3$$

From these examples it can be seen that the addition of two 2's raised to the same power gives rise to one 2 raised to the next highest power. Hence rule 3 applies, i.e. 0 down carry 1.

From Rules 2 and 3 together it can be seen that

$$1 + 1 + 1 = 1 \text{ carry } 1.$$

EXERCISES 4

1. Express the following as a single power of 2:
(a) $2 \times 2 \times 2$,   (b) $2^3 \times 2$,   (c) $2^2 \times 2^2$,

(d) $2^4 \times 2^3$,   (e) $\dfrac{2^6}{2^3}$,   (f) $\dfrac{2^3 \times 2^2}{2^2}$,

(g) $\dfrac{2 \times 2^2}{2^5}$,   (h) 8,   (i) 32,

(j) $\frac{1}{4}$,   (k) $\frac{1}{16}$,   (l) 1.

2. Express the following quantities with negative indices:

(a) 3^2,   (b) 5^3,   (c) $\dfrac{1}{6^4}$,

(d) $\sqrt{10}$,   (e) $\dfrac{1}{\sqrt{12}}$,   (f) $\sqrt[3]{7}$.

3. Use the laws of indices to simplify:
(a) $\dfrac{10^3}{10^{-1} \times 10^5}$,   (b) $\dfrac{10^4 \times 10^{-3} \times 10^2}{10^{-6} \times 10^5}$,

(c) $\dfrac{10^5 \times 10^2}{(10^2)^5}$,   (d) $\dfrac{10^6 \times 10^3}{(10^2)^4}$,

(e) $\dfrac{10^3 \times 10^{-2}}{10^{-1}}$.

4. Without using tables evaluate:
(a) $27^{\frac{2}{3}}$,   (b) $8^{\frac{2}{3}}$,   (c) $\left(\dfrac{8}{27}\right)^{\frac{2}{3}}$,   (d) $\left(\dfrac{16^{\frac{3}{4}}}{9^{\frac{3}{2}}}\right)^{\frac{1}{3}}$,

(e) $(2\frac{1}{4})^{\frac{1}{2}}$,   (f) $1000^{\frac{1}{3}}$,   (g) $\left(\dfrac{4}{25}\right)^{\frac{3}{2}}$,   (h) $(6\frac{1}{4})^{\frac{3}{2}}$.

5. Evaluate without using tables:
(a $\left(\dfrac{64}{27}\right)^{-\frac{1}{3}}$,   (b) $\left(\dfrac{8}{27}\right)^{-\frac{2}{3}}$,   (c) $4^{-\frac{1}{2}}$,   (d) $\left(\dfrac{2^2}{2^{-1}}\right)^2$,

(e) $(2\frac{1}{4})^{-\frac{1}{2}}$,   (f) $\left(\dfrac{16}{25}\right)^{-\frac{3}{2}}$,   (g) $\dfrac{1}{2^{-3}}$,   (h) $100^{-\frac{1}{2}}$,

(i) $\left(\dfrac{2^3}{3^2}\right)^{-2}$,   (j) 7^{-2},   (k) $(12\frac{1}{4})^{-\frac{1}{2}}$.

6. Find the numerical value of:
(a) $2\frac{1}{2} \times 2\frac{2}{3}$,   (b) $(16\frac{1}{2})^{-3}$.

(U.E.I.)

7. Write each of the following in its simplest form without indices:

(a) $(-1)^3$,   (b) $\dfrac{1}{(0.5)^2}$,   (c) $\dfrac{1}{2^{-4}}$.

(Y.H.C.F.E.)

8. Express the following in standard form:
(a) 100 000,   (b) 1 000 000,   (c) 17 000,
(d) 22 400,   (e) 13 600,   (f) 7200,
(g) 45 600,   (h) 760 000.

9. Convert the following to standard form:
(a) 0.000 582,   (b) 0.000 339,   (c) 0.003 04,
(d) 0.0042,   (e) 0.003 16,   (f) 0.000 011 9,
(g) 0.000 010 2.

10. Express the following in normal decimal form:
(a) 1.2×10^3,   (b) 2.35×10^4,   (c) 4.01×10^3,
(d) 8.34×10^5,   (e) 1.76×10^4,   (f) 1.16×10^5.

11. Convert the following from standard to decimal form:
(a) 5.6×10^{-4},   (b) 4.3×10^{-3},   (c) 2.55×10^{-6},
(d) 1.67×10^{-6},   (e) 1.3×10^{-5},   (f) 2.7×10^{-3},
(g) 1.1×10^{-2},   (h) 3.8×10^{-5}.

12. Evaluate the following expressing the answer in standard form:
(a) $1.7 \times 10^3 + 2.3 \times 10^3$,   (b) $2.34 \times 10^{-2} + 1.02 \times 10^{-2}$,
(c) $4.06 \times 10^6 + 7.1 \times 10^6$,   (d) $61 \times 10^3 - 2.1 \times 10^4$,
(e) $34.4 \times 10^5 - 1.4 \times 10^6$,   (f) $1.3 \times 10^6 + 2.7 \times 10^5$,
(g) $2.31 \times 10^{-4} - 1.1 \times 10^{-5}$, (h) $3.4 \times 10^6 + 0.17 \times 10^7$.

13. Convert each quantity to standard form and evaluate the quantities:

(a) $\dfrac{0.000\,81 \times 240\,000 \times 3000}{27\,000\,000 \times 0.000\,27}$,

(b) $\left(\dfrac{0.144 \times 10^5}{0.09 \times 10^{-2}}\right)^{\frac{1}{2}}$.

14. Express the following in standard form:

(a) $\dfrac{1}{400\,000}$,   (b) $\dfrac{1}{5000}$,

(c) $\dfrac{1}{8\,000\,000}$,   (d) $\dfrac{1}{20\,000}$.

15. Complete the following table:

Element	Electrochemical equivalent (z) g/C.	
	Normal decimal form	Standard form
Cadmium	0.000 582	5.82×10^{-4}
Chromium	0.000 089 8	
Copper		3.29×10^{-4}
Hydrogen	0.000 010 45	
Nickel	0.000 304	
Silver		1.118×10^{-3}
Zinc	0.000 339	

16. Complete the following table:

Material	Thermal coefficients of expansion (per °C)		
	Linear (α)	Superficial (2α)	Cubical (3α)
Aluminium	0.000 025 5	5.1×10^{-5}	7.65×10^{-5}
Brass		3.78×10^{-5}	
Copper			5.01×10^{-5}
Lead	0.000 029 1		
Nickel		2.56×10^{-5}	
Zinc	0.000 026 3		

17. Express the following binary numbers in denary form:
(a) 110, (b) 1011, (c) 1111, (d) 10101,
(e) 11011, (f) 100101, (g) 101011, (h) 110000,
(i) 110111, (j) 111111.

18. Convert the following denary numbers to binary form:
(a) 5, (b) 20, (c) 31, (d) 41,
(e) 46, (f) 52, (g) 59, (h) 62.

19. Find the sum of the following binary numbers:
(a) 101 + 1101, (b) 110 + 1010,
(c) 10110 + 010111, (d) 1011 + 10001,
(e) 100001 + 1101, (f) 101100 + 110,
(g) 10101 + 1010, (h) 11111 + 1111,
(i) 101010 + 10101, (j) 111001 + 110.

20. Read the four binary numbers off the computer tape, shown in Fig. 4.3, and convert into denary form.

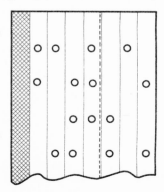

Fig. 4.3

21. Convert the following binary numbers to denary form:
(a) 10100.101, (b) 111.01, (c) 1101.111,
(d) 1001.001, (e) 111.011, (f) 1.0001,
(g) 101.1001, (h) 1001.11.

ANSWERS TO EXERCISES 4

1. (a) 2^3, (b) 2^4, (c) 2^4, (d) 2^7,
(e) 2^3, (f) 2^3, (g) 2^{-2}, (h) 2^3,
(i) 2^5, (j) 2^{-2}, (k) 2^{-4}, (l) 2^0.

2. (a) $1/3^{-2}$, (b) $1/5^{-3}$, (c) 6^{-4}, (d) $1/10^{-\frac{1}{2}}$,
(e) $12^{-\frac{1}{2}}$, (f) $1/7^{-\frac{1}{3}}$.

3. (a) 1/10, (b) 10^4, (c) $1/10^3$, (d) 10, (e) 10^2.

4. (a) 9, (b) 4, (c) 4/9, (d) 2/3,
(e) 3/2, (f) 10, (g) 8/125, (h) 125/8.

5. (a) 3/4, (b) 9/4, (c) 1/2, (d) 64,
(e) 2/3, (f) 125/64, (g) 8, (h) 1/10,
(i) 81/64, (j) 1/49, (k) 2/7.

6. (a) 8, (b) 1/64.

7. (a) −1, (b) 4, (c) 16.

8. (a) 1.0×10^5, (b) 1.0×10^6, (c) 1.7×10^4,
(d) 2.24×10^4, (e) 1.36×10^4, (f) 7.2×10^3,
(g) 4.56×10^4, (h) 7.6×10^5.

9. (a) 5.82×10^{-4}, (b) 3.39×10^{-4}, (c) 3.04×10^{-3},
(d) 4.2×10^{-3}, (e) 3.16×10^{-3}, (f) 1.19×10^{-5},
(g) 1.02×10^{-5}.

10. (a) 1200, (b) 23 500, (c) 4010,
(d) 834 000, (e) 17 600, (f) 116 000.

11. (a) 0.000 56, (b) 0.0043, (c) 0.000 002 55,
(d) 0.000 001 67, (e) 0.000 013, (f) 0.0027,
(g) 0.011, (h) 0.000 038.

12. (a) 4.0×10^3, (b) 3.36×10^{-2}, (c) 1.107×10^7,
(d) 4.0×10^4, (e) 2.04×10^6, (f) 1.57×10^6,
(g) 2.2×10^{-4}, (h) 5.1×10^6.

13. (a) 80, (b) 4000.

14. (a) 2.5×10^{-6}, (b) 2.0×10^{-4}, (c) 1.25×10^{-7},
(d) 5.0×10^{-5}.

15. 8.98×10^{-5}, 0.000 329, 1.045×10^{-5},
3.04×10^{-4}, 0.001 118, 3.39×10^{-4}.

16. 0.000 018 9, 5.67×10^{-5}, 0.000 016 7,
3.34×10^{-5}, 5.82×10^{-5}, 8.73×10^{-5},
0.000 012 8, 3.84×10^{-5}, 5.26×10^{-5},
7.89×10^{-5}.

17. (a) 6, (b) 11, (c) 15, (d) 21, (e) 27,
(f) 37, (g) 43, (h) 48, (i) 55, (j) 63.

18. (a) 101, (b) 10100, (c) 11111, (d) 101001,
(e) 101110, (f) 110100, (g) 111011, (h) 111110.

19. (a) 10010, (b) 10000, (c) 101101,
(d) 11100, (e) 101110, (f) 110010,
(g) 11111, (h) 101110, (i) 111111,
(j) 111111.

20. 1101010 (106), 1011001 (89),
0011100 (28), 0110101 (53).

21. (a) 20.625, (b) 7.25, (c) 13.875,
(d) 9.125, (e) 7.375, (f) 1.0625,
(g) 5.5625, (h) 9.75.

5 | Powers, roots, and reciprocals

5.1. POWERS

From Chapter 4 it will be remembered that in any number such as 10^3, 10 is known as the base of the number and 3 is the index or power. The index or power indicates the number of times the base must be multiplied by itself to give the number.

$$\textbf{Number} = \textbf{(base)}^{\textbf{power}}$$

EXAMPLE 5.1. Without using tables, find the value of :

(i) $(15)^2$, (ii) $(1.2)^3$, (iii) $(\frac{2}{5})^3$,
(iv) $(0.9)^4$, (v) $(1\frac{4}{5})^2$.

SOLUTION

(i) $15^2 = 15 \times 15 = 225$
(ii) $1.2^3 = 1.2 \times 1.2 \times 1.2 = 1.728$
(iii) $(\frac{2}{5})^3 = \frac{2}{5} \times \frac{2}{5} \times \frac{2}{5} = \frac{8}{125}$
(iv) $0.9^4 = 0.9 \times 0.9 \times 0.9 \times 0.9 = 0.6561$
(v) $(1\frac{4}{5})^2 = (\frac{9}{5})^2 = \frac{9}{5} \times \frac{9}{5} = \frac{81}{25} = 3\frac{6}{25}$

5.1.1. Table of squares. Suppose the square (second power) of a number such as 3.142 is required. Multiplying 3.142 by 3.142 gives 9.872 164. An alternative to the laborious and lengthy process of multiplying 3.142 by itself is to use a table of squares. Four-figure tables are generally used and are described here. Other tables, for example five-figure, are also available. An inspection of such tables will show that the position of the decimal point must be determined separately.

EXAMPLE 5.2. From mathematical tables, but without using logarithms, find the value of:

(i) $(3.142)^2$ and (ii) $(31.42)^2$.

SOLUTION

(i) The value of $(3.142)^2$ is obtained from the table of squares, the appropriate extract being given below.

The number to be squared, expressed to four significant figures when using four-figure tables, is split into

three parts, the first part being formed by the first two significant figures, and the two others being the remaining digits, in this example 3.1 4 2. The decimal point is then temporarily ignored and the table used as shown by the arrows.

Adding 9860 and 13 gives 9873 and the position of the decimal point must now be determined by inspection.

Rough check: $3.142 \approx 3$ and $3^2 = 9$

Thus $3.142^2 = 9.873$.

(ii) The value of 31.42^2 is found in exactly the same way as described in (i) above.

Rough check: $31.42 \approx 30$ and $30^2 = 900$

Thus $31.42^2 = 987.3$

It will be seen that by using four-figure tables the answer will always be obtained to an accuracy of four significant figures.

5.2. ROOTS

A root is the factor of a quantity which, multiplied by itself, gives that quantity.

In section 5.1 it was seen that

$$5^2 = 25 \quad (5 \times 5 = 25)$$
$$4^3 = 64 \quad (4 \times 4 \times 4 = 64)$$
$$2^4 = 16 \quad (2 \times 2 \times 2 \times 2 = 16)$$
$$3^5 = 243 \quad (3 \times 3 \times 3 \times 3 \times 3 = 243)$$

The square of 5 is 25 and of -5 is 25 $(- \times - = +)$ so that the square root of 25 is ± 5. The square root of a number is denoted by the sign $\sqrt{\ }$ (or sometimes $\sqrt[2]{\ }$). Thus $\sqrt{25} = \pm 5$. Similarly $25^{\frac{1}{2}} = \pm 5$.

In the same way the cube root of 64 is 4, and is shown as $\sqrt[3]{64}$ or $64^{\frac{1}{3}}$, the fourth root of 16 is ± 2 and is shown as $\sqrt[4]{16}$ or $16^{\frac{1}{4}}$, the fifth root of 243 is 3 and is shown as $\sqrt[5]{243}$ or $243^{\frac{1}{5}}$.

From the foregoing it will be seen that certain roots have positive *and* negative values, i.e. when an even number denotes the root, for example, $\sqrt{\ }$ (which represents $\sqrt[2]{\ }$), $\sqrt[4]{\ }$, etc.

5.2.1. Roots of negative numbers. When an odd number denotes a root, for example $\sqrt[3]{\ }$, $\sqrt[5]{\ }$, etc. the root of a negative quantity can be dealt with in the same way as for a positive quantity, but the root will be negative.

		Squares ·										Mean Differences							
	0	1	2	3	4	5	6	7	8	9	1	2	3	4	5	6	7	8	9
31					9860							13							

Consider, for example, $\sqrt[3]{-64}$. Since $(-4)\times(-4)\times(-4)=-64$, then $\sqrt[3]{-64}=-4$. Similarly $\sqrt[5]{-243}=-3$ because $(-3)\times(-3)\times(-3)\times(-3)\times(-3)=-243$.

Now, when an even number denotes the root (square root, fourth root, etc.), the root of a negative quantity cannot be found in the manner previously described. For practical reasons, only the square roots of negative numbers will be discussed here.

Since $(+2)\times(+2)=+4$ and $(-2)\times(-2)=+4$, the square root of -4 cannot be either $+2$ or -2 and must be another kind of number (known as an imaginary number).

Let the symbol j denote $\sqrt{-1}$. Then $\sqrt{-4}$ can be written as $\sqrt{(-1\times4)}$ or $\sqrt{-1}\times\sqrt{4}$, which is j multiplied by a real number.

Thus $\sqrt{-4}=j2$. Similarly, $\sqrt{-9}=j3$, $\sqrt{-10}=j3.162$, etc. Note that only the positive root of the real number is considered.

Imaginary numbers are of great importance to the engineer in a branch of mathematics known as complex numbers, such numbers being beyond the scope of this book. Now, when dealing with practical problems at the present level of studies it is unlikely that the student will be required to find the square root (or any other root) of a negative quantity. Therefore, in solving a problem, e.g. when using the formula for solving quadratic equations, if the student should stumble across the square root of a negative number it should be treated with much suspicion and careful search made for an almost certain error.

EXAMPLE 5.3. Find, without the use of tables,

(i) $\sqrt{81}$,   (ii) $\sqrt[3]{125}$,   (iii) $\sqrt{\frac{36}{49}}$,   (iv) $\sqrt[3]{\frac{8}{27}}$,
(v) $\sqrt[3]{3\frac{3}{8}}$,   (vi) $\sqrt{0.04}$.

SOLUTION

(i) $\sqrt{81}=\pm9$
   (Because $9\times9=81$ and $-9\times-9=81$).
(ii) $\sqrt[3]{125}=5$ (Since $5\times5\times5=125$).
(iii) $\sqrt{\frac{36}{49}}=\frac{\sqrt{36}}{\sqrt{49}}=\pm\frac{6}{7}$
(iv) $\sqrt[3]{\frac{8}{27}}=\frac{\sqrt[3]{8}}{\sqrt[3]{27}}=\frac{2}{3}$
   (Note that the root of a vulgar fraction equals the root of the numerator divided by the root of the denominator.)
(v) $\sqrt[3]{3\frac{3}{8}}=\sqrt[3]{\frac{27}{8}}=\frac{\sqrt[3]{27}}{\sqrt[3]{8}}$
   $=\frac{3}{2}=1\frac{1}{2}$
(vi) $\sqrt{0.04}=\pm0.2$
   (Note the number of decimal places as explained in section 2.2.2.)

Unless the root of a number is obvious, as in each of the above examples, it is advisable to use an aid to calculation such as tables, a slide rule, or a calculator.

5.2.2. Table of square roots. The square root of any positive number can be found from tables of square roots to an accuracy of at least four significant figures (depending on the tables used). An inspection of these tables will show that, in order to obtain the square root of a number, the first significant figure and the position of the decimal point must be determined by other means, such as a rough check.

Consider numbers whose significant figure value is 2768. Such values may occur in various forms as

$$0.2768,\ 0.000\ 276\ 8,\ \text{etc. or}$$

$$2.768,\ 276.8,\ \text{etc.}$$

By way of illustration consider determination of the square roots of three of these, say $\sqrt{0.2768}$, $\sqrt{0.000\ 276\ 8}$, and $\sqrt{2.768}$.

Starting from the decimal point place bars over pairs of figures as shown below:
(i) $0.\overline{27}\,\overline{68}$
(ii) $0.\overline{00}\,\overline{02}\,\overline{76}\,8$
(iii) $\overline{2}.\overline{76}\,8$

It will be seen that (ii) and (iii) are alike in the respect that the first significant figure '2' is alone under a bar, whereas in (i) the first two significant figures, that is '27', occur under the same bar. In cases such as (ii) and (iii) the square root is found from the first section of the tables whilst case (i) calls for the use of the second section. After extracting the significant figures from the tables, again consider the pairs and place a figure in the result for each pair as shown in the following examples:

EXAMPLE 5.4. Find the square roots of

(i) 0.2768, (ii) 0.000 276 8, and (iii) 2.768.

SOLUTION

The appropriate extract from the table of square roots is given below. Note the two sections.

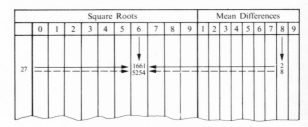

(i) $\sqrt{0.2768}$
Using the second section of the table as explained in 5.2.1. above:
5254 plus 8 gives 5262.
Then, number   0.27 68 00 00
square root   0.5   2   6   2
Thus $\sqrt{0.2768}=0.5262$

(ii) $\sqrt{0.000\,276\,8}$

Using the first section of the table as explained above:

1661 plus 2 gives 166<u>3</u>.

Then, number $0.00 \quad \overline{02} \quad \overline{76} \quad \overline{80} \quad \overline{00}$

$\qquad\qquad\qquad \downarrow \quad\; \downarrow \quad\; \downarrow \quad\; \downarrow \quad\; \downarrow$

square root $0.0 \qquad 1 \qquad 6 \qquad 6 \qquad 3$

Thus, $\sqrt{0.000\,276\,8} = 0.016\,63$.

(iii) $\sqrt{2.768}$

Again using the first section of the table:

1661 plus 2 gives 166<u>3</u>.

Then, number $2. \quad \overline{76} \quad \overline{80} \quad \overline{00}$

$\qquad\qquad\qquad\;\; \downarrow \quad\; \downarrow \quad\; \downarrow \quad\; \downarrow$

square root $1. \qquad 6 \qquad 6 \qquad 3$

Thus, $\sqrt{2.768} = 1.663$.

5.3. RECIPROCALS

The reciprocal of a number is defined as 1/(number) and is obtained by dividing the number into 1. For example, the reciprocal of 2 is $\frac{1}{2}$ or 0.5, the reciprocal of 4 is $\frac{1}{4}$ or 0.25, and the reciprocal of 10 is $\frac{1}{10}$ or 0.1.

5.3.1. Table of reciprocals. The reciprocal (expressed as a decimal fraction) of any number can be found from a table of reciprocals. However, care must be taken to *subtract* and not add the figure obtained from the 'differences' column of the table. The reason for this is that as numbers increase the corresponding reciprocals decrease as is shown above.

EXAMPLE 5.5. Find the value of (i) 1/2.345 and (ii) 1/23.45.

SOLUTION

(i) The value of 1/2.345 is obtained from the table of reciprocals, the appropriate extract being given below.

	Reciprocals										Subtract Mean Differences								
	0	1	2	3	4	5	6	7	8	9	1	2	3	4	5	6	7	8	9
2.3					↓.4274 ←									↓					9

The '9' shown in the right-hand column represents 0.0009.

Subtracting 0.0009 from 0.4274 gives 0.4265.

The position of the decimal point must now be verified by means of a rough check:

$$1/2.345 \simeq \tfrac{1}{2} \quad \text{(or } 0.5).$$

Thus $1/2.345 = 0.4265.$

(ii) The value of 1/23.45 is found in a similar manner to that described in (i) above. Again, a rough check is used

to determine the position of the decimal point:

$$1/23.45 \simeq \tfrac{1}{20} \quad \text{(or } 0.05).$$

Thus $1/23.45 = 0.04265.$

EXAMPLE 5.6. The resistance R ohms of three resistors connected in parallel, of values R_1, R_2, and R_3 ohms respectively, is given by

$$\frac{1}{R} = \frac{1}{R_1} + \frac{1}{R_2} + \frac{1}{R_3}$$

Find the value of R when R_1 is 3.5 ohms, R_2 is 4.5 ohms, and R_3 is 5.5 ohms.

SOLUTION

The value of R can be quickly found by using the table of reciprocals. Rough checks should be used throughout to verify that the decimal points have been correctly placed.

$$\frac{1}{R} = \frac{1}{3.5} + \frac{1}{4.5} + \frac{1}{5.5}$$

$$= 0.2857 + 0.2222 + 0.1818$$

$$= 0.6897$$

$$\therefore\; R = \frac{1}{0.6897}$$

$$= 1.449$$

(N.B. Remember to subtract the 'difference'.)

The values of R_1, R_2, and R_3 were given to an accuracy of two significant figures. The value of R will likewise be expressed to the same accuracy.

$$\therefore\; R = 1.4 \text{ ohms.}$$

EXERCISES 5

The following exercises should be worked using mathematical tables, but without the use of logarithms. As an additional exercise the answers obtained may be checked by means of a slide rule or a calculator.

1. Find the square of each of the following numbers:
   (a) 8.376,   (b) 0.6543,   (c) 0.04567.

2. Find the square roots of each of the following numbers:
   (a) 5.037,   (b) 0.007 624,   (c) 0.4246.

3. Evaluate each of the following:
   (a) $(16.38)^2 - \sqrt{16.38}$
   (b) $(4.8 \times 3.7)^2 + \sqrt{2468}$
   (c) $\sqrt{\left(\dfrac{1}{0.1176} + 1.8708^2\right)}.$

4. Find the value of each of the following:
   (a) $\dfrac{1}{\dfrac{1}{6.73} + \dfrac{1}{5.26}}$ (b) $1 - \dfrac{1}{1.661}$ (c) $\dfrac{1}{(0.00765)^2}$

5. By using a table of reciprocals, find the value of:

$$\frac{1}{3.61}+\frac{3}{9.72}-\frac{2}{8.42}$$

6. If $\dfrac{1}{v}=\dfrac{1}{f}-\dfrac{1}{u}$, calculate the value of v when $f=20$ and $u=100$.

7. Determine the value of R to three significant figures, given by $\dfrac{1}{R}=\dfrac{1}{R_1}+\dfrac{1}{R_2}$, when $R_1=9.87$ and $R_2=12.45$.

ANSWERS TO EXERCISES 5

1. (a) 70.16, (b) 0.4281, (c) 0.002 085.
2. (a) ±2.245, (b) ±0.087 31, (c) ±0.6516.
3. (a) 264.253 or 272.347,
   (b) 365.08 or 265.72,
   (c) ±3.464.
4. (a) 2.95, (b) 0.398, (c) 17 100.
5. 0.348.
6. 25.
7. 5.51.

6 | Logarithms

6.1. INDICES AND LOGARITHMS

Indices form the basis of a section of mathematics known as logarithms, in which the multiplication and division of numbers are achieved by the more straight-forward process of addition and subtraction of indices. These indices (or powers) are known as logarithms.

The *logarithm* of a *number* is the *power* to which the *base* must be raised in order to equal that number.

The number corresponding to a given logarithm is called its *antilogarithm*.

$$base^{power\ (logarithm)} = number\ (antilogarithm).$$

By applying the above definition of a logarithm and using a base equal to a it is possible to write any number in terms of a power of a. For example, using a base of 10, any number can be written as a power of 10.

Consider the following statements:

$1 = 10^0$, i.e. the logarithm of 1 to base 10 equals 0
$10 = 10^1$, the logarithm of 10 to base 10 equals 1
$100 = 10^2$, the logarithm of 100 to base 10 equals 2
$1000 = 10^3$, the logarithm of 1000 to base 10 equals 3

The numbers chosen, i.e. 1, 10, 100, and 1000, are all exact whole number powers of 10. If however a number lying between 10 and 100 were chosen then the value of its logarithm must lie between 1 and 2.

For example, the logarithm of 50 to base 10 equals 1.6990. Written as a power this may be expressed as

$$50 = 10^{1.6990},$$

i.e. the logarithm of 50 to base 10 equals 1.6990.

The above examples are an indication of how all numbers may be expressed as a power of 10. This method of expressing a number as a power of 10 is the basis of common logarithms.

The logarithm of any number x to base a may be represented by the symbol $\log_a x$.

The natural logarithm† (base approximately equal to 2.718 and represented by the symbol e) of any number x is symbolized by $\ln x$ and $\log_e x$.

Approved symbols for the common logarithm (base 10) of any number x are $\lg x$ and $\log_{10} x$. The symbol $\log x$ is very often used, the base 10 being omitted.

The antilogarithm, i.e. the number corresponding to a given logarithm, say m, is represented symbolically by antilog m.

---

† Natural logarithms are beyond the scope of the present book but are mentioned here because of their great importance in science and technology.

6.1.1. Characteristic and mantissa. The logarithm of a number is made up of two parts:
 (i) the whole number part, which is known as the characteristic, and
 (ii) the decimal fraction part which is called the man-tissa.

For example, the common logarithm of 50.0 is 1.6990. For numbers greater than 1.0 the characteristic is obtained by inspection and its value is equal to the number of figures (digits) before the decimal point minus one. (Note. For numbers less than 1.0 see section 6.5.) In this case the characteristic of lg 50.0 is 1.(0) and the mantissa is (0).6990. The mantissa for any number is obtained from tables of logarithms.

EXAMPLE 6.1. Write the numbers 3 and 81 as powers of 9 and hence find the logarithms of (i) 3 and (ii) 81 to the base 9.

SOLUTION
 (i) $3 \times 3 = 9$
   $3 = \sqrt{9} = 9^{\frac{1}{2}}$ (see section 4.1.3)
   But, number = base^{logarithm}
   $\therefore \log_9 3 = \frac{1}{2}$ or 0.5
   Note. The characteristic is 0.(0) and the mantissa is (0).5 so that $\log_9 3 = 0.5$.
   (See section 6.1.1.)
 (ii) $9 \times 9 = 81$
   $\therefore 9^2 = 81$
   so that $\log_9 81 = 2.0$
   Note. The characteristic is 2.(0) and the mantissa is (0).0 so that $\log_9 81 = 2.0$.
   (Again see section 6.1.1.)

6.2. LOGARITHMIC TABLES

6.2.1. Tables of common logarithms. The common logarithms used in this chapter and throughout the text are four-figure logarithms, i.e. the mantissa contains four figures. It should be appreciated however that although answers are generally quoted to four significant figures, the last digit is frequently inaccurate. If greater accuracy from logarithmic tables is required they are also available in the form of five-figure and seven-figure tables.

It must be remembered that the logarithm of a number is made up of two parts: the characteristic, which is found by inspection, and the mantissa, which is obtained from the tables. The method of finding the common logarithm of a number from logarithmic tables is explained in example 6.2, which follows.

EXAMPLE 6.2. Find, using tables, the common logarithms of:
(a) 564.2, (b) 56.42, and (c) 5.642.

SOLUTION
(a) log 564.2.
(i) To find the characteristic.
   The number of figures before the decimal point = 3 (i.e. 564)
   ∴ the characteristic = 3 − 1 = 2. (See section 6.1.1.)
(ii) To find the mantissa.
   The mantissa, or decimal part, of the logarithm is obtained from tables, the appropriate extract being given below.

	Common Logarithms										Mean Differences								
	0	1	2	3	4	5	6	7	8	9	1	2	3	4	5	6	7	8	9
56					7513							2							

The number whose common logarithm is required is split into three parts, the first part being formed by the first two significant figures, in this example 564.2.

The first two significant figures, 56, are found in the left-hand column as shown. In the row of figures at the top of the table the third significant figure, 4, is found and by descending this column to the row containing 56 the number 7513 (i.e. 0.7513) is reached. This is the major part of the required mantissa but in order to complete the logarithm it is necessary to add to 7513 the figure appearing under the difference column headed by the fourth significant figure, 2, and in the row containing 7513. The required addition is 2 (i.e. 0.0002). Note that the decimal point is usually omitted from the tables except at the beginning of each row. The figure 2 obtained from the difference column is in fact 0.0002. The required mantissa is, therefore, 0.7513 + 0.0002.

Hence log 564.2 = characteristic + mantissa
$$= 2 + 0.7513 + 0.0002$$
$$∴ log\ 564.2 = 2.7515$$

(b) log 56.42
(i) To find the characteristic.
   The number of figures before the decimal point = 2 (i.e. 56)
   ∴ the characteristic = 2 − 1 = 1.
(ii) To find the mantissa.
   The value of the mantissa for 56.42 is exactly the same as that for 564.2.
   It is purely the characteristic which distinguishes log 56.42 from log 564.2.
   ∴ log 56.42 = 1.7515.

(c) Log 5.642
(i) To find the characteristic.
   The number of figures before the decimal point = 1 (i.e. 5)
   ∴ the characteristic = 1 − 1 = 0.
(ii) To find the mantissa.
   The mantissa for 5.642 is identical to that for 56.42 and 564.2.
   ∴ log 5.642 = 0.7515.

6.2.2. Tables of antilogarithms. At the end of a calculation in which common logarithms have been used it is generally necessary to convert the final logarithm back into a number. This simple conversion is generally carried out by using tables of antilogarithms. If preferred, however, ordinary logarithm tables may also be used to convert from logarithm to number. In this case remember to reverse the process throughout the whole operation.

Consider the following example.

EXAMPLE 6.3. Convert the following common logarithms into the appropriate numbers:
(a) 0.4972, (b) 1.4972, and (c) 3.4972.

SOLUTION
(a) 0.4972
   Characteristic = 0, mantissa = .4972.

Initially only the mantissa is used in converting the logarithm into a number. The method used is similar to that used in determining the logarithm of a number. Below is the appropriate extract taken from a table of antilogarithms.

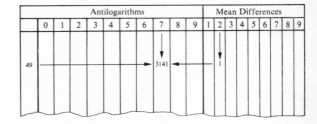

	Antilogarithms										Mean Differences								
	0	1	2	3	4	5	6	7	8	9	1	2	3	4	5	6	7	8	9
49								3141				1							

The first two decimal places in the mantissa, .49, are found in the extreme left-hand column as shown. In the row of figures at the top of the table the third decimal place, 7, is found and by descending this column to the row containing .49 the number 3141 is reached. This is the major part of the required number but in order to complete the number it is necessary to add to 3141 the figure appearing under the mean difference column headed by the fourth decimal place, 2, and in the row containing 3141. The required addition is 1.

Hence 3141 + 1 = 3142.

The characteristic 0 is now used to identify the correct position of the decimal point. Since the characteristic is 0 there will be one figure in front of the decimal point in the antilogarithm. This is the reverse of the process used in finding the logarithm.

∴ antilog 0.4972 = 3.142

(b) 1.4972

Characteristic = 1, mantissa = .4972
The antilog of .4972 = 3142 (see part a)
The characteristic 1 indicates there will be two figures in front of the decimal point.
∴ antilog 1.4972 = 31.42.

(c) 3.4972

Characteristic = 3, mantissa = .4972
The antilog of .4972 = 3142 (as for parts a and b)
The characteristic 3 indicates there will be four figures in front of the decimal point.
∴ antilog 3.4972 = 3142.0.

A simple rule for finding the position of the decimal point after the antilogarithm has been obtained is as follows:

The number of figures in front of the decimal point = characteristic + 1.

This applies when the characteristic is greater than or equal to 0.

(Note. For negative characteristics, see section 6.5.)

6.3. MULTIPLICATION OF NUMBERS USING LOGARITHMS

Since logarithms are indices (powers) it follows that they obey the laws of indices referred to in Chapter 4.

Therefore the multiplication of numbers may be achieved by the simpler process of the addition of logarithms (see law 1, section 4.1.1).

multiplication of numbers: add the logarithms

EXAMPLE 6.4. Evaluate, using common logarithms, $67.32 \times 2.63 \times 13.7$.

SOLUTION

Method 1. This method indicates the way in which a calculation of this kind may be set out.

The logarithmic tables are used as previously described in examples 6.2 and 6.3.

Number	Logarithm
67.32 $\longrightarrow$	1.8281
2.63 $\longrightarrow$	0.4200 (Add)
13.7 $\longrightarrow$	1.1367
Antilog = 2425.0 $\longleftarrow$	3.3848

Thus, $67.32 \times 2.63 \times 13.7 = 2425 = 2430$ to 3 sig. figs. (The fourth significant figure is not reliable, and in any case two of the factors are only given to three figures.)

Method 2. This method of presentation is included purely to illustrate and emphasise the relationship between logarithms and indices (powers).

Each of the numbers can be expressed as a power of 10, thus

$$67.32 = 10^{1.8281}$$
$$2.63 = 10^{0.4200}$$
$$13.7 = 10^{1.1367}$$
$$\therefore 67.32 \times 2.63 \times 13.7 = 10^{1.8281} \times 10^{0.4200} \times 10^{1.1367}$$

Using the law of indices relating to multiplication, the powers are now added together, giving

$$10^{1.8281} \times 10^{0.4200} \times 10^{1.1367} = 10^{(1.8281+0.4200+1.1367)}$$
$$= 10^{3.3848}$$

From tables of common logarithms the value of $10^{3.3848}$ is obtained, giving

$$10^{3.3848} = 2425$$

Again, $67.32 \times 2.63 \times 13.7 = 2425 = 2430$ to 3 sig. figs.

6.4. DIVISION OF NUMBERS USING LOGARITHMS

Referring again to Chapter 4, the division of numbers containing powers was achieved by subtracting the indices. Therefore the division of numbers can be carried out by the simpler process of the subtraction of logarithms (see law 2, section 4.1.1).

division of numbers: subtract the logarithms

EXAMPLE 6.5. Use common loagrithms to evaluate $\dfrac{338.6}{24.21}$

SOLUTION

Method 1. The tables of logarithms and antilogarithms are used as described in examples 6.2 and 6.3.

In practice the form of presentation is as follows:

Number	Logarithm
338.6 $\longrightarrow$	2.5289
24.21 $\longrightarrow$	1.3840 (Subtract)
Antilog = 13.96 $\longleftarrow$	1.1449

Thus, $338.6 \div 24.21 = 13.96 = 14.0$ to 3 sig. figs.

Method 2. Again this method is not used in practice but serves to illustrate the relationship between logarithms and indices (powers).

Written as powers of 10:

$$338.6 = 10^{2.5289}$$

$$24.21 = 10^{1.3840}$$

$$\therefore \ \frac{338.6}{24.21} = \frac{10^{2.5289}}{10^{1.3840}}$$

Applying the laws of indices relating to division,

$$\frac{10^{2.5289}}{10^{1.3840}} = 10^{(2.5289-1.3840)}$$

$$= 10^{1.1449}$$

From logarithm tables $10^{1.1449} = 13.96$.
Again, $338.6 \div 24.21 = 13.96 = 14.0$ to 3 sig. figs.

EXAMPLE 6.6. Use common logarithms to evaluate

$$\frac{201.3 \times 6.24}{31.6 \times 10.7}$$

SOLUTION

In an example of this type logarithms are used to find the values of the numerator and denominator (i.e. each a multiplication exercise) and then, before finding any antilogarithms, the logarithm of the denominator is subtracted from the logarithm of the numerator. This process then completes the division of numerator by denominator.

The logarithmic tables are used as in examples 6.2 and 6.3.

DENOMINATOR

Number	Logarithm
31.6 →	1.4997
10.7 →	1.0294 (Add)
	2.5291

NUMERATOR

Number	Logarithm
201.3 →	2.3038 (Add)
6.24 →	0.7952
(Log. of numerator)	3.0990 (Subtract)
(Log. of denominator)	2.5291
Antilog = 3.714 ←	0.5699

The result is 3.714, or 3.71 to 3 sig. figs.

As was stated in section 1.5, whenever possible it is advisable to carry out a rough check to establish that the answer arrived at is of the right order.

In example 6.5 just considered it would be sufficient to write $\frac{200 \times 6}{30 \times 10} = 4$. This confirms that the answer is 3.71 and not 0.371, 37.1, 371, etc.

6.5. LOGARITHMS OF NUMBERS LESS THAN 1.0

Logarithms of numbers less than 1.0 are dealt with separately in order to introduce the idea of negative characteristics.

Referring to the definition of a logarithm and its relationship with indices it was shown that, for example,

$$100 = 10^2, \text{ i.e. the logarithm}_{10} 100 = 2$$
$$10 = 10^1 \quad \text{the logarithm}_{10} 10 = 1$$
$$1 = 10^0 \quad \text{the logarithm}_{10} 1 = 0$$

If this process is continued for numbers less than 1, then

$$0.1 = \tfrac{1}{10} = 10^{-1}, \text{ i.e. the logarithm}_{10} \ 0.1 = -1$$
$$0.01 = \frac{1}{100} = \frac{1}{10^2} = 10^{-2}, \text{ i.e. the logarithm}_{10} \ 0.01 = -2,$$

and so on.

Thus the logarithm of any number less than 1 could be expressed as a wholly negative quantity.

However both for convenience and simplicity it is better to express the logarithm of a number less than 1 as the sum of two parts:
(a) a *negative characteristic* and
(b) a *positive mantissa*.

The following worked example illustrates this more fully:

EXAMPLE 6.7. Find the common logarithms of (i) 0.03, (ii) 0.0075.

SOLUTION

(i) 0.03 may be written as $\frac{3}{100} = 3 \times \frac{1}{100}$
Expressed as powers of 10, $3 = 10^{0.4771}$ (obtained from log. tables)
and $\frac{1}{100} = \frac{1}{10^2} = 10^{-2}$
$\therefore \ 3 \times \frac{1}{100} = 10^{0.4771} \times 10^{-2}$
Using the law of indices for multiplication, $10^{0.4771} \times 10^{-2} = 10^{(-2+0.4771)}$
$\therefore \ 0.03 = 10^{(-2+0.4771)}$
i.e. logarithm$_{10}$ 0.03 $= -2 + 0.4771$.

As $-2 + 0.4771$ is an inconvenient method of writing a logarithm, $-2 + 0.4771$ is written as $\bar{2}.4771$ indicating that the negative sign relates to the characteristic, 2, only. The negative characteristic $\bar{2}$ is expressed as 'bar 2'.

Therefore, log $0.03 = \bar{2}.4771$.

Note. The common logarithm of 0.03 could not be written as -2.4771 as this would imply that both characteristic and mantissa were negative.

SOLUTION

(ii) As in the previous example, $0.0075 = 7.5 \times \frac{1}{1000}$

Expressing 7.5 and $\frac{1}{1000}$ as powers of 10,

$7.5 \times \frac{1}{1000} = 10^{0.8751} \times \frac{1}{10^3}$ (the value 0.8751 is obtained from log. tables).

Again $10^{0.8751} \times \frac{1}{10^3} = 10^{0.8751} \times 10^{-3} = 10^{(-3+0.8751)}$

(see laws of indices)

Therefore the common logarithm of $0.0075 = \bar{3}.8751$.

Note. The characteristic '3' is negative (bar 3) whilst the mantissa 0.8751 is positive.

The above examples have been fully worked in order to show the meaning of negative characteristics. In practice when it is required to find the value of the characteristic for a number less than 1.0 the following simple rule is used.

For numbers less than 1.0 the (negative) characteristic is obtained by inspection and its numerical value is one more than the number of zeros between the decimal point and the first non-zero figure.

The mantissa is obtained from logarithm tables as before.

EXAMPLE 6.8. What are the characteristics for the common logarithms of the following numbers (i) 0.016, (ii) 0.13, (iii) 0.006, (iv) 0.0007?

SOLUTION

Characteristic of (i) $0.016 = \bar{2}$ ('bar 2')
(ii) $0.13 = \bar{1}$ ('bar 1')
(iii) $0.006 = \bar{3}$ ('bar 3')
(iv) $0.0007 = \bar{4}$ ('bar 4')

EXAMPLE 6.9. Find the common logarithms of (a) 0.34, (b) 0.0034, and (c) 0.034.

SOLUTION

(a) (i) To find the characteristic of log 0.34.
The number of zeros between the decimal point and the first non-zero figure $= 0$.
$\therefore$ the characteristic $= \bar{1}$.
(ii) The mantissa or decimal part of log 0.34 is obtained from tables in the normal way.
$\therefore$ the mantissa $= .5315$.
The common logarithm of 0.34 is thus $\bar{1} + 0.5315$
$\therefore$ log $0.34 = \bar{1}.5315$.

(b) (i) To find the characteristic of log 0.0034.
The number of zeros between the decimal point and the first non-zero figure $= 2$
$\therefore$ the characteristic $= \bar{3}$.
(ii) The mantissa is the same as for part (a), i.e. .5315
$\therefore$ log $0.0034 = \bar{3}.5315$.

(c) (i) To find the characteristic of log 0.034.
The number of zeros between the decimal point and the first non-zero figure $= 1$
$\therefore$ the characteristic $= \bar{2}$.
(ii) The mantissa is the same as for parts (a) and (b), i.e. .5315
$\therefore$ log $0.034 = \bar{2}.5315$.

EXAMPLE 6.10. Evaluate, using common logarithms, 0.8146×0.0056.

SOLUTION

The logarithmic tables used are described in examples 6.2 and 6.3.

No.	Log.
0.8146 $\longrightarrow$	$\bar{1}.9109$ (Add)
0.0056 $\longrightarrow$	$\bar{3}.7482$
Antilog $= 0.004561 \longleftarrow$	$\bar{3}.6591$

Note. The 1 carried forward when 0.9 and 0.7 are added is positive, since the decimal part is always positive. The characteristic is obtained by the addition of $-3-1+1$, i.e. $-4+1 = -3$ or $\bar{3}$. The $\bar{3}$ indicates two zeros after the decimal point.

The result is 0.004 561, or 0.004 56 to 3 sig. figs.

EXAMPLE 6.11. Evaluate, using common logarithms, $\frac{0.9462}{0.0053}$.

SOLUTION

See examples 6.2 and 6.3 for the use of logarithmic tables.

No.	Log.
0.9462 $\longrightarrow$	$\bar{1}.9760$ (Subtract)
0.0053 $\longrightarrow$	$\bar{3}.7243$
Antilog $= 178.5 \longleftarrow$	2.2517

Note. The characteristic 2 is obtained by the subtraction of -3 from -1 as follows:

$$-1 - (-3) = -1 + 3 = 2.$$

The result is 178.5, or 179 to 3 sig. figs.

To assist in confirming that the correct characteristic has been obtained it is always worthwhile to apply a rough check to the calculations. In this case $\dfrac{9462}{53}$ $\left(\text{which is roughly } \dfrac{9500}{50}=190\right)$ equals a number somewhere between 100 and 200. Hence the characteristic is of the right order.

EXAMPLE 6.12. Evaluate $\dfrac{0.00361 \times 13.6}{9.81 \times 0.291}$

SOLUTION

The procedure is as described in example 6.6.

NUMERATOR

No.	Log.
0.00361 $\longrightarrow$	$\bar{3}.5575$
13.6 $\longrightarrow$	1.1335 (Add)
	$\bar{2}.6910$

DENOMINATOR

No.	Log.
9.81 $\longrightarrow$	0.9917
0.291 $\longrightarrow$	$\bar{1}.4639$ (Add)
	0.4556

	Log
Log numerator	$\bar{2}.6910$ (Subtract)
Log denominator	0.4556
Antilog = 0.01719 $\longleftarrow$	$\bar{2}.2354$

The result is 0.01719, or 0.0172 to 3 sig. figs.

Rough check: $\dfrac{0.004 \times 15}{10 \times 0.3} = \dfrac{0.004 \times 15}{3}$
$= 0.004 \times 5$
$= 0.02$

This indicates that the first answer is of the right order.

6.6. ROOTS AND POWERS OF NUMBERS USING LOGARITHMS

6.6.1. Roots of numbers. Logarithms provide a convenient means of obtaining any root of a number.

Consider the following two statements.
Statement 1: Since $\sqrt{9} \times \sqrt{9} = 9$ (i.e. $3 \times 3 = 9$)
$\log \sqrt{9} + \log \sqrt{9} = \log 9$
i.e. $2 \log \sqrt{9} = \log 9$
$\therefore \log \sqrt{9} = \tfrac{1}{2} \log 9$
or $\log 3 = \tfrac{1}{2} \log 9$
Statement 2: Since $\sqrt[3]{8} \times \sqrt[3]{8} \times \sqrt[3]{8} = 8$ (i.e. $2 \times 2 \times 2 = 8$)
$\log \sqrt[3]{8} + \log \sqrt[3]{8} + \log \sqrt[3]{8} = \log 8$
i.e. $3 \log \sqrt[3]{8} = \log 8$
$\therefore \log \sqrt[3]{8} = \tfrac{1}{3} \log 8$
or $\log 2 = \tfrac{1}{3} \log 8$
Statement 1 indicates that the $\log \sqrt{9}$ equals half of $\log 9$.
Statement 2 illustrates that the $\log \sqrt[3]{8}$ equals one-third of $\log 8$.

In general, therefore, to find the root of a number using logarithms, divide the logarithm of the number by the figure denoting the required root and find the antilogarithm.

EXAMPLE 6.13. Using logarithms find $\sqrt{89.23}$.

SOLUTION

Steps to be taken are:
(i) Find $\log 89.23$ from tables.
(ii) Divide this logarithm by 2 ($\sqrt{} = \sqrt[2]{}$, i.e. square root).
(iii) Antilog the result from step (ii).

No.	Log.
89.23 $\longrightarrow$	1.9505
$\sqrt{89.23} \longrightarrow$	$\dfrac{1.9505}{2} = 0.97525$ *

Antilog $0.9753 = 9.448$
$\therefore \sqrt{89.23} = 9.448 = 9.45$ to 3 sig. figs.

*Note the method of division: 2 into 1 put 0, carry 1 then 2 into 19 goes 9 carry 1, etc.

Rough check: $9 \times 9 = 81$ which is of the right order.

EXAMPLE 6.14. Using logarithms find $\sqrt[4]{7614}$

SOLUTION

The method used is as summarised in section 6.6.1.

No.	Log.
7614 $\longrightarrow$	3.8816
$\sqrt[4]{7614} \longrightarrow$	$\dfrac{3.8816}{4} = 0.9704$

Antilog $0.9704 = 9.342$
$\therefore \sqrt[4]{7614} = 9.342 = 9.34$ to 3 sig. figs.

Rough check: $9 \times 9 \times 9 \times 9 = 6561$

$\qquad\qquad 10 \times 10 \times 10 \times 10 = 10\,000$

The result 9.34 is therefore of the right order.

In the following three examples (6.15, 6.16, and 6.17) the roots of numbers less than 1.0 are calculated. Some variation in the method of division of the logarithm is required in these examples as the characteristic is negative and the mantissa is positive. The following procedure is therefore adopted.

Rearrange the logarithm so that the negative characteristic is exactly divisible by the figure denoting the root. The alteration of the negative characteristic is then adjusted to its original value by the introduction of the appropriate positive number. For example,

$\dfrac{\bar{1}.}{2}$ becomes $\dfrac{\bar{2}+1.}{2}$, i.e. $\bar{2}$ is exactly divisible by 2, also minus 2 plus 1 = minus 1.

$\dfrac{\bar{2}.}{3}$ becomes $\dfrac{\bar{3}+1.}{3}$, i.e. $\bar{3}$ is exactly divisible by 3, also minus 3 plus 1 = minus 2.

$\dfrac{\bar{4}.}{3}$ becomes $\dfrac{\bar{6}+2.}{3}$, i.e. $\bar{6}$ is exactly divisible by 3, also minus 6 plus 2 = minus 4.

EXAMPLE 6.15. Using logarithms find $\sqrt{0.144}$.

SOLUTION

The method used is as summarised in section 6.6.1 and as shown above.

No.	Log.
0.144 $\longrightarrow$	$\bar{1}.1584$
$\sqrt{0.144}$ $\longrightarrow$	$\dfrac{\bar{1}.1584}{2} = \dfrac{\bar{2}+1.1584^{*}}{2}$
	$= \bar{1}.5792$

Antilog $\bar{1}.5792 = 0.3795$

$\therefore \sqrt{0.144} = 0.3795 = 0.380$ to 3 sig. figs.

*Note the method of division: 2 into $\bar{2}$ equals $\bar{1}$. Next step is 2 into 11 = 5 remainder 1, etc.

Rough check: $0.37 \simeq 0.4$ $\therefore 0.4 \times 0.4 = 0.16$. Hence 0.37 is of the correct order.

EXAMPLE 6.16. Use logarithms to find the value of $\sqrt[3]{0.000\,621}$.

SOLUTION

No.	Log.
0.000 621 $\longrightarrow$	$\bar{4}.7931$
$\sqrt[3]{0.000\,621}$ $\longrightarrow$	$\dfrac{\bar{4}.7931}{3} = \dfrac{\bar{6}+2.7931}{3}$
	$= \bar{2}.9310$

Antilog $\bar{2}.9310 = 0.085\,31$

$\therefore \sqrt[3]{0.000\,621} = 0.085\,31 = 0.0853$ to 3 sig. figs.

A rough check indicates that the cube root of 0.000 621 lies between 0.08 and 0.09.

EXAMPLE 6.17. Using logarithms calculate $\sqrt[4]{0.915}$.

SOLUTION

The method is similar to that used in example 6.16.

No.	Log.
0.915 $\longrightarrow$	$\bar{1}.9614$
$\sqrt[4]{0.915}$ $\longrightarrow$	$\dfrac{\bar{1}.9614}{4} = \dfrac{\bar{4}+3.9614}{4}$
	$= \bar{1}.9904$

Antilog $\bar{1}.9904 = 0.9782$

$\therefore \sqrt[4]{0.915} = 0.9782 = 0.978$ to 3 sig. figs.

6.6.2. Powers of numbers. The method of calculating the power of a number using logarithms may be illustrated by using similar reasoning to that applied for obtaining the root of a number.

Consider the following two statements.

Statement 1: Since $5 \times 5 = 5^2$

$\qquad\qquad \log 5 + \log 5 = \log 5^2$

$\qquad\qquad$ i.e. $2 \log 5 = \log 5^2$.

Statement 2: Since $3 \times 3 \times 3 = 3^3$

$\qquad\qquad \log 3 + \log 3 + \log 3 = \log 3^3$

$\qquad\qquad$ i.e. $3 \log 3 = \log 3^3$.

Statement 1 indicates that $\log 5^2$ equals twice $\log 5$. Statement 2 illustrates that $\log 3^3$ equals three times $\log 3$.

In general, therefore, to find the power of a number using logarithms multiply the logarithm of the number by the index of the power and find the antilogarithm.

EXAMPLE 6.18. Using logarithms calculate $(3.142)^2$.

SOLUTION

The method of solution is described in section 6.6.2.

No.	Log.
3.142 $\longrightarrow$	0.4972
3.142^2 $\longrightarrow$	0.4972×2 $\quad$ i.e. $\log 3.142^2 = 2 \log 3.142$
	$= 0.9944$

Antilog $0.9944 = 9.872$

$\therefore (3.142)^2 = 9.872 = 9.87$ to 3 sig. figs.

EXAMPLE 6.19. Calculate, using logarithms, $(26.4)^3$.

SOLUTION

Proceed as explained in section 6.6.2.

No.	Log.
26.4 ⟶	1.4216
26.4^3 ⟶	$1.4216 \times 3 = 4.2648$
	i.e. $\log 26.4^3 = 3 \log 26.4$

Antilog $4.2648 = 18\,400$
$\therefore (26.4)^3 = 18\,400$ (3 sig. figs.).

EXAMPLE 6.20. Use logarithms to find the value of $(0.0036)^4$.

SOLUTION

The procedure is explained in sections 6.5 and 6.6.2.

No.	Log.
0.0036 ⟶	$\bar{3}.5563$
$(0.0036)^4$ ⟶	$\bar{3}.5563 \times 4 = \overline{10}.2252$
	i.e. $\log (0.0036)^4 = 4 \log (0.0036)$.

Note: $\bar{3} \times 4 = \overline{12}$. $\overline{12} + 2$ carried forward from mantissa equals $\overline{10}$.
Antilog $\overline{10}.2252 = 0.000\,000\,000\,167\,9$
$\therefore (0.0036)^4 = 0.000\,000\,000\,168$ to 3 sig. figs.

EXAMPLE 6.21. Using logarithms find the value of $(9.81)^2 \times (0.051)^3$.

SOLUTION

The procedure is as given in sections 6.2 and 6.3.

No.	Log.
9.81 ⟶	0.9917
9.81^2 ⟶	$0.9917 \times 2 = 1.9834$ ⎤
0.051 ⟶	$\bar{2}.7076$ (Add)
0.051^3 ⟶	$\bar{2}.7076 \times 3 = \bar{4}.1228$ ⎦
	$\bar{2}.1062$

Antilog $\bar{2}.1062 = 0.012\,77 = 0.012\,8$ to 3 sig. figs.

EXAMPLE 6.22. Evaluate $\sqrt{87.6} + (0.141)^2$.

SOLUTION

In this example each part must be worked independently and then the separate parts are added together.

No.	Log.
87.6 ⟶	1.9425
$\sqrt{87.6}$ ⟶	$\dfrac{1.9425}{2} = 0.971\,25$

Antilog $0.9713 = 9.361$
$\therefore \sqrt{87.6} = 9.36$ to 3 sig. figs.

No.	Log.
0.141 ⟶	$\bar{1}.1492$
0.141^2 ⟶	$\bar{1}.1492 \times 2 = \bar{2}.2984$

Antilog $\bar{2}.2984 = 0.019\,87$
$\therefore 0.141^2 = 0.0199$ to 3 sig. figs.

Thus, $\sqrt{87.6} + (0.141)^2 = 9.36 + 0.0199 = 9.38$ to 3 sig. figs.

6.6.3. Negative powers of numbers. In section 4.1.2 it was shown that a number raised to a negative power is equal to the inverse of the number raised to the same (numerically equal) positive power. Thus, when using logarithms to evaluate a number raised to a negative power it is first necessary to express the number in terms of the equivalent positive power. The procedure is then as explained in section 6.6.2 and is as demonstrated in examples 6.23 and 6.24.

EXAMPLE 6.23. Use logarithms to evaluate $(2.31)^{-2}$.

SOLUTION
Invert $(2.31)^{-2}$ as explained in section 4.1.2. Then

$$(2.31)^{-2} = \frac{1}{(2.31)^2}$$

No.	Log.	No.	Log.
2.31 ⟶	0.3636	1 ⟶	0.0000
2.31^2 ⟶	0.7272 ⟶	2.31^2 ⟶	0.7272
			(Subtract)
			$\bar{1}.2728$

Antilog $\bar{1}.2728 = 0.1874$
$\therefore (2.31)^{-2} = 0.187$ to 3 sig. figs.

EXAMPLE 6.24. Find the value of $\left(\dfrac{0.324}{4.76\times6.3}\right)^{-3}$.

SOLUTION

The first step is as shown in example 6.23.

$$\left(\frac{0.324}{4.76\times6.3}\right)^{-3}=\left(\frac{4.76\times6.3}{0.324}\right)^{3}$$

(See section 4.1.2.)

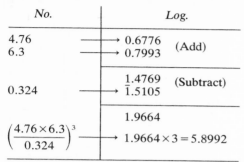

No.		Log.
4.76	→	0.6776
6.3	→	0.7993 (Add)
		1.4769 (Subtract)
0.324	→	1.5105
		1.9664
$\left(\dfrac{4.76\times6.3}{0.324}\right)^{3}$	→	$1.9664\times3=5.8992$

Antilog $5.8992 = 792\,900$.
∴ Value of expression $= 793\,000$ to 3 sig. figs.

6.7. MISCELLANEOUS EXAMPLES

The following worked examples (6.25, 6.26, 6.27, and 6.28) are included to provide a greater understanding of the manipulation of logarithms.

EXAMPLE 6.25. If $\log_{10}2 = 0.3010$, find, without tables, the value of $4\log_{10}2 + \log_{10}8 - \log_{10}4$.

(U.E.I.)

SOLUTION

$4\log_{10}2 = 4\times0.3010 = 1.2040$
$\log_{10}8 = \log_{10}2^{3} = 3\log_{10}2 = 3\times0.3010 = 0.9030$
$\log_{10}4 = \log_{10}2^{2} = 2\log_{10}2 = 2\times0.3010 = 0.6020$
∴ $4\log_{10}2 + \log_{10}8 - \log_{10}4$
$\qquad = 1.2040 + 0.9030 - 0.6020 = 1.3050$

EXAMPLE 6.26. Evaluate without tables $\log_{10}56 + \log_{10}50 - \log_{10}28$.

(E.M.E.U.)

SOLUTION

In this example it is important to note that the addition of logarithms indicates multiplication of numbers and subtraction of logarithms, division of numbers.
∴ $\log_{10}56 + \log_{10}50 - \log_{10}28$
means $\log_{10}\left(\dfrac{56\times50}{28}\right) = \log_{10}100$
∴ $\log_{10}56 + \log_{10}50 - \log_{10}28 = \log_{10}100 = 2$
∴ $\log_{10}56 + \log_{10}50 - \log_{10}28 = 2$.

EXAMPLE 6.27. If $\log 2 = 0.3010$ and $\log 3 = 0.4771$, without using tables determine the values of (a) log 6 (b) log 16 (c) log 18 (d) log 1.5.

SOLUTION
(a) $2\times3 = 6$
∴ $\log 2 + \log 3 = \log 6$
i.e. $0.3010 + 0.4771 = 0.7781$
∴ $\log 6 = 0.7781$.
(b) $2^{4} = 16$
∴ $\log 2^{4} = \log 16$
i.e. $4\log 2 = \log 16$
$4\times0.3010 = \log 16$
$\log 16 = 1.2040$.
(c) $3^{2}\times2 = 18$
$\log 3^{2} + \log 2 = \log 18$
$2\log 3 + \log 2 = \log 18$
$2\times0.4771 + 0.3010 = \log 18$
$0.9542 + 0.3010 = \log 18$
∴ $\log 18 = 1.2552$.
(d) $1.5 = \frac{3}{2}$
∴ $\log 3 - \log 2 = \log 1.5$
$0.4771 - 0.3010 = \log 1.5$
∴ $\log 1.5 = 0.1761$.

EXAMPLE 6.28. Evaluate $(3.46)^{1.4}$.

SOLUTION

$1.4\log 3.46 = 1.4\times0.5391$
$\qquad\qquad = 0.7547$
Antilog $0.7547 = 5.685$
∴ $(3.46)^{1.4} = 5.69$ to 3 sig. figs.

EXERCISES 6

1. Use tables to find the common logarithm of each of the following numbers:
   (a) 3.142   (b) 9.81   (c) 7820   (d) 46 000
   (e) 2.16   (f) 2.16×10^{4} (g) 216 900   (h) 16.32.

2. Use tables to find the antilogarithms of each of the following common logarithms:
   (a) 1.8388   (b) 0.4771   (c) 2.3010   (d) 2.9917
   (e) 3.7782   (f) 1.7784   (g) 1.0496   (h) 2.3224

3. Use logarithms to evaluate:
   (a) 3.142×83 (b) $2\times3.142\times76.13$
   (c) 9.81×116.4 (d) $46.1\times1.72\times6$
   (e) $3.4\times17\times10^{6}$ (f) $4.12\times37.1\times10^{4}$
   (g) $99.2\times16.3 - 407$ (h) $63.9 - 3.71\times7.42$.

4. Evaluate using logarithms:
   (a) $\dfrac{17.3}{5.46}$ (b) $\dfrac{873.2}{19.7}$ (c) $\dfrac{104.7}{9.81}$
   (d) $\dfrac{3176}{18.74}$ (e) $\dfrac{191.7}{13.8}$ (f) $\dfrac{23.46\times10^{3}}{347.1}$
   (g) $\dfrac{6.1}{3.7}+\dfrac{9.4}{8.3}$ (h) $\dfrac{27.14}{5.2}-\dfrac{13.9}{3.4}$

5. Find the common logarithms of each of the following numbers:
   (a) 0.6990   (b) 0.0069   (c) 0.06948
   (d) 0.000 83   (e) 0.000 011   (f) 23×10^{-6}
   (g) 1.2×10^{-6} (h) 1.9×10^{-5} (i) 0.000 017.

6. Find the antilogarithm of each of the following common logarithms:

(a) $\bar{1}.4686$ (b) $\bar{4}.2304$ (c) $\bar{4}.0414$
(d) $\bar{2}.7324$ (e) $\bar{3}.9914$ (f) $\bar{3}.3619$
(g) $\bar{2}.0049$ (h) $\bar{5}.1463$.

7. Use logarithms to evaluate:

(a) 3.142×0.7346 (b) 0.46×0.7633
(c) 0.037×0.2819 (d) $0.0037 \times 0.000\,812$
(e) 0.92×0.0019 (f) $9.81 \times 0.17 \times 0.871$
(g) $0.008\,13 \times 0.15$ (h) 0.0111×0.0046

8. Evaluate using logarithms:

(a) $\dfrac{0.764}{0.029}$ (b) $\dfrac{0.0471}{0.0034}$ (c) $\dfrac{1.371}{0.9191}$

(d) $\dfrac{13.6}{0.6112}$ (e) $\dfrac{0.742}{8.36}$ (f) $\dfrac{27.8 \times 0.16}{0.461}$

(g) $\dfrac{0.0084}{0.172}$ (h) $\dfrac{0.005 \times 0.34}{3.76}$

9. Calculate using logarithms:

(a) $\sqrt{259}$ (b) $\sqrt[3]{94}$ (c) $\sqrt{8.7}$ (d) $\sqrt[4]{144}$
(e) $\sqrt[3]{17.26}$ (f) $\sqrt{0.016}$ (g) $\sqrt[3]{0.0027}$ (h) $(19.2)^{\frac{1}{2}}$
(i) $(0.0136)^{\frac{1}{4}}$ (j) $(14.8)^{\frac{3}{2}}$ (k) $(0.298)^{\frac{1}{3}}$ (l) $(0.76)^{\frac{1}{3}}$

10. Evaluate, using logarithms:

(a) $(22.3)^2$ (b) $(8.91)^3$ (c) $(19.84)^3$
(d) $(0.41)^2$ (e) $(0.013)^3$ (f) $(0.0026)^4$
(g) $(1.7 \times 10^{-4})^3$ (h) $(1.2 \times 10^{-3})^2$ (i) $(1.24 \times 10^{-6})^3$

11. Use logarithms to evaluate:

$$\frac{9\,810\,000}{3.14 \times (0.06)^2 \times 0.000\,75}$$

stating the answer in standard form.   (Y.H.C.F.E.)

12. Use logarithms to evaluate, correct to three significant figures. $\sqrt{(38.45)^3}$, stating the answer in standard form. (N.C.T.E.C.)

13. Evaluate using logarithms:

(a) $\dfrac{(1.74)^3 + (0.625)^2}{0.0066}$

(b) $(6.451)^{\frac{3}{2}}$ (Y.H.C.F.E.)

14. Evaluate, using tables $\sqrt[3]{(7.819)^2}$.

(C.G.L.I.)

15. Use mathematical tables to evaluate:

(i) $\dfrac{7.93 \times (0.832)^2}{6.57}$

(ii) $\sqrt{0.0573}$.   (U.E.I.)

16. Evaluate by means of logarithms:
(i) $\sqrt{0.928}$
(ii) $(2.865)^{1.4}$.   (E.M.E.U.)

17. Evaluate:

(a) $\sqrt[3]{\dfrac{10.47 \times 0.6589}{172.4}}$

(b) $(14.46)^{1.4}$.   (U.L.C.I.)

18. Use logarithms to evaluate:

(i) $\dfrac{\sqrt{0.762}}{1.893}$

(ii) $\dfrac{1}{(0.00765)^2}$ (U.E.I.)

19. Evaluate, using tables of logarithms:
(a) $5278 \times 9.346 \times 0.002\,15$

(b) $\dfrac{0.002351}{0.01784}$

(c) $(0.005\,432)^{\frac{1}{3}}$
(d) $(9.762)^7$ (E.M.E.U.)

20. Use tables to evaluate the following:

(a) $\dfrac{12.72 \times 0.0869}{1.286}$

(b) $(9.242)^{\frac{2}{3}}$

(c) $\dfrac{1}{0.1819}$ (E.M.E.U.)

21. Using tables find the value of $\dfrac{28.6 \times 0.063}{10^2}$ in standard form. (N.C.T.E.C.)

22. Evaluate, using logarithms:

(a) $\dfrac{1}{16.18 \times \sqrt{120}}$

(b) $(0.001\,442)^{\frac{1}{2}}$

(c) $4\pi \sqrt[3]{\left(\dfrac{49.27 \times 3}{4\pi}\right)^2}$ (E.M.E.U.)

23. Evaluate, without using tables:
$$\log_{10}60 - \log_{10}12 + \log_{10}2$$

24. Find without tables the value of:
$$5\log_{10}2 + \log_{10}16 - \log_{10}4$$

25. Find, without using tables, the value of:
$$4\log_{10}3 - \log_{10}27 + \log_{10}\tfrac{1}{3} - \log_{10}\sqrt{3}$$
(N.C.T.E.C.)

26. Calculate, without using tables:
$$\log_{10}30 + \log_{10}50 - \log_{10}15$$

27. Given $\lg 2 = 0.3010$, $\lg 3 = 0.4771$, and $\lg 5 = 0.6990$, determine, without the use of logarithm tables, $\lg 2.5$, $\lg 6$, $\lg 22.5$, and $\lg 75$.

28. Given $\lg 2 = 0.3010$, $\lg 3 = 0.4771$, and $\lg 7 = 0.8451$, find, without using logarithm tables, $\lg 1.5$, $\lg 3.5$, $\lg 8$, and $\lg 63$.

29. Write the numbers 2 and 64 as powers of 4 and hence find $\log_4 2$ and $\log_4 64$.

30. (a) Using logarithm tables, write the number 4.5 as a power of 10. Hence write 4.5^3 as a power of 10.
(b) Using $\lg 4.5$ from part (a) above, find $\lg 45\,000$ and hence find $\sqrt{45\,000}$ to 4 sig. figs.

31. If $\lg A = a$, $\lg B = b$, and $\lg C = c$, write $\lg A^2BC$ and $\lg AB/\sqrt{C}$ in terms of a, b, and c.

32. Given that $\lg W = 2\lg I + \lg R + \lg t$, write a formula for W.

33. From the formula $W = V^2t/R$, write an equation for $\lg W$.

34. The area of a circle is given by the equation $A = \pi D^2/4$. Write a formula for $\lg A$. Use logarithm tables to simplify the formula.

35. Determine $\lg 243$ given that $\log_3 243 = 5.0$.

36. Given that lg $\pi = 0.4972$, find $\log_e \pi$ where e = 2.718.

37. The formula $A = \sqrt{\{s(s-a)(s-b)(s-c)\}}$ gives the area of a triangle when the lengths of the three sides, a, b, and c are known. Given that $s = (a+b+c)/2$, use logarithm tables to find the area of a triangle whose sides are $a = 37.1$, $b = 44.2$, and $c = 61.3$ millimetres respectively.

38. When a material is heated its thermal coefficient of linear expansion (α) is given by

$$\alpha = \frac{\text{increase in length}}{\text{original length} \times \text{temp. rise}} \text{ mm/mm/}°C$$

(Note: This unit is generally abbreviated to /°C which means 'per °C'.)
A steel rod, 500 mm long at a temperature of 20 °C, expands by 0.45 mm when heated to 95 °C.
(a) Use logarithm tables to determine the thermal coefficient of linear expansion for the steel.
(b) Express the value of α in standard form.

ANSWERS TO EXERCISES 6

1. (a) 0.4972 (b) 0.9917 (c) 3.8932 (d) 4.6628 (e) 0.3345 (f) 4.3345 (g) 5.3363 (h) 1.2127.

2. (a) 69.0 (b) 3 (c) 200 (d) 981 (e) 6000 (f) 60.03 (g) 11.21 (h) 210.1

3. (a) 260.8 (b) 478.4 (c) 1142 (d) 475.8 (e) 57 800 000 (f) 1 528 000 (g) 1210 (h) 34.4.

4. (a) 3.168 (b) 44.32 (c) 10.67 (d) 169.5 (e) 13.89 (f) 67.6 (g) 2.78 (h) 1.161.

5. (a) 0.5 (b) $\bar{3}.8388$ (c) $\bar{2}.8419$ (d) $\bar{4}.9191$ (e) $\bar{5}.0414$ (f) $\bar{5}.3617$ (g) $\bar{6}.0792$ (h) $\bar{5}.2788$ (i) $\bar{5}.2304$.

6. (a) 0.2942 (b) 0.000 17 (c) 0.000 11 (d) 0.054 (e) 0.009 804 (f) 0.002 301 (g) 0.010 11 (h) 0.000 014 01

7. (a) 2.308 (b) 0.3512 (c) 0.010 43 (d) 0.000 003 005 (e) 0.001 748 (f) 1.452 (g) 0.001 219 (h) 0.000 051 06.

8. (a) 26.34 (b) 13.85 (c) 1.492 (d) 22.25 (e) 0.088 76 (f) 9.646 (g) 0.048 84 (h) 0.000 452 2.

9. (a) 16.09 (b) 4.546 (c) 2.949 (d) 3.464 (e) 2.584 (f) 0.1265 (g) 0.1392 (h) 4.381 (i) 0.3415 (j) 56.93 (k) 0.6679 (l) 0.9124.

10. (a) 497.2 (b) 707.5 (c) 7807 (d) 0.1681 (e) 0.000 002 197 (f) 4.571×10^{-11} (g) 4.811×10^{-12} (h) 1.44×10^{-6} (i) 1.906×10^{-18}.

11. 1.157×10^{12}.

12. 5.685×10^4.

13. (a) 857 (b) 16.38

14. 3.94.

15. (i) 0.8353 (ii) 0.2394.

16. (i) 0.9632 (ii) 4.366.

17. (a) 0.3421 (b) 42.11.

18. (i) 0.4611 (ii) 17090.

19. (a) 106 (b) 0.1318 (c) 0.1758 (d) 8.443×10^6.

20. (a) 0.8595 (b) 4.403 (c) 5.497.

21. 1.801×10^{-2}.

22. (a) 0.005 641 (b) 0.037 98 (c) 65.

23. 10.

24. 128.

25. $\dfrac{1}{\sqrt{3}}$.

26. 100.

27. 0.3980, 0.7781, 1.3522, 1.8751.

28. 0.1761, 0.5441, 0.9030, 1.7993.

29. $4^{\frac{1}{2}}$, 4^3, 0.5, 3.0.

30. (a) $10^{0.6532}$, $10^{1.9596}$ (b) 4.6532, 212.1.

31. $2a+b+c$, $a+b-\dfrac{c}{2}$.

32. $W = I^2 Rt$.

33. lg $W = 2$ lg $V + $lg $t - $lg R.

34. lg $A = $lg $\pi + 2$ lg $D - $lg $4 = 2$ lg $D - 0.1049$.

35. 2.3855.

36. 1.145.

37. 812.9 mm².

38. (a) 0.000 012/°C (b) 1.2×10^{-5}/°C.

7 | Calculators

7.1. SLIDE RULE

7.1.1. Introduction. It is easy to use a slide rule even though it may take practice to become really familiar with it. In using the various scales it will be found helpful to work out a simple problem which can be checked mentally before going on to more complicated calculations. In this way confidence and a proper understanding of the scales is quickly built up, together with an appreciation of the very great use which can be made of the slide rule.

The main parts of the slide rule are shown in Fig. 7.1.

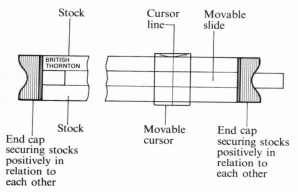

Fig. 7.1

A slide rule can be regarded normally as giving the answer to a calculation to an accuracy of three significant figures (although sometimes a fourth significant figure can be read off). (See sections 1.4 and 2.3.)

Usually the approximate value of an answer is known and, therefore, also the position of the decimal point. If, however, there is any doubt a rough check should be carried out. (See also section 1.5.)

Each of the scales on a slide rule serves a particular purpose, and the number of scales may vary from one type of slide rule to another. Details of the basic scales included on all slide rules are given in the following table.

7.1.2. C and D scales. These two scales are the most frequently used on a slide rule and are the basic scales normally used for multiplication, division, ratios etc. An inspection of these C and D scales will show that they are numbered from left to right viz., 1, 11, 12 and so on 2, 3, 4, 5, to 10. It will probably be easier to imagine the numbering as 100, 110, 120...200, 300, 400,

TABLE 7.1

Scales	Application	Functional symbol of scales	Division of scales
C and D	Multiplication, division, proportion.	x	1–10
C1	Reciprocals, Continuous multiplication with C and D scales	$\dfrac{1}{x}$	10–1
A and B	Squares and square roots	x^2	1–100

500...to 1000 as this will help in reading and setting the first three significant figures of numbers. Fig. 7.2 shows the settings for various significant figure values. It will be noticed how values between adjacent lines sub-dividing the scale change from left to right along the scale. At the beginning the sub-divisions run 1, 101, 102, 103, 104, 105 etc up to 110—thus giving a change of 1 in the third significant figure—and continue in this way up to the 2 position. The scale then runs 2, 202, 204 etc., thus giving a change of 2 in the third significant figure and further along the scale the change in third significant figure is 5. These changes in the values of sub-divisions on the various scales of the slide rule must be constantly observed.

The C and D scales are logarithmic scales numbered naturally. This accounts for the fact that the distance between 1 and 2 is greater than the distance between 2 and 3 which in turn is greater than the distance between 3 and 4 and so on to 10. But the important thing to realise is that these logarithmic scales are of uniform proportional accuracy. A displacement of the C scale in relation to the D scale gives a fixed proportional relationship for all points in alignment. This can be seen by moving the slide to the right so that 1 on C scale is over 2 on D scale and observing that opposite 2 on C scale is

```
1      11   12   13  2            25  8       9      10
|.....|....|....|....|     |....|....|....|   |....|....|....|.....|
  :    :   :    :           :   :    :    :     :    :    :
101 1075 115 122          202 210 225 241     805 850 917
```
Fig. 7.2

4 on D scale, opposite 3 on C is 6 on D, etc., thereby giving a portion of the two times table. Similarly by setting 1 on C scale over 3 on D scale a portion of the three times table is obtained.

7.1.3. Division. This is carried out by subtracting one logarithmic length (the divisor) from another (the dividend).

EXAMPLE 7.1. Evaluate $\dfrac{84}{24}$.

SOLUTION

Set the cursor at 84 on the D scale (referred as D_{84}) and move the slide so that 24 on the C scale (referred to as C_{24}) aligns with the cursor line. At 1 on C scale (referred to as C_1) read 35 on the D scale i.e. the significant figures of the answer. Considering the position of the decimal point gives 3.5.

EXAMPLE 7.2. Evaluate $\dfrac{30.6}{68}$.

SOLUTION

Set the cursor at 306 on the D scale and move the slide so that 68 on the C scale aligns with the cursor line. At 10 on C scale read 45 on the D scale, the significant figures of the answer. The decimal point considered gives 0.45.

The two examples only differ in the respect that in example 7.1 the answer aligns with C_1 on the D scale and in example 7.2 the result is found at C_{10}.

7.1.4. Multiplication. This is carried out by adding together the logarithmic lengths which correspond to the numbers.

EXAMPLE 7.3. Evaluate 2.6×3.5.

SOLUTION

Move the slide bringing C_1 to D_{26}, set the cursor at C_{35} and read on the D scale 91, the significant figures of 2.6×3.5. Considering the position of the decimal point gives 9.1.

EXAMPLE 7.4. Evaluate 3.25×4.4.

SOLUTION

Cursor to D_{325}, C_{10} to cursor, cursor to C_{44} and read 143 on the D scale the significant figure value of 3.25×4.4. The position of the decimal point considered gives 14.3.

Again it will be noted that the only difference between examples 7.3 and 7.4 is in respect of applying either C_1 or C_{10}, the choice being such as to bring the second factor within the D scale range.

7.1.5. Compound multiplication and division. The same principle applies of adding and subtracting logarithmic lengths corresponding to the numbers.

The general rule is—the *first* numerator value is set on the D scale. *All other* numerator and denominator values are set on the slide (thus adding or subtracting them from the logarithmic length of the first numerator value). The *answer* is read on the D scale.

Note. Movement of the *cursor* carries out *multiplication*. Movement of the *slide* carries out *division* and these operations must take place *alternately*. If the *cursor* is moved last the result is read at the cursor on D scale. If the *slide* is moved last the result is read on the D scale against the C_1 or C_{10} line.

EXAMPLE 7.5. Find the value of:

$$\frac{161 \times 923 \times 152}{258 \times 172}.$$

SOLUTION

Instruction	Stage	Significant figures of result on D scale at:		
		C_1	C_{10}	Cursor
(i) Set cursor at D_{161}	161			
(ii) Move slide bringing C_{258} to the cursor	$\dfrac{161}{258}$		624	
(iii) Cursor to C_{928}	$\dfrac{161}{258} \times 923$			576
(iv) Move slide bringing C_{172} to the cursor	$\dfrac{161 \times 923}{258 \times 172}$	335		
(v) Cursor to C_{152}	$\dfrac{161 \times 923 \times 152}{258 \times 172}$			509

Taking the position of the decimal point into consideration, by doing a rough check, gives 509.0.

EXAMPLE 7.6. Find the value of:

$$\frac{0.0535 \times 741.0 \times 4.87}{0.1925 \times 0.0524}.$$

SOLUTION

In this example, if factors are taken in the order in which they occur, alternating from numerator to denominator etc., what is known as an 'end switch' occurs as one of the factors on the slide to which it is desired to move the cursor extends beyond the end of the stock of the rule. The method involved for end switching is simply as follows:

When the slide protrudes to the left of the stock move the cursor to C_{10} and then 'end switch' the slide by bringing C_1 to the cursor. If the slide protrudes to the right of the stock move the cursor to C_1 and then 'end switch' the slide by bringing C_{10} to the cursor.

'End switching' does not affect the accuracy of the answer as it is simply the equivalent of multiplying or dividing by 1 or 10 and the significant figures remain the same.

Instruction	Stage	Significant figures of result on D scale at:		
		C_1	C_{10}	Cursor
(i) Set cursor at D_{535}	535			
(ii) Move slide C_{1925} to cursor	$\dfrac{535}{1925}$	278		
(iii) 'End switch'. Cursor to C_1				
(iv) Move slide C_{10} to cursor				
(v) Cursor to C_{741}	$\dfrac{535 \times 741}{1925}$			206
(vi) Move slide C_{524} to cursor	$\dfrac{535 \times 741}{1925 \times 524}$		393	
(vii) Cursor to C_{487}	$\dfrac{535 \times 741 \times 487}{1925 \times 524}$			1914

Placing the decimal point, by a rough check, gives 19 140.0.

7.1.6. Reciprocals. In Chapter 5, the reciprocal of a number was defined as 1/(number) and was obtained by dividing the number into 1.

Using a slide rule, the reciprocal of a number can be obtained by cursor projection from the C to the C1 scale. Particular care must be taken, when using the Reciprocal of C scale (C1), to keep in mind the reverse direction of ascending significant figures.

EXAMPLE 7.7. Find the value of 1/2.345.

SOLUTION

Set the cursor at 2345 on the C scale and read 4265 on the C1 scale, i.e. the significant figures of the answer. Considering the position of the decimal point gives 0.4265.

7.1.7. Square roots and squares. It will be observed that Scale A, of two $\frac{1}{2}$-unit sections, (viz 1 to 10 and 10 to 100) is arranged in relation to the D scale (unit length) so that:

$$A_1 \text{ aligns with } D_1$$
$$A_{100} \text{ aligns with } D_{10}$$

Using the cursor for projection from D scale to A scale

the following alignments can be observed:
(a) for involution

D	1	2	3	4	5	etc	10
A	1	4	9	16	25	etc	100

i.e. 'squares' of values on D are in alignment on A.
(b) for evolution, a reverse process provides 'square roots' of the values on A in alignment with D scale.

Since each section of the A scale provides a full cycle of signficant figure range, in the case of 'square roots' the user has to decide which of the two sections is applicable to any particular evaluation.

Consider numbers whose significant figure value is 2788. Such values may occur in various forms as 0.000 278 8, 0.002 788, etc. or 278.8, 278 800, etc.

By way of illustration consider determination of the square roots of three of these say

$$\sqrt{0.000\ 278\ 8}, \quad \sqrt{278.8} \quad \text{and} \quad \sqrt{278\ 800}.$$

Starting from the decimal point arrange bars over pairs of numbers as shown.

$$0.\overline{00}\ \overline{02}\ \overline{78}\ \overline{80} \qquad (1)$$
$$\overline{2}\ \overline{78}.\overline{80} \qquad (1a)$$
$$\overline{27}\ \overline{88}\ \overline{00}. \qquad (2)$$

(1) and (1a) are alike in the respect that the first significant figure 2 is alone under a bar, whereas in (2) the first two significant figures, that is '27', occur under the same bar. In cases such as (1) or (1a) projection is from the first section of the A scale whilst case (2) calls for projection from the 2nd Section.

EXAMPLE 7.8. Evaluate $\sqrt{0.000\ 278\ 8}$.

SOLUTION

Starting from the decimal point arrange bars over pairs of number as shown.

$$\sqrt{0.\overline{00}\ \overline{02}\ \overline{78}\ \overline{8}}$$

The first significant figure '2' is alone under a bar and projection is from the first section of scale A.

Set the cursor to 2788 on the first section of scale A and read 167 on the D scale. Again consider the pairs, and with cipher or figure in the result for each pair:

$$\sqrt{0.\overline{00}\ \overline{02}\ \overline{78}\ \overline{8}}$$
$$\downarrow \quad \downarrow \quad \downarrow \quad \downarrow$$
$$0.0 \quad 1 \quad 6 \quad 7$$

Thus the result is 0.0167.

EXAMPLE 7.9. Evaluate $\sqrt{278.8}$.

SOLUTION

Proceed as described in example 7.8 above.

$$\sqrt{\overline{2}\ \overline{78}.\overline{80}}$$
$$\downarrow \quad \downarrow \quad \downarrow$$
$$1 \quad 6. \quad 7$$

Cursor to 2788 on 1st Section of A and read on D scale 167. This significant figure value 167, decimal point considered, becomes 16.7. The result is, therefore, 16.7.

EXAMPLE 7.10. Evaluate $\sqrt{278\,800}$.

SOLUTION

Proceed as described in example 7.8 above.

$$\sqrt{27\ \overline{88}\ \overline{00}}.$$

The first two significant figures '27' occur under the same bar. Projection is from the second section of scale A.

$$\sqrt{27\ \overline{88}\ \overline{00}}$$
$$\downarrow\ \downarrow\ \downarrow$$
$$5\quad 2\quad 8$$

Cursor to 2788 on the 2nd Section of A scale and read on D scale 528. This significant figure group 528, decimal point considered, becomes 528.0. Thus the result is 528.0.

EXAMPLE 7.11. Find the value of π^2.

SOLUTION

Set the cursor to π on the D scale and read 9873 on scale A. Taking the position of the decimal point into consideration gives 9.873. Thus π^2 equals 9.873.

7.2. ELECTRONIC CALCULATOR

7.2.1. Introduction. There are many different models of electronic calculator on the market, varying from those which will perform only the simplest of arithmetical processes to models which will carry out many mathematical processes. An important consideration of any display calculator is its capacity: the larger its capacity, the greater its accuracy and performance.

When switched to the 'on' position the display will show ▢ 0.▢. A number is entered, just as written, using the keys (0) to (9) together with the decimal key (.) when appropriate.

7.2.2. Keyboard. Fig. 7.3 shows the keyboard of a versatile calculator, but the use of only those basic keys found on most calculators will be described here.

(C) The **Clear Entry/Clear** key.
Pressing this key during or immediately after a numerical entry will clear the display. Only prior entries are retained intact. Pressing the key in all other cases clears the calculator. (Note. Memories are not cleared.)

(×) The **Multiplication** key.
The use of this key completes any previous calculation

Fig. 7.3

displays the immediate result and stores the current multiplication function.

(÷) The **Division** key.
Pressing this key completes any previous calculation, displays the immediate result, and stores the current 'divide' command.

(+) The **Addition** key.
Using this key completes any previous calculation, displays the immediate result, and stores the current 'add' command.

(−) The **Subtraction** key.
The use of this key completes any previous calculation, displays the immediate result, and stores the current 'subtract' command.

(+/−) The **Change Sign** key.
Pressing this key commands the calculator to change the sign of the quantity appearing in the display. The key can be pressed at any time, before, during or after the entry of a number to effect the sign change.

(=) The **Result** (Equals) key.
The use of this key completes any previous calculation and displays the result of the calculation.

(.) The **Decimal** key.
Pressing this key enters a decimal point.

(π) The **Pi** key.
Using this key enters the value of Pi (π) to ten significant digits into a calculation. The display will read 3.141592654.

(1/x) The **Reciprocal** key.
Pressing this key commands the calculator to divide the numeral 'one' by the number displayed and display the result.

(x^2) The **Square** key.
The use of this key commands the calculator to determine the square of the displayed number, i.e. to multiply the displayed number by itself. the answer is automatically displayed.

$(\sqrt{x})$ The **Square Root** key.
Using this key commands the calculator to compute the square root of the displayed number, i.e. to determine that number, which when multiplied by itself, equals the currently displayed number. The answer is automatically displayed.

(y^x) $(\sqrt[x]{y})$ The **y to the Power of x** keys.
Pressing either of these keys instructs the calculator to raise the number displayed to the required power (or root).

EXAMPLE 7.12. Find the value of $6.59+0.03$.

SOLUTION

Enter	Depress function key	Read
6.59	+	6.59
.03	=	6.62

The result is 6.62.

EXAMPLE 7.13. Find the value of $0.0072-63.4-12.88$.

SOLUTION

Enter	Depress function key	Read
.0072	−	0.0072
63.4	−	−63.3928
12.88	=	−76.2728

The result is −76.2728.

EXAMPLE 7.14. Find the value of 35.86×11.45.

SOLUTION

Enter	Depress function key	Read
35.86	×	35.86
11.45	=	410.597

The result is 410.597.

EXAMPLE 7.15. Evaluate $91.0\div7.35$.

SOLUTION

Enter	Depress function key	Read
91	÷	91.
7.35	=	12.38095238

The result is 12.38095238.

EXAMPLE 7.16. Evaluate $2.1\times(-3.2)$.

SOLUTION

Enter	Depress function key	Read
2.1	×	2.1
	+/−	−0.
3.2	=	−6.72

The result is −6.72.

EXAMPLE 7.17. Find the value of $1/4.2$.

SOLUTION

Enter	Depress function key	Read
4.2	1/x	0.238095238

ALTERNATIVE

Enter	Depress function key	Read
1	÷	1.
4.2	=	0.238095238

The result is 0.238095238.

EXAMPLE 7.18. Find the value of $3\pi^2$.
SOLUTION
Notes: (i) $3\pi^2$ is NOT the same as $(3\pi)^2$.
(ii) $3\pi^2$ can be written as $\pi^2\times3$.

Enter	Depress function key	Read
π	x^2	9.869604404
	×	
3	=	29.60881321

The result is 29.60881321.

EXAMPLE 7.19. Evaluate $4.1+\sqrt{3}$.

SOLUTION

Enter	Depress function key	Read
4.1	+	4.1
3		3.
	$\sqrt{x}$	1.732050807
	=	5.832050807

The result is $\boxed{5.832050807}$.

EXAMPLE 7.20. Find the value of 0.9^4.

SOLUTION

Enter	Depress function key	Read
.9	y^x	0.9
4	=	0.656099999

The result is $\boxed{0.656099999}$.

7.3. COMPARISON OF AIDS TO CALCULATIONS

Some of the uses of a slide rule and of an electronic calculator have been described in sections 7.1 and 7.2, while in Chapters 5 and 6 the uses of various four-figure mathematical tables have been explained. A few of the relative advantages and disadvantages of these several aids to calculations are summarized in Table 7.2.

EXERCISES 7

The following exercises should be worked using a slide rule and/or an electronic calculator. As an additional exercise, the answers obtained may be checked by the use of mathematical tables.

The answers to the exercises are generally given to an accuracy of four significant figures.

1. Evaluate each of the following:
   (a) 8.381^2 (b) 0.6538^2 (c) $0.045\,74^2$ (d) 27.35^2.

2. Find the value of each of the following:
   (a) $\sqrt{0.4634}$ (b) $\sqrt{0.001\,638}$ (c) $\sqrt{808.7}$ (d) $\sqrt{83.83}$.

3. Determine the value of each of the following:
   (a) $1/0.3927$ (b) $1/6.817$ (c) $1/45.22$ (d) $1/246.8$.

4. Evaluate each of the following:
   (a) 70.24×0.4275.
   (b) $748.0\times0.002\,092$.
   (c) $3.821\times7.398\times21.82$.
   (d) $62.43\times1.782\times11.28$.

5. Compute each of the following:
   (a) $0.7521\div0.0305$.
   (b) $967.0\div13.21$.
   (c) $75.75\div733.4$.
   (d) $8.667\div273.6$.

TABLE 7.2.

Aid to Calculations	Advantages	Disadvantages
Four-figure tables	Very cheap.	Accuracy to four significant figures at most. Slow in use.
Slide rule	Quicker in use than tables.	Accuracy generally to three significant figures only. Position of decimal point in answer not given.
Electronic calculator	High-speed in use. More versatile than tables and slide rule. Very accurate. (A machine with a ten digit number display and two digit exponent can handle values as small as 1.0×10^{-99} up to 9.999999999×10^{99} which affords far greater precision than is known for most of the physical constants in the universe).	Requires some maintenance. (Batteries to recharge or replace).

6. Determine the value of each of the following:
   (a) $\dfrac{1.658\times29.31}{14.08}$
   (b) $\dfrac{5.384\times16.57}{110.8}$
   (c) $\dfrac{36.42}{9.28\times48.06}$
   (d) $\dfrac{84.3}{5.768\times0.7308}$.

7. Evaluate each of the following:
   (a) $\sqrt{(4.86\div7.491)}$
   (b) $\sqrt{(8.672^2+17.37)}$
   (c) $(3.7\times4.8)^2+\sqrt{2468}$
   (d) $\sqrt{(6.82+17.81)}-\pi^2$.

8. If $\dfrac{1}{f}=\dfrac{1}{u}+\dfrac{1}{v}$, calculate the value of f when $u=1000$ mm and $v=250$ mm.

9. Given that $\dfrac{1}{R}=\dfrac{1}{R_1}+\dfrac{1}{R_2}+\dfrac{1}{R_3}$, find the value of R when $R_1=9\Omega$, $R_2=18\Omega$ and $R_3=36\Omega$.

10. If $r=\sqrt{\dfrac{hR^2}{h+d}}$, calculate the value of r when $h=0.52$, $R=8.5$ and $d=0.3$.

11. If a triangle has sides of length a, b and c, and s is the semi-perimeter $\left(\text{i.e. } s=\dfrac{a+b+c}{2}\right)$, the area A of the triangle can be obtained using the formula
$$A=\sqrt{s(s-a)(s-b)(s-c)}.$$
Find the area A when $a=10.4$, $b=16.9$ and $c=21.3$ millimetres.

(C.G.L.I.)

12. The Brinell hardness number H of a material may be determined from the formula

$$H = \frac{W}{\frac{\pi D}{2}[D - \sqrt{(D^2 - d^2)}]}$$

where W is the dead load, in kilogrammes, applied to the ball, D is the diameter of the ball and d is the diameter of the indentation, both diameters being measured in millimetres.

Calculate the Brinell hardness number H when $W = 3000$ kg, $D = 10$ mm, $d = 2.45$ mm and $\pi = 3.142$.

(U.E.I.)

13. When applying a flattening test to boiler tubes, a section of tube is compressed between flat platens. The distance H between platens to which a mild steel tube of outside diameter D and wall thickness t must be flattened without failure is given by

$$H = \frac{1.09t}{0.09 + \frac{t}{D}}$$

Find H when $t = 3.2$ mm and $D = 51$ mm.

(C.G.L.I.)

14. If a solid strut of diameter S is replaced by a tubular strut having an outside diameter of D and an inside diameter of d, the cross-sectional areas of the struts being equal, the ratio B of their stiffnesses can be obtained from the formula

$$B = \frac{D^4 - d^4}{DS^3}$$

Find B, to two significant figures, when $D = 25$, $d = 15$ and $S = 20$ millimetres.

(C.G.L.I.)

15. When a projectile is discharged with a velocity V at an angle θ to the horizontal, the theoretical range R is given by the formula

$$R = \frac{2V^2 \sin \theta \cos \theta}{g}.$$

Calculate the value of R, in metres to three significant figures, when $V = 80$ m/s, $\theta = 40°$ and $g = 9.81$m/s^2.

(C.G.L.I.)

16. When a closely-coiled helical spring is subjected to compressive loading, the maximum outside diameter of the spring increases, the greatest value occurring when the spring is compressed solid.

If
D = nominal mean diameter of spring
p = pitch of coils
d = diameter of wire
and
C = maximum outside diameter when compressed solid,
then

$$C = d + \sqrt{\left(\frac{p^2 + 4D^2 - d^2}{4}\right)}.$$

(a) Find C when $D = 22$ mm, $p = 10$ mm and $d = 4$ mm.
(b) By what percentage has the maximum outside diameter increased when the spring is compressed solid?

(C.G.L.I.)

ANSWERS TO EXERCISES 7

1. (a) 70.24 (b) 0.4275 (c) 0.002 092 (d) 748.0
2. (a) 0.6807 (b) 0.040 47 (c) 28.44 (d) 9.156
3. (a) 2.546 (b) 0.1467 (c) 0.022 11 (d) 0.004 052
4. (a) 30.03 (b) 1.565 (c) 616.8 (d) 1255.0
5. (a) 24.66 (b) 73.20 (c) 0.1033 (d) 0.031 68
6. (a) 3.451 (b) 0.8052 (c) 0.081 66 (d) 20.00
7. (a) 0.8055 (b) 9.622 (c) 365.1 (d) −4.907
8. 200 mm.
9. 5.143 Ω
10. 6.769
11. 86.59 mm^2
12. 626.2
13. 22.75 mm
14. 1.7
15. 630 m
16. (a) 26.47 mm (b) 1.81 %

8 | Basic algebra

8.1. FUNDAMENTAL LAWS

Algebra is a branch of mathematics in which symbols, usually letters, represent numbers. The letters are used either to express general relationships, as for example in Chapter 4 where $a^m \times a^n = a^{m+n}$ (a, m, and n representing any numbers), or to indicate quantities satisfying certain conditions.

All the laws of arithmetic apply equally to algebra.

Three of the fundamental laws, which it will be seen are already familiar from Chapter 1, are now given.

8.1.1. The commutative laws:
(a) For addition.

From a knowledge of arithmetic it is known that

$$4 + 7 = 7 + 4,$$

or, in words, adding 4 to 7 is equivalent to adding 7 to 4. Similarly, in algebra, where the letters a and b may represent any number,

$$a + b = b + a.$$

The commutative law applied to addition merely indicates that the numbers or letters may be added in any order.

(b) For multiplication.

Similarly in arithmetic

$$2 \times 3 = 3 \times 2;$$

again in words, the product of 2 by 3 is equivalent to multiplying 3 by 2.

Applied to algebra, where a and b represent any numbers,

$$a \times b = b \times a.$$

The commutative law applied to multiplication simply indicates that the numbers or letters may be multiplied in any order.

8.1.2. The associative laws:
(a) For addition.

In arithmetic

$$9 + 6 + 4 = (9 + 6) + 4 = 9 + (6 + 4).$$

This statement indicates the order in which the three numbers are added will not make any difference to the final result. Expressed in another way $9 + 6 + 4 = 15 + 4 = 19$ or $9 + 10 = 19$. Applying this law to algebra where a, b, c represent any numbers

$$(a + b) + c = a + (b + c).$$

The associative law applied to addition simply indicates that these operations may be carried out in any order.

(b) For multiplication.

In arithmetic

$$3 \times 4 \times 6 = (3 \times 4) \times 6 = 3 \times (4 \times 6).$$

Applied to algebra where a, b, c represent any numbers then

$$a \times b \times c = (a \times b) \times c = a \times (b \times c).$$

The associative law applied to multiplication indicates that the multiplication of any numbers may take place in any order.

In practical terms the associative laws indicate that in order to add or multiply three numbers it is immaterial which pair of numbers is initially operated upon.

8.1.3. The distributive law
This law applies where both multiplication and addition are involved, for example

$$3 \times (4 + 5) = 3 \times 4 + 3 \times 5.$$

The left hand side of the equation indicates 'add $4 + 5$' then 'multiply the result by 3' and this is equivalent to multiplying each number separately by 3 and then adding the results.

Note. On the right-hand side of the example multiplication must be completed before addition.

Applying this law to algebra where a, b, c are any numbers the distributive law is expressed as

$$a \times (b + c) = a \times b + a \times c.$$

In practice the distributive law states that to multiply an expression in a bracket by a number, multiply each term in the bracket by the number and remove the brackets.

Note. Again on the right-hand side of the expression do not attempt to add b to a.

The operations $a \times b$ and $a \times c$ must take place before addition.

8.2. ALGEBRAIC EXPRESSIONS
The basic language used in algebra is perhaps more easily demonstrated by reference to a worked example.

EXAMPLE 8.1. To maintain an adequate number of small tools in the stores of an engineering workshop an order was made for drills, taps, and reamers. It was necessary to order five times as many 1.5 mm drills and twice as many 3.5 mm as 7.5 mm drills. The taps were all of one size as also were the reamers.

If x is the number of 7.5 mm drills required, y the number of taps required, and z the quantity of reamers ordered, find in terms of x, y, z,
  (i) the number of 1.5 mm drills ordered,
 (ii) the number of 3.5 mm drills required,
(iii) the total number of drills required,
(iv) the total number of small tools ordered.

SOLUTION

  (i) Since x is the number of 7.5 mm drills ordered, then five times x will be the number of 1.5 mm drills required.
  $\therefore$ Number of 1.5 mm drills $= 5 \times x = 5x$.
 (ii) Similarly, the number of 3.5 mm drills ordered $= 2 \times x = 2x$.
(iii) The total number of drills required is obtained by adding together
$$x + 2x + 5x = 8x.$$
  Total number of drills required $= 8x$.
(iv) The total number of small tools required will be,

number of drills + number of taps + number of reamers.

i.e. $8x$ (drills) $+ y$ (taps) $+ z$ (reamers) or simply $8x + y + z$.

A number of important general definitions and facts arising from this example are now considered.

DEFINITIONS

1. *Expression.* In example 8.1 (solution part iv), the statement $8x + y + z$ is called an algebraic expression. The expression uses letters and multiples of letters to express certain conditions.

2. *Term.* Each part of the expression connected by a $+$ or $-$ sign is called a term. For example, $8x$, y, and z are called terms of the expression $8x + y + z$.

   In part (iii) of the solution to example 8.1, the terms x, $2x$, and $5x$ are said to be like terms, as they only differ from one another by a numerical quantity. In such cases, like terms can be added or subtracted and reduced to a single term.

   The terms of the expression $8x + y + z$ are unlike terms and therefore the expression cannot be further reduced.

3. *Factors.* The terms $5x$ and $2x$ are made up of factors. the factors of $5x$ are 5 and x and of $2x$, 2, and x.

4. *Coefficient.* Any one of the factors of a term may be called the coefficient of the other(s). In the case of $5x$ the coefficient may be the 5 or the x, although it is generally accepted that the numerical factor is the coefficient.

Points to note.

1. In parts (i) and (ii) of the solutions to example 8.1 it

can be seen that $5 \times x$ and $2 \times x$ were shortened to $5x$ and $2x$ respectively. This is standard practice in algebra whereas in arithmetic the omission of a multiplication sign would obviously lead to much confusion. For example, the number 25 represents $20 + 5$ not 2×5.

Frequently in algebra a dot is also used to denote multiplication. In this sense $2 \cdot 2x$ means $2 \times 2x = 4x$.

2. The coefficients of the terms y and z in the expression $8x + y + z$ are 1, i.e. $1y$ and $1z$. However the coefficient 1 is normally omitted from a term. hence $1z$ is written as z and $1y$ is written as y.

EXAMPLE 8.2. Reduce the following expression to three terms and state the coefficients of p, q, and r in the final expression
$$p + 3q + 4p + 2r + 6q + 3r.$$

SOLUTION

Collecting like terms (p), $p + 4p = 5p$
$\qquad\qquad\qquad (q)$, $3q + 6q = 9q$
$\qquad\qquad\qquad (r)$, $2r + 3r = 5r$
Hence $p + 3q + 4p + 2r + 6q + 3r = 5p + 9q + 5r$.
The coefficient of $p = 5$, $q = 9$ and $r = 5$.

8.3. ALGEBRAIC ADDITION

In science plus and minus signs are frequently used to distinguish between movements or actions taking place in opposite directions. Consider the following simple illustration taken from mechanics.

EXAMPLE 8.3. Two forces act on a body as shown in Fig. 8.1. Find the magnitude and direction of the resultant in each case.

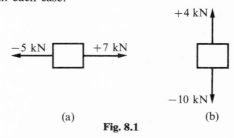

(a)   (b)

Fig. 8.1

SOLUTION

(a) To find the resultant it is necessary to add together the forces acting on the body. However since it is also necessary to take into account the directions in which they act, the forces acting to the left are prefixed by a minus sign and forces acting to the right are prefixed by a plus sign.

By algebraic addition, resultant $= -5$ kN $+ 7$ kN
$$= +2 \text{ kN}.$$

$\therefore$ The magnitude of the resultant force $= 2$ kN.
The plus sign of the 2 kN force simply indicates that if the body were free to move it would do so towards the right or positive(+) direction.

(b) In this case the resultant is also obtained by algebraic addition.

$$\therefore \text{ resultant} = -10 \text{ kN} + 4 \text{ kN}$$
$$= -6 \text{ kN}.$$

Magnitude or size of force = 6 kN

The minus sign here indicates that if the body were free to move it would do so in a downward direction.

In this example it should be noted that the + and − signs were used to indicate direction.

In a similar manner plus and minus signs are used in algebra to denote direction in a general sense. It is therefore essential to understand and to be able to manipulate negative (−) and positive (+) quantities.

The following example illustrates, by using numbers, how negative and positive quantities are added algebraically.

EXAMPLE 8.4. Find the average value of the following pairs of temperatures.
(a) 18 °C and 10 °C
(b) 11 °C and −5 °C
(c) −4 °C and −2 °C
(d) −6 °C and 4 °C.

SOLUTION
The average or mean temperature in all these cases is found by adding together the two temperatures and dividing the result by 2.

(a) The average of 18 °C and 10 °C $= \dfrac{18\,°C + 10\,°C}{2}$

$$= \dfrac{28\,°C}{2} = 14\,°C.$$

It should be noted that in the absence of a plus or minus sign the quantity, in this case temperature, is deemed to be positive (+)

i.e. 18 °C = +18 °C and 10 °C = +10 °C.

(b) Average temperature $= \dfrac{11\,°C + (-5\,°C)}{2}$

$$= \dfrac{11\,°C - 5\,°C}{2} \quad \text{(see rule for addition)}$$

$$= \dfrac{6\,°C}{2} = 3\,°C.$$

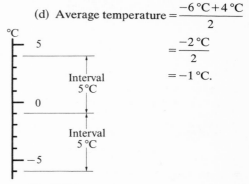

Fig. 8.2(a)

Note. The temperature intervals in Fig. 8.2(a) confirm this answer.

(c) Average temperature $= \dfrac{-4\,°C + (-2\,°C)}{2}$

$$= \dfrac{-4\,°C - 2\,°C}{2}$$

$$= \dfrac{-6\,°C}{2}$$

$$= -3\,°C.$$

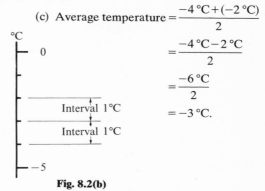

Fig. 8.2(b)

Note. Again Fig. 8.2(b) confirms this result.

(d) Average temperature $= \dfrac{-6\,°C + 4\,°C}{2}$

$$= \dfrac{-2\,°C}{2}$$

$$= -1\,°C.$$

Fig. 8.2(c)

Note. From Fig. 8.2(c) it can be seen that there are 5 temperature intervals between −1 °C and −6 °C and −1 °C and 4 °C, hence confirming the result of −1 °C as the average temperature.

The algebraic addition which has been carried out in example 8.4, although applied to numbers, also applies equally to the addition of positive and negative quantities involving letters.

The method of algebraic addition applied to example 8.2 is now given as a general rule.

(1) *Quantities having the same sign.*
When adding quantities together having the same sign, i.e. either both plus or both minus, add them as in arithmetic and prefix the final result with the sign which is common to both quantities.

e.g. add −7 − 2 = −9

add 7 + 2 = +9 = 9.

(2) *Quantities having opposite signs.*
Where the quantities have oppostie signs, i.e. one plus and one minus, find the difference between the quantities and prefix the result with the sign of the greater

quantity.

e.g. add $3a - 7a = -4a$

add $7a - 3a = +4a = 4a$.

EXAMPLE 8.5. Find the sum of the following expressions

(a) $-3x + 2x - 8x + 7x$
(b) $3a - 4a - 2a + a$
(c) $-7p + 4q + 3p + 5q$

SOLUTION

(a) Collect all the terms having like signs

$$-3x - 8x = -11x$$
$$+2x + 7x = +9x$$
$$\therefore -3x - 8x + 2x + 7x = -11x + 9x$$
$$= -2x.$$

(b) In similar manner to (a) collect terms having like signs

$$3a + a = 4a$$
$$-4a - 2a = -6a$$
$$\therefore 3a - 4a - 2a + a = 4a - 6a$$
$$= -2a.$$

(c) In this example the answer will contain two unlike terms. Consider the terms containing p, then

$$-7p + 3p = -4p$$

Secondly

$$4q + 5q = 9q$$
$$\therefore -7p + 4q + 3p + 5q = -4p + 9q.$$

8.4. ALGEBRAIC SUBTRACTION

The idea of algebraic subtraction is again illustrated by reference to a temperature scale.

EXAMPLE 8.6. Find the difference between the following pairs of temperatures
(a) 6 °C and 4 °C
(b) 5 °C and −2 °C
(c) −2 °C and −5 °C

SOLUTION

(a) To find the difference between the two temperatures it is necessary to subtract the lower temperature from the higher one.

$$\therefore \text{ temperature difference} = 6\,°C - (+4\,°C)$$

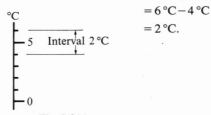

$$= 6\,°C - 4\,°C$$
$$= 2\,°C.$$

Fig. 8.3(a)

(b) Again temperature difference

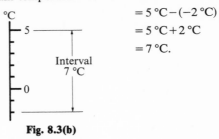

$$= 5\,°C - (-2\,°C)$$
$$= 5\,°C + 2\,°C$$
$$= 7\,°C.$$

Fig. 8.3(b)

(c) In this case the higher temperature is represented by −2 °C. The temperature difference is therefore obtained by subtracting −5 °C from −2 °C.

$$\therefore \text{ temperature difference} = -2\,°C - (-5\,°C)$$

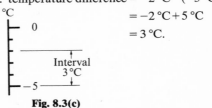

$$= -2\,°C + 5\,°C$$
$$= 3\,°C.$$

Fig. 8.3(c)

The algebraic subtraction carried out in each of the parts, a, b, c will show agreement with the temperature differences shown in Fig. 8.3(a–c). The general rule applied to algebraic subtraction will help to clarify the operations carried out in example 8.6.

When subtracting one quantity from another change the sign of the quantity to be subtracted and proceed as in algebraic addition.

Note. In example 8.6 part (a) +4 °C became −4 °C, part (b) −2 °C became +2 °C, and part (c) −5 °C became +5 °C.

EXAMPLE 8.7. Subtract $4x + 3y$ from $8x + 2y$.

SOLUTION

For simplicity the quantity to be subtracted is placed under the quantity from which it is to be subtracted, like terms being placed under like terms.

$$\begin{array}{r} 8x + 2y \\ 4x + 3y \\ \hline 4x - y \\ \hline \end{array}$$

Step 1: Change the sign of $+3y$ to $-3y$ and algebraically add $+2y$ and $-3y$. It is inadvisable to physically change the sign as this may lead to confusion. Answer $-y$.

Step 2: Change the sign of $4x$ to $-4x$ and algebraically add to $8x$. Answer $4x$. (Again the change of sign is only performed mentally)

$$\therefore 8x + 2y \text{ minus } 4x + 3y = 4x - y.$$

EXAMPLE 8.8. Subtract $4a+3b-c$ from $7a+2b$.

SOLUTION

$7a+2b$

$4a+3b-c$

Again change the sign of the quantity to be subtracted and add algebraically.

Step 1: $-c$ from $0=+c$, (there are no terms involving c on the top line)

Step 2: $3b$ from $2b=-b$, (change sign of $3b$ to $-3b$ and add algebraically)

Step 3: $4a$ from $7a=3a$, (change sign of $4a$ to $-4a$ and add to $7a$ algebraically)

$$\therefore \ 7a+2b \text{ minus } 4a+3b-c = 3a-b+c.$$

8.5. ALGEBRAIC MULTIPLICATION

Apart from adding or subtracting positive or negative terms or quantities, it is also necessary to be able to multiply and divide such quantities. The following rules must therefore be applied when multiplying quantities having similar or dis-similar signs.

1. *When quantities or terms having the same sign are multiplied together the resulting quantity is positive.*
2. *When quantities or terms having opposite signs are multiplied together the resulting quantity is negative.*
   To emphasise these two rules they may be expressed in the following way:
   (a) $(+)\times(+)=+$
   (b) $(-)\times(-)=+$
   (c) $(-)\times(+)=-$

EXAMPLE 8.9. Simplify $8x \times 3y$.

SOLUTION

'Simplify' means express in a more compact form. Since both terms are positive the final result will be positive.

Step 1: Multiply together the numerical coefficients of the two quantities.

Step 2: Multiply together x and y

$$\therefore \ 8x \times 3y = 24 \times x \times y.$$

Earlier in the chapter it was stated that the multiplication sign may be omitted between letters and between letters and numbers.

$$\text{Hence } 24 \times x \times y = 24xy.$$

EXAMPLE 8.10. Simplify $-3a \times 5bc$

SOLUTION

In this example the quantities are of opposite sign

$$\therefore \ -3a \times 5bc = -15abc$$
$$(-)\times(+)=(-)$$

Note. $-15abc = -15 \times a \times b \times c$.

EXAMPLE 8.11. Simplify $2a \times 3a \times 4a$

SOLUTION

This is the first example to include a common letter in each term i.e. 'a'. Reference should be made to the chapter on indices (Chapter 4).

Step 1: Multiply together the three coefficients 2, 3, and 4.

$$2 \times 3 \times 4 = 24$$

Step 2: Multiply $a^1 \times a^1 \times a^1 = a^{1+1+1}$ (i.e. add the powers of a^1)

$$\therefore \ a \times a \times a = a^3$$
$$\therefore \ 2a \times 3a \times 4a = 24a^3.$$

EXAMPLE 8.12. Simplify $-3x^2 \times 4x^3 \times -2x$.

SOLUTION

Step 1: Multiply together the numerical coefficients

$$-3 \times 4 = -12$$
$$(-)\times(+)=(-)$$

then

$$-12 \times -2 = 24$$
$$(-)\times(-)=(+)$$

Step 2: Applying law of indices to the powers of x

$$x^2 \times x^3 \times x = x^{2+3+1} = x^6$$
$$\therefore \ -3x^2 \times 4x^3 \times -2x = 24x^6.$$

EXAMPLE 8.13. Simplify $-3a^2b \times 5abc \times 2c$.

SOLUTION

One method of proceeding is to multiply together two of the terms and multiply the result by the third term.

Step 1: $-3a^2b \times 5abc$
$$= -3 \times 5 \times a^2 \times a \times b \times b \times c$$
$$= -15a^3b^2c \quad (\text{since } a^2 \times a = a^3 \text{ and } b \times b = b^2)$$

Step 2: $-15a^3b^2c \times 2c$
$$= -15 \times 2 \times a^3 \times b^2 \times c \times c$$
$$= -30a^3b^2c^2 \quad (\text{since } c \times c = c^2).$$

The following two examples show the method of procedure when the multiplicand or multiplier contains more than one term.

EXAMPLE 8.14. Multiply $x-y$ by $2+x$

SOLUTION

Step 1: Multiply $x-y$ by 2

$$(x-y)\times 2 = 2x-2y$$

Step 2: Multiply $x - y$ by the second term x and add the result to $2x - 2y$

$$(x - y) \times x = x^2 - xy$$

Step 3: $2x - 2y$ plus $x^2 - xy$

$$= x^2 - xy + 2x - 2y$$

Note. $x - y$ and $2 + x$ are called the factors of $x^2 - xy + 2x - 2y$.

EXAMPLE 8.15. Multiply $a - 2b$ by $a^2 - 2ab$.

SOLUTION

Step 1: Multiply $a - 2b$ by a^2

$$(a - 2b) \times a^2 = a^3 - 2a^2b$$

Step 2: Multiply $a - 2b$ by $-2ab$

$$(a - 2b)x - 2ab$$
$$= -2a^2b + 4ab^2$$

Step 3: Add $a^3 - 2a^2b$ and $-2a^2b + 4ab^2$

$$\therefore (a - 2b) \times (a^2 - 2b) = a^3 - 4a^2b + 4ab^2.$$

Note 1. In the final expression although all the terms contain 'a' as a factor they cannot be added together since: (1) all the powers of 'a' are different and (2) some of the terms contain powers of b. In other words all the terms of this expression are unlike.

Note 2. $a - 2b$ and $a^2 - 2ab$ are factors of the final expression.

8.6. ALGEBRAIC DIVISION

The rules of signs applied to multiplication also apply to division.

1. *When a term or quantity is divided by another term or quantity having the same sign the resulting answer is positive.*
2. *When a term or quantity is divided by another term or quantity having the opposite sign the resulting answer is negative.*

These rules may be expressed in the following manner:

(a) $\dfrac{(+)}{(+)} = (+)$

(b) $\dfrac{(-)}{(-)} = (+)$

(c) $\dfrac{(+)}{(-)} = (-)$

(d) $\dfrac{(-)}{(+)} = (-)$

These rules are now applied to a number of examples.

EXAMPLE 8.15. Simplify $\dfrac{6x^3}{2x}$

SOLUTION

Step 1: Divide the coefficient of $6x^3$, i.e. 6, by the coefficient of $2x$, i.e. 2.

then

$$\frac{6x^3}{2x} = \frac{3x^3}{x} \qquad \frac{(+)}{(+)} = (+)$$

Step 2: Divide x^3 by x using the rule of indices for division, i.e. subtract the power of x from the power of x^3

then

$$\frac{3x^3}{x} = 3x^{3-1} = 3x^2$$

Hence

$$\frac{6x^3}{2x} = 3x^2.$$

EXAMPLE 8.16. Divide $-8a^4$ by $2a^2b$.

SOLUTION

Step 1: Divide coefficients:

then

$$\frac{-8a^4}{2a^2b} = \frac{-4a^4}{a^2b} \qquad \frac{(-)}{(+)} = (-)$$

Step 2: Divide a^2 into a^4 using law of indices:

then

$$\frac{-4a^{4-2}}{b} = \frac{-4a^2}{b}.$$

Note 1. The factor 'b' does not change.

Note 2. It should be understood that

$$\frac{-4a^2}{b} = -\frac{4a^2}{b} = \frac{4a^2}{-b},$$

i.e. the fraction is negative irrespective of the position of any of the three $(-)$ signs.

EXAMPLE 8.17. Divide $9a^3bc$ by $-3a^2b^2c^3$.

SOLUTION

Step 1: Divide coefficient 9 by coefficient -3:

then

$$\frac{9a^3bc}{-3a^2b^2c^3} = \frac{-3a^3bc}{a^2b^2c^3}.$$

Step 2: Use the law of indices for division to simplify the powers of a, b, and c:

then

$$\frac{-3a^3bc}{a^2b^2c^3} = \frac{-3a^{3-2}}{b^{2-1}c^{3-1}}$$

Note. In order to keep the powers of b and c positive, b and c on the top line have been cancelled into the powers of b and c on the bottom line.

$$\therefore \frac{-3a^{3-2}}{b^{2-1}c^{3-1}} = \frac{-3a}{bc^2}.$$

EXAMPLE 8.18. Simplify $\dfrac{2a^3 - 4a^2 - a}{a}$

SOLUTION

In this case each term is divided separately by a.

$$\frac{2a^3 - 4a^2 - a}{a} = 2a^2 - 4a - 1$$

In those cases where there is more than one term in the divisor and dividend the procedure shown in example 8.19 is followed.

EXAMPLE 8.19. Divide $x^2 - 7x + 12$ by $x - 3$.

SOLUTION

The procedure is similar to that used in arithmetic for long division.

Step 1: Arrange the dividend and divisor in descending powers of x and set out in the form of a normal arithmetical long division problem.

$$\begin{array}{r} x-4 \\ x-3\overline{\smash{\big)}\ x^2-7x+12} \\ \underline{x^2-3x} \\ -4x+12 \\ \underline{-4x+12} \end{array}$$

Step 2: Divide x^2 by x to find part of quotient x.

Step 3: Multiply whole of divisor by x to obtain $x^2 - 3x$ and place this expression under corresponding terms in the dividend.

Step 4: Subtract $x^2 - 3x$ from $x^2 - 7x$ to obtain $-4x$.

Step 5: Bring down next term in the dividend, 12, giving $-4x + 12$.

Step 6: Divide x into $-4x$ to give -4 which is next part of quotient.

Step 7: Multiply divisor by -4 to give $-4x + 12$ and subtract from $-4x + 12$.

Hence $x^2 - 7x + 12 \div x - 3 = x - 4$.

Note. $x-3$ and $x-4$ are factors of $x^2 - 7x + 12$, i.e. $(x-3)(x-4) = x^2 - 7x + 12$.

EXAMPLE 8.20. Divide $2a^2 - 3ab - 44b^2 + 1$ by $a + 4b$.

SOLUTION

$$\begin{array}{r} 2a-11b \\ a+4b\overline{\smash{\big)}\ 2a^2-3ab-44b^2+1} \\ \underline{2a^2+8ab} \\ -11ab-44b^2 \\ \underline{-11ab-44b^2} \\ \text{Remainder is} +1 \end{array}$$

$$\therefore \frac{2a^2-3ab-44b^2+1}{a+4b} = 2a-11b \text{ remainder 1}$$

or

$$2a-11b+\frac{1}{a+4b}.$$

8.7. USE OF BRACKETS

8.7.1. Brackets. Brackets indicate that all the terms, or quantities, inside the bracket must be operated upon by the term, or quantity, outside the bracket when the latter is removed.

Two important points emerge when brackets are removed from an expression.
1. *If a bracket is multiplied by a positive (+) quantity the sign of the terms within the bracket remain unchanged when the bracket is removed.*
2. *If a bracket is multiplied by a negative (−) quantity all the signs within the bracket must be changed from + to −, or − to + on removal of the bracket.*

EXAMPLE 8.21. Simplify the expression $3(a+b)-2(3a-4b)$

SOLUTION

To simplify the expression it is necessary to remove the brackets and then collect together like terms.
$3(a+b)$ becomes $3a+3b$ on removal of brackets.
$-2(3a-4b)$ becomes $-6a+8b$ on removal of brackets.
Note. The -2 changes $3a$ into $-6a$ and $-4b$ into $+8b$.
Hence $3(a+b)-2(3a-4b) = 3a+3b-6a+8b$
Collecting like terms $3a+3b-6a+8b = -3a+11b$
$\therefore 3(a+b)-2(3a-4b) = -3a+11b$.

EXAMPLE 8.22. Simplify $-(2x^2+3x-1)+(2x^2+4x-1)$.

SOLUTION

The apparent absence of a quantity in front of the bracket simply indicates that quantity is equal to 1.

$$\therefore -(2x^2+3x-1) = -1(2x^2+3x-1) = -2x^2-3x+1$$

i.e. all the signs in the brackets change.

$$+(2x^2+4x-1) = +1(2x^2+4x-1) = 2x^2+4x-1$$

i.e. no signs change on removal of the bracket.

$$\therefore -(2x^2+3x-1)+(2x^2+4x-1)$$
$$= -2x^2-3x+1+2x^2+4x-1.$$

Collecting like terms $-2x^2-3x+1+2x^2+4x-1 = x$.

$$\therefore -(2x^2+3x-1)+(2x^2+4x-1) = x.$$

8.7.2. Multiple Brackets. It is frequently necessary to use more than one set of brackets in an expression. The main types of brackets used are (round), [square] and {curly}.

To simplify an expression which contains more than one set of brackets multiply out the pairs of brackets in order, starting with the innermost pair.

EXAMPLE 8.23. Simplify $2\{a + 5[2a - 4(3 - 2a)]\}$.

SOLUTION

Step 1: Remove (round) brackets.
Expression becomes $2\{a + 5[2a - 12 + 8a]\}$.
Step 2: Remove [square] brackets.
giving $2\{a + 10a - 60 + 40a\}$.
Step 3: Remove {curly} brackets and simplify.

$$2a + 20a - 120 + 80a$$
$$= 102a - 120.$$

8.8. ALGEBRAIC FRACTIONS

In arithmetic before two or more fractions having different denominators, can be added or subtracted it is necessary to find the lowest common multiple of the fractions. This same principle is applied in algebra.

EXAMPLE 8.24. Express as a single fraction

$$\frac{1}{R_1} + \frac{1}{R_2} + \frac{1}{R_3}.$$

SOLUTION
The L.C.M. of R_1, R_2, and R_3 is $R_1 \times R_2 \times R_3$ or $R_1 R_2 R_3$.

$$\therefore \frac{1}{R_1} + \frac{1}{R_2} + \frac{1}{R_3} = \frac{R_2 R_3 + R_1 R_3 + R_1 R_2}{R_1 R_2 R_3}.$$

Note. R_1 divides into $R_1 R_2 R_3$, $R_2 R_3$ times
R_2 divides into $R_1 R_2 R_3$, $R_1 R_3$ times
R_3 divides into $R_1 R_2 R_3$, $R_1 R_2$ times.

EXAMPLE 8.25. Simplify $\dfrac{3u - v}{2v} - \dfrac{v - 2u}{4u}$.

SOLUTION
Step 1: Find the L.C.M. of the denominators $2v$ and $4u$ which is $4uv$.
Step 2: Divide $4uv$ by $2v$: result equals $2u$. Multiply numerator $(3u - v)$ by $2u$.
Step 3: Divide $4uv$ by $4u$: result equals v. Multiply numerator $(v - 2u)$ by $-v$, the minus sign $(-v)$ being the one prefixing the second fraction.
Hence

$$\frac{3u - v}{2v} - \frac{v - 2u}{4u} = \frac{2u(3u - v) - v(v - 2u)}{4uv}.$$

Step 4: Multiply out the brackets of the numerator and simplify:

$$\frac{2u(3u - v) - v(v - 2u)}{4uv} = \frac{6u^2 - 2uv - v^2 + 2uv}{4uv}$$
$$= \frac{6u^2 - v^2}{4uv}.$$

EXERCISES 8

Algebraic addition.

1. Given the following pairs of moments find the magnitude and direction of their resulting moment. Clockwise moments are considered to be positive and anticlockwise moments negative:
   (a) $6\,\text{N m} - 3\,\text{N m}$ (b) $-8\,\text{N m} + 5\,\text{N m}$ (c) $1\,\text{N m} + 3\,\text{N m}$
   (d) $-6\,\text{N m} - 5\,\text{N m}$ (e) $-5\,\text{N m} + 5\,\text{N m}$

2. Find the mean value of the following pairs of temperatures:
   (a) $5\,°\text{C}$ and $9\,°\text{C}$ (b) $3\,°\text{C}$ and $-5\,°\text{C}$
   (c) $10\,°\text{C}$ and $-2\,°\text{C}$ (d) $-6\,°\text{C}$ and $-4\,°\text{C}$
   (e) $20\,°\text{C}$ and $-20\,°\text{C}$.

3. Find an expression for the mean value of the following pairs of temperatures given in $°\text{C}$:
   (a) a and b (b) $-x$ and y (c) $2y$ and $8y$
   (d) $-t$ and $7t$ (e) $6a$ and $-7b$ (f) $-7x$ and $-13x$

Simplify the expressions given in questions 4–20.

4. $3x + 8x - 2x$

5. $4a + 3a - 7a$

6. $9y - 4y - 7y$

7. $4xy + 7xy - 8xy$

8. $3ab + 2ab - 6ab$

9. $4ba + 2ab + 5ba$

10. $-4abc + 6abc - 8abc$

11. $7x + 8xy + 8y - 4xy - 3y$

12. $2ax + 4xy - 3ax - 2xy$

13. $3a^2 + 4b^2 - 3c^2 - 2a^2 - 3b^2 + 2c^2$

14. $3x^2y + 4x^2 - x^2y - 2x^2$

15. $-3 + 4ac - 7 - ac$

16. $-8 + 7x^2y + 6xy^2 + 4 - 7xy^2 + 3x^2y$

17. $7T_1 - 5T_2 + 8T_1 + 6T_2$

18. $5R_1 - 6R_2 + R_3 - 5R_1 + 3R_2$

19. $\dfrac{3v}{I} - \dfrac{4v}{I} + \dfrac{6v}{I}$

20. $3Al + 5Al - 2Al$

Algebraic subtraction

21. Find the difference between the following pairs of temperatures:
    (a) $10\,°\text{C}$ and $2\,°\text{C}$ (b) $8\,°\text{C}$ and $-4\,°\text{C}$
    (c) $-9\,°\text{C}$ and $7\,°\text{C}$ (d) $-8\,°\text{C}$ and $-4\,°\text{C}$
    (e) $9\,°\text{C}$ and $-9\,°\text{C}$.

22. Find an expression for the temperature difference between the following pairs of temperatures given in °C.
(a) a and b (b) $2a$ and $-4a$
(c) $-2x$ and $-4x$ (d) $-2t$ and $-12t$

In questions 23 to 40 subtract:

23. $2a+b$ from $3a+2b$

24. $2x+y$ from $7x-y$

25. $3v+4u$ from $5u+3v$

26. $4T_1+T_2$ from $8T_1-2T_2$

27. $-3v_1+2v_2$ from $-3v_1+3v_2$

28. $-6+y$ from $6+2y$

29. $-a^2+2b^2$ from $2a^2+3b^2$

30. $3x-5y-2z$ from $2x-3y+4z$

31. $gt-2u^2$ from $3gt+u^2$

32. $15-200a-b$ from $20-400a-b$

33. $4R^2-3R+2$ from $6R^2-2R+2$

34. $90+B-C$ from $180-B-C$

35. $4m^2+2m-6$ from $3m^2+2m-3$

36. $3abc-2bc+b^2$ from $2cab+2bc+b^2-4$

37. $\dfrac{2V}{R_1}-\dfrac{E}{R_2}$ from $\dfrac{5V}{R_1}-\dfrac{4E}{R_2}$

38. $\frac{1}{2}gt^2-2s$ from $-\frac{1}{2}gt^2+s$

39. $\dfrac{z}{4}+\dfrac{z^2}{3}$ from $z+z^2$

40. $\dfrac{5L}{2}+7$ from $3L+7$

Algebraic multiplication

In questions 41 to 60 multiply out and simplify, where necessary.

41. 2 by $5y$

42. $3x$ by $4y$

43. $3x$ by $2x$

44. $-3z$ by $5z$

45. $-3a$ by $(-4a\times 6a)$

46. $4x^2$ by $3x^3$

47. $-a^3$ by $6a^2$

48. $a-b$ by $b-a$

49. $-3abc$ by $2ab$

50. $3a^2+a-6$ by $a-3$

51. $2x-3$ by $2x-3$

52. $x-y$ by $x+y$

53. $2\pi R$ by R

54. $\dfrac{A}{l}$ by $\dfrac{A}{l^2}$

55. $3-a$ by $3+a$

56. $a+b$ by $c+d$

57. $x+y$ by $a-b$

58. v^2-2gs by $3t+2$

59. $3t^3-5t+6$ by $2t^2-3t+1$

60. $8y^3x-3xy+4$ by $3xy-2y$

Algebraic division.

In questions 61 to 80 divide:

61. $3x$ by 3

62. $6x^2$ by x

63. $10y^3$ by $2y^2$

64. $-5z^2$ by z

65. $-9t^2$ by $-3t$

66. $-12x^2$ by $4x$

67. $10x^3y^2$ by $-2x^2y$

68. $-20a^2b^3c^2$ by $-5abc$

69. $\dfrac{4\pi r^3}{3}$ by $2\pi r^2$

70. $-\frac{3}{5}x^2y$ by $\frac{3}{20}xy^2$

71. $-15a^3bc$ by $-3a^2b^2c^2$

72. $9abc$ by $18a^2b^2c^2$

73. $2x^2-3x-9$ by $x-3$

74. $2x^3-x^2-12x-9$ by $x+1$

75. $5a^2x+4ax-15a-12$ by $5a+4$

76. x^2-9 by $x-3$

77. $25a^2-4x^2$ by $5a-2x$

78. $6x^2-5x-4$ by $3x-4$

79. $3a^4-10a^3+15a^2-20a+12$ by a^2-3a+2

80. $36x^2-16$ by $6x-4$

In questions 81 to 95 remove brackets and simplify, where possible.

81. $I(R+r)$

82. $t(u+\frac{1}{2}at)$

83. $u(v+v^2)-u(u+v)$

84. $2a-3b+2(a-2b)-2(2a-b)$

85. $3t^2-(a^2+t^2)+(t^2-a^2)$

86. $3x+[(z-1)-(x-1)]$

87. $20\times 2.5(\theta-65)$

88. $12-[(5+2x)-5]$

89. $3x-\{5y+2x-[9y-(3x+2y)]\}$

90. $4s-3[s-(1-s)+2(1+s)]$

91. $2(x-4)+3(x-1)-4(x+1)$

92. $-2a^3(1-a^2-2a)$

93. $a^2-\{b^2-[a^2-(a^2+b^2)]\}$

94. $\{2t-[(a+b)-t]-[2a+2b]\}$

95. $5\times 4.2(100-20)+0.9\times 5\times 2260$

Simplify the expressions given in questions 96 to 109.

96. $\dfrac{x}{2}+\dfrac{x}{3}$

97. $\dfrac{t}{4}-\dfrac{t}{8}$

98. $\dfrac{t+1}{2}+\dfrac{t-2}{4}$

99. $\dfrac{x+3}{5}-\dfrac{2x+1}{3}$

100. $\dfrac{y+3}{2y}-\dfrac{y^2-3}{2}$

101. $\dfrac{1}{R}+\dfrac{2}{R}+\dfrac{3}{R}$

102. $\dfrac{x-1}{2}+\dfrac{x-2}{3}+\dfrac{x-3}{3}$

103. $x+\dfrac{2x-1}{3}+\dfrac{x-1}{4}$

104. $\dfrac{3v+1}{u}-\dfrac{2u+1}{v}$

105. $\dfrac{1}{3R}+\dfrac{1}{2R}+\dfrac{2}{5R}$

106. $\dfrac{3(t-1)}{4}-\dfrac{2(3+t)}{t}$

107. $\dfrac{v+u}{2}-\dfrac{u-v}{u}$

108. $\dfrac{2}{3t}+\dfrac{3}{5t}-\dfrac{1}{10t}$

109. $\dfrac{s}{2}-\dfrac{2(s-1)}{3}$

ANSWERS TO EXERCISES 8

1. (a) 3 Nm; C,   (b) −3 Nm; A/C,   (c) 4 Nm; C
   (d) −11 Nm; A/C,   (e) 0
2. (a) 7 °C   (b) −1 °C   (c) 4 °C   (d) −5 °C   (e) 0 °C
3. (a) $\dfrac{a+b}{2}$,   (b) $\dfrac{-x+y}{2}$,   (c) 5y   (d) 3t   (e) $\dfrac{6a-7b}{2}$
   (f) −10x
4. 9x
5. 0
6. −2y
7. 3xy
8. −ab
9. 11ab
10. −6abc
11. $7x+4xy+5y$
12. $-ax+2xy$
13. $a^2+b^2-c^2$
14. $2x^2y+2x^2$
15. $-10+3ac$
16. $-4+10x^2y-xy^2$
17. $15T_1+T_2$
18. $-3R_2+R_3$
19. $\dfrac{5v}{I}$

20. $6Al$
21. (a) 8 °C   (b) 12 °C   (c) 16 °C   (d) −4 °C   (e) 18 °C
22. (a) $a-b$ (b) $6a$ (c) $2x$ (d) $10t$
23. $a+b$
24. $5x-2y$
25. u
26. $4T_1-3T_2$
27. V_2
28. $12+y$
29. $3a^2+b^2$
30. $-x+2y+6z$
31. $2gt+3u^2$
32. $5-200a$
33. $2R^2+R$
34. $90-2B$
35. $-m^2+3$
36. $-abc+4bc-4$
37. $\dfrac{3V}{R_1}+\dfrac{3E}{R_2}$
38. $-gt^2+3s$
39. $\dfrac{3z}{4}+\dfrac{2z^2}{3}$
40. $\dfrac{l}{2}$
41. $10y$
42. $12xy$
43. $6x^2$
44. $-15z^2$
45. $72a^3$
46. $12x^5$
47. $-6a^5$
48. $2ab-a^2-b^2$
49. $-6a^2b^2c$
50. $3a^3-8a^2-9a+18$
51. $4x^2-12x+9$
52. x^2-y^2
53. $2\pi R^2$
54. $\dfrac{A^2}{L^3}$
55. $9-a^2$
56. $ac+bc+ad+bd$
57. $ax+ay-bx-by$
58. $3v^2t-6gst+2v^2-4gs$
59. $6t^5-9t^4-7t^3+27t^2-23t+6$
60. $24x^2y^4-9x^2y^2+12xy-16y^4x+6xy^2-8y$
61. x
62. $6x$
63. $5y$

64. $-5z$

65. $3t$

66. $-3x$

67. $-5xy$

68. $4ab^2c$

69. $\dfrac{2r}{3}$

70. $\dfrac{4x}{y}$

71. $\dfrac{5a}{bc}$

72. $\dfrac{1}{2abc}$

73. $2x+3$

74. $2x^2-3x-9$

75. $ax-3$

76. $x+3$

77. $5a+2x$

78. $2x+1$

79. $3a^2-a+6$

80. $6x+4$

81. $IR+Ir$

82. $ut+\frac{1}{2}at^2$

83. uv^2-u^2

84. $-5b$

85. $3t^2-2a^2$

86. $2x+z$

87. $50\theta-3250$

88. $12-2x$

89. $-2x+2y$

90. $-8s-3$

91. $x-15$

92. $2a^5+4a^4-2a^3$

93. a^2-2b^2

94. $3t-3a-3b$

95. 11850

96. $\dfrac{5x}{6}$

97. $\dfrac{t}{8}$

98. $\dfrac{3t}{4}$

99. $\dfrac{-7x+4}{5}$

100. $\dfrac{-y^3+4y+3}{2y}$

101. $\dfrac{6}{R}$

102. $\dfrac{7x-13}{6}$

103. $\dfrac{19x-11}{12}$

104. $\dfrac{3v^2+v-2u^2-u}{uv}$

105. $\dfrac{37}{30R}$

106. $\dfrac{3t^2-11t-24}{4t}$

107. $\dfrac{uv^2+u^2-2u+2v}{2u}$

108. $\dfrac{35}{30t}$

109. $\dfrac{-s+4}{6}$

9 | Algebraic factors

9.1. FACTORS

If a quantity is contained an exact number of times in another it is said to be a factor of that other quantity. Thus the numbers 3 and 7 are factors of 21. In the same way the product of $(x-5)$ and $(x+3)$ is $x^2-2x-15$ so that the factors of the expression $x^2-2x-15$ are $(x-5)$ and $(x+3)$. From the foregoing it will be seen that to factorise an algebraic expression, quantities must be found which when multiplied together give the original expression.

Not all algebraic expressions have factors, just as in arithmetic a number such as 179 is said to be prime because it has no factors (other than itself and unity).

There are various methods of factorisation. When factorising any expression, an obvious factor should first be looked for, the factors then being examined in turn to see if they will factorise further.

9.1.1. Single-term common factor. Whatever is common to all terms in an expression is a factor of that expression. Consider, for example, the expression $2x+2y$. Each term contains 2, which is, therefore, a factor of the expression. The common factor is written outside a pair of brackets, inside which is the quotient resulting from the original expression being divided throughout by the common factor. Thus $2x+2y=2(x+y)$ so that 2 and $(x+y)$ are factors of the original expression $2x+2y$. In some cases, when a common factor has been extracted, it will be found that the factor contained in the brackets can itself be factorised.

9.1.2. Factors of certain binomials. A binomial is an algebraic expression consisting of two terms joined by a plus $(+)$ or a minus $(-)$ sign. The binomial should be carefully examined to see if it will factorise and is of a type the factors of which are known. If there is a common factor to the two terms it should be taken out first.

(a) *The difference of two squares.*

Consider Fig. 9.1 which shows a square $ABCD$ with a smaller square $DEFG$ removed from one corner.
Area of large square $ABCD = a \times a = a^2$.
Area of small square $DEFG = b \times b = b^2$.
∴ L-shaped area remaining $= a^2 - b^2$
    (which is the difference of two squares).
By rearranging the L-shaped section as shown its area is seen to be given by a rectangle whose sides are $(a+b)$ and $(a-b)$. Thus $a^2-b^2=(a+b)(a-b)$, so that $(a+b)$· and $(a-b)$ are factors of a^2-b^2.

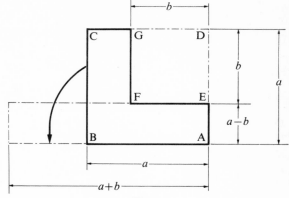

Fig. 9.1

In words, the difference of the squares of two quantities is equal to the product of their sum and their difference.

$$a^2 - b^2 = (a+b)(a-b).$$ These factors should be memorised.

(b) *The sum of two squares*

There are no rational factors for the sum of the squares of two quantities, i.e. a^2+b^2 cannot be factorised in the same way as a^2-b^2.

$$a^2 + b^2 \quad \textbf{has no factors.}$$

(c) *The difference of two cubes*

The product of $(a-b)$ and (a^2+ab+b^2) is a^3-b^3. It follows, therefore, that the factors of a^3-b^3 are $(a-b)$ and (a^2+ab+b^2).

$$a^3 - b^3 = (a-b)(a^2+ab+b^2)$$ These factors should be memorised.

(d) *The sum of two cubes*

The product of $(a+b)$ and (a^2-ab+b^2) is a^3+b^3. Thus the factors of a^3+b^3 are $(a+b)$ and (a^2-ab+b^2).

$$a^3 + b^3 = (a+b)(a^2-ab+b^2)$$ These factors should be memorised.

EXAMPLE 9.1. Evaluate $150^2 - 144^2$ by using factors.

SOLUTION

150^2-144^2 is the difference of two squares. [See section 9.1.2(a).]

$$\therefore \ 150^2 - 144^2 = (150+144)(150-144)$$
$$= 294 \times 6$$
$$= 1764.$$

The result is 1764.

EXAMPLE 9.2. Factorise $9x^2 - 4y^2$.

SOLUTION

The given expression shows the difference of two squares because

$$9x^2 = (3x)^2 \quad \text{and} \quad 4y^2 = (2y)^2.$$
$$\therefore \ 9x^2 - 4y^2 = (3x + 2y)(3x - 2y).$$

9.1.3. Factors of certain trinomials. A trinomial is an algebraic expression consisting of three terms connected by plus (+) or minus (−) signs. In general, the factors of a trinomial are found by inspection (i.e. by trial and error), the resulting factors then being checked by multiplication. The factors of a trinomial are often two binomials. It is sometimes possible first to simplify the trinomial by taking out any factor common to the three terms.

Note. A trinomial expression such as $6x^2 - 13x + 5$ is seen to contain only one unknown (x) and its greatest power is the second (x^2). Such an expression is often referred to as a 'quadratic' expression. The expressions $y^2 + 7y + 10$ and $3z^2 + 13z - 10$ are also examples of quadratic expressions.

The methods of factorising trinomials as described in sections 9.1.3(a) and (b) below will be found useful when solving certain quadratic equations such as $4x^2 - 11x = 3$, which can be rewritten as $4x^2 - 11x - 3 = 0$, showing a trinomial on one side of the equals sign. The solution of quadratic equations is, however, outside the scope of the present book.

(a) *When the coefficient of x^2 is unity and the factors are binomials*

Consider, for example, the trinomial $x^2 - 2x - 15$. The object is to fill in the brackets in the statement $x^2 - 2x - 15 = (\ )(\ )$. In such a case the first term in each binomial is x since their product must give x^2. It is then required to find two numbers such that their product is the absolute term (i.e. -15) in the given trinomial and their sum is the coefficient of x (i.e. -2) in the given trinomial. The possibilities to be considered are, therefore,

(i) $(x + 15)(x - 1) = x^2 + 14x - 15$
[not the given trinomial]

(ii) $(x - 15)(x + 1) = x^2 - 14x - 15$
[not the given trinomial]

(iii) $(x + 5)(x - 3) = x^2 + 2x - 15$
[not the given trinomial]

(iv) $(x - 5)(x + 3) = x^2 - 2x - 15$
[which is the given trinomial].

Check:

$x \times x = x^2$ [the first term in the given trinomial]

$-5 \times 3 = -15$ [the third term in the given trinomial]

$-5 + 3 = -2$ [the coefficient of the second term].

It will be noticed that the sign of the given absolute term is −(minus) and that the second terms in each factor are of opposite signs so that numerically the coefficient of x in the trinomial is their difference.

In the same way, when the sign of the absolute term is +(plus) the second terms is each factor are of the same sign as each other and numerically the coefficient of x in the trinomial is their sum.

(b) *When the coefficient of x^2 is not unity and the factors are binomials*

Consider, for example, the trinomial $3x^2 + 13x - 10$. The object is to fill in the brackets in the statement $3x^2 + 13x - 10 = (\ )(\ )$. In this case the first term in one of the binomials is $3x$ and in the other is x since their product must give $3x^2$. It is then required to find two numbers such that their product is the absolute term (i.e. -10) in the given trinomial. A suitable combination of all the terms in the factors must then be found to equal the second term (i.e. $13x$) in the given trinomial. The possibilities to be considered are, therefore,

(i) $(3x - 10)(x + 1) = 3x^2 - 7x - 10$
[not the given trinomial]

(ii) $(3x + 10)(x - 1) = 3x^2 + 7x - 10$
[not the given trinomial]

(iii) $(x - 10)(3x + 1) = 3x^2 - 29x - 10$
[not the given trinomial]

(iv) $(x + 10)(3x - 1) = 3x^2 + 29x - 10$
[not the given trinomial]

(v) $(3x - 5)(x + 2) = 3x^2 + x - 10$
[not the given trinomial]

(vi) $(3x + 5)(x - 2) = 3x^2 - x - 10$
[not the given trinomial]

(vii) $(x - 5)(3x + 2) = 3x^2 - 13x - 10$
[not the given trinomial]

(viii) $(x + 5)(3x - 2) = 3x^2 + 13x - 10$
[which is the given trinomial].

From the above results it follows that, in general terms,

$$(ax + b)(cx + d) = ac(x^2) + (ad + bc)x + bd,$$

where ac is the coefficient of x^2, $(ad + bc)$ is the coefficient of x, and bd is the absolute term. It is essential that correct mathematical signs are used throughout.

Check: $1 \times 3 = 3$ [the coefficient of x^2]

$(1 \times -2) + (5 \times 3) = -2 + 15 = 13$
[the coefficient of x]

$5 \times -2 = -10$ [the absolute term].

Note. In the examples considered in sections 9.1.3(a) and (b), all the possibilities were shown. In practice, as

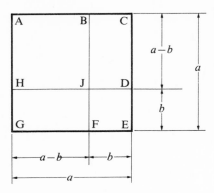

Fig. 9.2

soon as the correct factors are found, the trial and error exercise is discontinued.

(c) *The square of the difference of two terms.*

Consider Fig. 9.2 which shows a square $ACEG$ containing two squares $JHAB$ and $JDEF$ and two rectangles $JBCD$ and $JFGH$ all meeting at J.

Area of square $ACEG = a \times a = a^2$.

Area of square $JDEF = b \times b = b^2$.

Area of square $JHAB = (a-b) \times (a-b) = (a-b)^2$
    [which is the square of the difference of two terms].

Area of rectangle $JBCD = b \times (a-b) = ab - b^2$.

Area of rectangle $JFGH = b \times (a-b) = ab - b^2$.

It will be seen that

area $JHAB$ = area $ACEG$ − area $JDEF$
                        − area $JBCD$ − area $JFGH$,

$$(a-b)^2 = a^2 - b^2 - (ab - b^2) - (ab - b^2),$$
$$= a^2 - b^2 - ab + b^2 - ab + b^2,$$
$$= a^2 + b^2 - ab - ab,$$
$$= a^2 + b^2 - 2ab.$$

Thus $(a-b)$ and $(a-b)$ are factors of the trinomial $a^2 + b^2 - 2ab$.

In words, the square of the **difference** of two quantities is equal to the sum of their squares **minus** twice their product.

$$(a-b)^2 = a^2 + b^2 - 2ab.$$ This result should be memorised.

Note. The factors $(a-b)^2$ are said to form a 'perfect square'.

(d) *The square of the sum of two terms*

The product of $(a+b)$ and $(a+b)$ is $a^2 + b^2 + 2ab$. Thus $(a+b)$ and $(a+b)$ are factors of the trinomial $a^2 + b^2 + 2ab$.

In words, the square of the **sum** of two quantities is equal to the sum of their squares **plus** twice their product.

$$(a+b)^2 = a^2 + b^2 + 2ab.$$ This result should be memorised.

Note. Fig. 9.2 represents geometrically the statement $(a-b)^2 = a^2 + b^2 - 2ab$. The corresponding figure may be drawn to show $(a+b)^2 = a^2 + b^2 + 2ab$.

The factors $(a+b)^2$, like the factors $(a-b)^2$, are said to form a 'perfect square'.

EXAMPLE 9.3. Evaluate 1.002^2.

SOLUTION

1.002^2 may be written as $(1+0.002)^2$ which is the square of the sum of two terms. [See section 9.1.3(d).]

$$\therefore (1+0.002)^2 = 1^2 + 0.002^2 + 2 \times 1 \times 0.002,$$
$$= 1 + 0.000\,004 + 0.004,$$
$$= 1.004\,004.$$

Thus $1.002^2 = 1.004\,004$.

EXAMPLE 9.4. Factorise $4x^2 - 12x + 9$.

SOLUTION

An inspection of this expression shows that

$$4x^2 = (2x)^2 \qquad \text{Note:} \quad \text{Let } 2x = a$$
$$9 = (3)^2 \qquad\qquad\qquad \text{and } 3 = b$$
$$12x = 2 \times 2x \times 3 \qquad\quad \text{then } 12x = 2ab.$$

Thus $4x^2 - 12x + 9$ is of the form $a^2 - 2ab + b^2$ the factors of which are known to be $(a-b)^2$. [See section 9.1.3(c).]

The factors of $4x^2 - 12x + 9$ are, therefore, $(2x-3)^2$.

EXAMPLE 9.5. Simplify

$$\frac{x^2 - 5x}{2x^2 - 9x + 9} \times \frac{x^2 - 9}{x^2 - x - 20} \div \frac{x+3}{2x^2 + 5x - 12}.$$

by using factors.

SOLUTION

In section 2.1.3 it was shown that the division of vulgar fractions is carried out by inverting the divisor and then proceeding as for multiplication. Thus the given expression can be written as

$$\frac{x^2 - 5x}{2x^2 - 9x + 9} \times \frac{x^2 - 9}{x^2 - x - 20} \times \frac{2x^2 + 5x - 12}{x+3}.$$

Each of the numerators and denominators is now

inspected and factorised as found appropriate.

$$x^2 - 5x = x(x - 5).$$

$$\begin{bmatrix} \text{Common factors,} \\ \text{see section 9.1.1.} \end{bmatrix}$$

$$x^2 - 9 = (x + 3)(x - 3).$$

$$\begin{bmatrix} \text{Difference of two squares,} \\ \text{see section 9.1.2(a).} \end{bmatrix}$$

$$2x^2 + 5x - 12 = (2x - 3)(x + 4).$$
$$2x^2 - 9x + 9 = (2x - 3)(x - 3)$$

$$\begin{bmatrix} \text{Trinomials with coefficient} \\ \text{of } x^2 \text{ greater than unity,} \\ \text{see section 9.1.3(b).} \end{bmatrix}$$

$$x^2 - x - 20 = (x - 5)(x + 4).$$

$$\begin{bmatrix} \text{Trinomial with coefficient} \\ \text{of } x^2 \text{ equal to unity,} \\ \text{see section 9.1.3(a).} \end{bmatrix}$$

$x + 3$ will not factorise.

The expression is now written as

$$\frac{x(x - 5)}{(2x - 3)(x - 3)} \times \frac{(x + 3)(x - 3)}{(x - 5)(x + 4)} \times \frac{(2x - 3)(x + 4)}{x + 3}$$

and by cancelling in the usual way the result is found to be x.

9.1.4. Factors of certain polynomials. The name 'binomial' has been given to algebraical expressions consisting of two terms joined by a plus $(+)$ or a minus $(-)$ sign, and 'trinomial' to algebraical expressions consisting of three terms connected by plus $(+)$ or minus $(-)$ signs. When the number of terms exceed three, the expression is called a polynomial. In factorising any polynomial, if all the terms contain a common factor it should be taken out first.

(a) *Polynomials of four terms.*

Certain algebraical expressions containing four terms may be factorised by grouping the terms in two pairs so that each pair has a common factor. The other factor is then found by division. (See example 9.6.)

(b) *Polynomials of five terms*

Certain algebraical expressions containing five terms, and certain polynomials of four terms which will not factorise by grouping, may be factorised if three of the terms form a trinomial having factors. (See example 9.7.)

EXAMPLE 9.6. Factorise $ax + ay - bx - by$.

SOLUTION

An inspection of the given expression shows that there is no factor common to all four terms. But

$$ax + ay - bx - by = (ax + ay) - (bx + by),$$
$$= a(x + y) - b(x + y).$$

The common factor is $(x + y)$, and the second factor, $(a - b)$, is found by division. Thus

$$ax + ay - bx - by = (x + y)(a - b).$$

EXAMPLE 9.7. Factorise $x^2 + y^2 + 2xy + x + y$.

SOLUTION

An inspection of the given expression shows that there is no factor common to all five terms. But

$$x^2 + y^2 + 2xy + x + y = (x^2 + y^2 + 2xy) + x + y$$

where the trinomial in brackets has the factors $(x + y)$ and $(x + y)$, i.e. $(x + y)^2$ which is the square of the sum of two terms. [See section 9.1.3(d).]

$$\therefore \ x^2 + y^2 + 2xy + x + y = (x + y)^2 + x + y,$$
$$= (x + y)^2 + (x + y),$$
$$= (x + y)(x + y + 1).$$

The required factors are $(x + y)(x + y + 1)$.

EXERCISES 9

1. Factorise: (a) $3m^2n - mn^2 + 2mn$,
   (b) $9x^3y - 12x^2y^2 + 6x^2yz$.
2. Factorise: (a) $15y^4 - 5y^2$,
   (b) $2w^2xyz - 2wx^2yz - 2wxy^2z + 6wxyz^2$.
3. Factorise: (a) $x^2 - 16$, (b) $4 - 25x^2$.
4. Factorise: (a) $x^4 - 16$, (b) $108 - 3x^2$.
5. Factorise: (a) $4a^2 + 20a + 25$, (b) $9b^2 - 12b + 4$.
6. Factorise: (a) $4c^2 + 12cd + 9d^2$, (b) $9e^2 - 24ef + 16f^2$.
7. Factorise: (a) $ax^2 + 2axy + ay^2$, (b) $2.5m^2 + 2.5n^2 - 5mn$.
8. Factorise: (a) $8x^3 + 27y^3$, (b) $64t^3 - 1$.
9. Factorise: (a) $a^2 + 6a + 8$, (b) $b^2 - 11b + 10$.
10. Factorise: (a) $c^2 + 4c - 12$, (b) $d^2 - 3d - 10$.
11. Factorise: (a) $36e^2 - 13e + 1$, (b) $2f^2 - 17f + 21$.
12. Factorise: (a) $12h^2 + 7h - 10$, (b) $12 + k - 6k^2$.
13. Factorise: (a) $2m^2 + 7mn - 22n^2$, (b) $4r^2 + 13rs + 3s^2$.
14. Factorise: (a) $11uv - 3v^2 - 6u^2$, (b) $11w^2 - 86wx + 63x^2$.
15. Factorise: (a) $11e^2 - 9ef + 11e - 9f$,
    (b) $ax^2 + bx^2 - 4a - 4b$.
16. Factorise: (a) $a^2 - ax - 3a + 2x + 2$,
    (b) $x^2 - 4x - y^2 + 4$.
17. Simplify $(2x^2 - 8x)/(x^2 - 16)$.
18. Simplify $\dfrac{x^2 + 4x + 3}{x^2} \times \dfrac{2x}{3x + 9}$.
19. Simplify $\dfrac{x - 8}{2x^2 + 3x - 2} + \dfrac{3}{2x - 1} - \dfrac{1}{x + 2}$.
20. Simplify $\dfrac{x\{x^2 + 2(x + 1)\}}{x - 2} + \dfrac{2x(x^2 - 1)}{x^2 - 3x + 2}$.

ANSWERS TO EXERCISES 9

1. (a) $mn(3m-n+2)$, (b) $3x^2y(3x-4y+2z)$.

2. (a) $5y^2(3y^2-1)$, (b) $2wxyz(w-x-y+3z)$.

3. (a) $(x+4)(x-4)$, (b) $(2+5x)(2-5x)$.

4. (a) $(x^2+4)(x+2)(x-2)$, (b) $3(6+x)(6-x)$.

5. (a) $(2x+5)^2$, (b) $(3x-2)^2$.

6. (a) $(2x+3y)^2$, (b) $(3e-4f)^2$.

7. (a) $a(x+y)^2$, (b) $2.5(m-n)^2$.

8. (a) $(2x+3y)(4x^2-6xy+9y^2)$,
(b) $(4t-1)(16t^2+4t+1)$.

9. (a) $(a+4)(a+2)$, (b) $(b-10)(b-1)$.

10. (a) $(c+6)(c-2)$, (b) $(d-5)(d+2)$.

11. (a) $(1-4e)(1-9e)$, (b) $(2f-3)(f-7)$.

12. (a) $(4h+5)(3h-2)$, (b) $(3-2k)(4+3k)$.

13. (a) $(2m+11n)(m-2n)$, (b) $(4r+s)(r+3s)$.

14. (a) $(2u-3v)(v-3u)$, (b) $(w-7x)(11w-9x)$.

15. (a) $(11e-9f)(e+1)$, (b) $(a+b)(x+2)(x-2)$.

16. (a) $(a-2)(a-x-1)$, (b) $(x+y-2)(x-y-2)$.

17. $\dfrac{2x}{x+4}$.

18. $\dfrac{2(x+1)}{3x}$.

19. $\dfrac{1}{x+2}$.

20. $\dfrac{x(x+2)(x+2)}{x-2}$.

10 | Formulae

10.1. CONSTRUCTION OF FORMULAE

An equation is an algebraic statement in which two quantitative expressions are equal to each other: the sign of equality ($=$) means that the expression which precedes it is equal to the expression which follows it. In an equation, such as $6x = 12$, the unknown (x) has a particular value. For the equation $6x = 12$, it will be seen that the value of x can only be 2 because only $6 \times 2 = 12$.

A formula is a generalized equation in which symbols are used to denote numbers. Consider, for example, the area of a rectangle. In every case

the area of a rectangle = its length × its breadth.

Let A = the area of a rectangle, l = the length of the rectangle, and b = the breadth of the rectangle.

Then the above statement can be written in the abbreviated form of

$$A = lb.$$

Such an abbreviated statement is called a formula. The equation $A = lb$ is true for all rectangles and provided that any two of the three quantities A, l, and b are known, the value of the third can be easily determined.

The construction of formulae is further demonstrated in the examples 10.1 and 10.2 which follow.

EXAMPLE 10.1. A steel drum has a mass of m kilograms when empty. When full it contains n kilograms of lubricating oil. Construct a formula for the total mass of D drums full of oil.

SOLUTION

Mass of an empty steel drum = m kilograms.
Mass of oil in one drum = n kilograms.
Total mass of one full drum = $(m + n)$ kilograms.
Total mass of D full drums = $D(m + n)$ kilograms.
Let T = the total mass of the D drums full of oil.
Then $T = D(m + n)$ kilograms.
The formula $T = D(m + n)$ may now be used to find the total mass of any number of drums full of oil when the values of D, m, and n are known.

EXAMPLE 10.2. A vehicle is uniformly accelerated along a straight road so that its velocity increases from u m/s to v m/s in t seconds. Develop a formula for the distance travelled by the vehicle during the period of acceleration.

SOLUTION

$$\text{Average velocity} = \frac{\text{initial velocity} + \text{final velocity}}{2},$$
$$= \frac{u + v}{2} \text{ metres per second.}$$

Distance travelled = average velocity × time.
Let s = the distance travelled in metres.

Then $s = \dfrac{u + v}{2}$ (m/s) × t (s),

$$= \frac{(u + v)t}{2} \text{ metres.}$$

The formula $s = \dfrac{(u + v)t}{2}$ is a very useful one. In physics and in engineering science it is known as one of the 'speed equations' for uniform acceleration.

10.2. EVALUATION OF FORMULAE

When a formula is to be used, and numerical values are to be substituted for the symbols contained in it, the fundamental rules for addition, subtraction, multiplication, and division must be strictly obeyed. Furthermore, it is very important to be consistent in the use of units. For example, if the symbol v in the formula $v = u + at$ represents velocity in metres per second (m/s), then, if the numerical value given for velocity is in kilometres per hour (km/h), a conversion to the proper unit must be made before evaluation.

It has previously been stated that units like the metre (m) or ampere (A) are called base units, while units such as metres per second (m/s) or kilograms per cubic metre (kg/m^3) are called derived units (see section 1.1). In the evaluation of formulae it is often convenient to include all units throughout the expression, preferably in the form of products or quotients of base units, and then to give the units the same treatment as that given to the corresponding numerical values. This will assist in determining the final unit when there is any doubt.

EXAMPLE 10.3. The force on a current-carrying conductor lying in and at right-angles to a magnetic field of flux is given by the formula $F = BIl$ newtons (N) where B is the flux density in tesla (T), I is the current in amperes (A) and l is the effective length of the conductor in metres (m).

A conductor having an effective length of 250 mm and carrying a current of 75 A lies in and at right-angles to a magnetic field of flux density 80 mT. Calculate the force acting on this conductor.

SOLUTION

The first step is to convert to the proper units where appropriate.

$F = BIl$ where $B = 80\,\text{mT} = 0.08\,\text{T}$

$$I = 75\,\text{A}$$
$$l = 250\,\text{mm} = 0.25\,\text{m}.$$

Then $F = 0.08 \times 75 \times 0.25,$

$$= 1.5.$$

The force acting on the conductor is 1.5 newtons.

EXAMPLE 10.4. The kinetic energy possessed by a moving body is given by the formula $W = mv^2/2$, where m is the mass of the body in kilograms and v is its velocity in metres per second.

A locomotive of mass 200 tonnes is travelling at a velocity of 54 km/h. Calculate the kinetic energy of the locomotive.

SOLUTION

The first step is to ensure that units are properly expressed. Mass, $m = 200$ tonnes $= 200\,000$ kg. (See section 1.2.2.)

Velocity, $v = 54\,\text{km/h}$

$$= \frac{54 \times 1000\,\text{metres}}{3600\,\text{seconds}} = 15\,\text{m/s}.$$

The numerical values, together with the corresponding units, can now be substituted for the symbols in the formula

$$W = \frac{mv^2}{2},$$

$$= \frac{200\,000\,\text{kg} \times 15^2\,\text{m}^2/\text{s}^2}{2},$$

$$= 22\,500\,000\,\text{kg m}^2/\text{s}^2.$$

But $1\,\text{N} = 1\,\text{kg m/s}^2$ (see section 1.2.9) so that

$$W = 22\,500\,000\,\text{N m or joules (J)}$$

$$\therefore\ W = 22.5\ \text{megajoules}.$$

The kinetic energy possessed by the locomotive is 22.5 MJ.

10.3. TRANSPOSITION OF FORMULAE

It is often found that a formula must be rearranged in order to solve a particular problem. In transposing any formula it is essential that the equality of the two expressions be maintained throughout the operation.

10.3.1. Formulae involving multiplication and division only. Consider the formula for the power developed by

a torque,

$$P = \frac{2\pi NT}{60}\ \text{watts.}$$

The symbol N represents the rotational speed in revolutions per minute and T represents the torque in newton-metres. As it stands, the formula allows for the calculation of P when the values of N and T are given. Suppose that it is required to make T the subject of the formula, i.e. to isolate T on one side of the sign of equality. The given formula may be written with that part containing T (the required subject) on the left-hand side thus:

$$\frac{2\pi NT}{60} = P.$$

The present left-hand side must now be multiplied by 60 and divided by 2, π, and N in order that T stands alone. Exactly the same processes must also be applied to the present right-hand side of the formula so that the equality of the two sides is maintained.

Therefore $\dfrac{2\pi NT}{60} \times \dfrac{60}{2\pi N} = P \times \dfrac{60}{2\pi N},$

from which, $T = \dfrac{60P}{2\pi N}$

or $T = \dfrac{30P}{\pi N}.$

EXAMPLE 10.5. A formula used in connection with the expansion of gases is

$$\frac{p_1 V_1}{T_1} = \frac{p_2 V_2}{T_2},$$

where p, V, and T represent respectively the absolute pressure, volume, and thermodynamic temperature of the gas. Transpose the formula making T_2 the subject.

SOLUTION

$$\frac{p_1 V_1}{T_1} = \frac{p_2 V_2}{T_2}.$$

Cross-multiplication gives

$$p_1 V_1 T_2 = p_2 V_2 T_1.$$

In order to isolate T_2 it is now necessary to divide the present left-hand side by p_1 and V_1, not forgetting to do exactly the same to the right-hand side. Thus

$$\frac{p_1 V_1 T_2}{p_1 V_1} = \frac{p_2 V_2 T_1}{p_1 V_1}.$$

Now, by cancelling where appropriate, the required formula is

10.3.2. Formulae involving addition and subtraction only.

Consider the formula for the total resistance in a series circuit,

$$R = R_1 + R_2 + R_3 \text{ ohms,}$$

and suppose that it is required to make R_3 the subject of the formula. In order to isolate R_3 it will be seen that both R_1 and R_2 must be subtracted from the right-hand side of the given formula. Exactly the same treatment must also be given to the left-hand side so that the expressions remain equal. Therefore

$$R - R_1 - R_2 = R_1 + R_2 + R_3 - R_1 - R_2,$$
$$= R_3.$$

The required formula is $R_3 = R - R_1 - R_2$.

It will be noticed that, in the case of a formula containing only addition and subtraction of terms, when a term changes sides its sign also changes.

EXAMPLE 10.6. The formula for the terminal potential difference of a cell is

$$V = E - Ir \text{ volts,}$$

where E represents the electromotive force of the cell in volts, I represents the current supplied by the cell in amperes and r represents the internal resistance of the cell in ohms.

Transpose the formula making r the subject.

SOLUTION

$$V = E - Ir$$

It is seen that r is a factor of the term Ir so that the first step must be to subtract E from the right-hand side of the formula, not forgetting to do likewise to the left-hand side. Therefore,

$$V - E = E - Ir - E,$$
$$= -Ir.$$

The term containing r is negative and can now be made positive by multiplying both sides by -1. Then

$$-V + E = Ir$$

which can be written as $Ir = E - V$.

As explained in section 10.3.1, the present left-hand side must now be divided by I in order to isolate r. It is then also necessary to divide the right-hand side by I so that the expressions remain equal. Then

$$\frac{Ir}{I} = \frac{E - V}{I}$$

which gives

$$r = \frac{E - V}{I}.$$

Note. The original formula was $V = E - Ir$. Remembering the methods described in sections 10.3.1 and

10.3.2, the process of transposition may be quickly carried out as follows.

$$V = E - Ir$$
$$Ir = E - V$$
$$r = \frac{E - V}{I}.$$

10.3.3. Formulae involving powers and roots.

Many formulae contain a symbol or group of symbols raised to a power or root. The power or root may be removed at the most convenient stage in the transformation of the formula. In cases where the symbol which is to become the new subject is alone raised to a power in the given formula, it is generally found best to remove the power or root at the final stage. In cases where the power or root applies to a group of symbols, the power or root should be removed as early as possible.

EXAMPLE 10.7. Transpose the formula $W = V^2 t/R$ making V the subject.

SOLUTION

$$W = \frac{V^2 t}{R}.$$

Cross-multiplication (multiplying both sides by R) gives

$$WR = V^2 t.$$

Dividing both sides by t gives

$$\frac{WR}{t} = V^2.$$

Extracting the square root of both sides gives

$$V = \sqrt{\frac{WR}{t}}$$

which is the required formula.

EXAMPLE 10.8. Transpose the formula $v = \sqrt{\frac{\gamma P}{\rho}}$ making ρ the subject.

SOLUTION

$$v = \sqrt{\frac{\gamma P}{\rho}}.$$

Squaring both sides to remove the square root sign gives

$$v^2 = \frac{\gamma P}{\rho}.$$

Cross-multiplication (multiplying both sides by ρ) gives

$$\rho v^2 = \gamma P.$$

Dividing both sides by v^2 gives

$$\rho = \frac{\gamma P}{v^2},$$

which is the required formula.

10.3.4. Formulae involving brackets. The use of brackets has been explained in sections 1.8 and 8.7. When the symbol which is to become the new subject of a formula is, together with other terms, contained in a pair of brackets it is generally convenient to isolate the bracketed terms before attempting to remove the brackets.

EXAMPLE 10.9. Transpose the formula

$$P = \frac{2\pi rN(F_1 - F_2)}{60},$$

making F_1 the subject.

SOLUTION

$$P = \frac{2\pi rN(F_1 - F_2)}{60}.$$

Cross-multiplication gives

$$60P = 2\pi rN(F_1 - F_2).$$

Dividing both sides by $2\pi rN$ isolates the brackets when they can be removed giving

$$\frac{60P}{2\pi rN} = F_1 - F_2.$$

Adding F_2 to both sides gives

$$\frac{60P}{2\pi rN} + F_2 = F_1.$$

Cancelling the 2, the required formula is, therefore,

$$F_1 = \frac{30P}{\pi rN} + F_2.$$

10.3.5. Formulae involving factorisation. In many formulae the symbol which is to become the new subject occurs in more than one term. The terms in which the required new subject appears must be collected together, in a suitable manner, on one side of the formula and the symbol then extracted as a common factor.

EXAMPLE 10.10. Transpose the formula

$$\frac{R_1}{R_2} = \frac{1 + \alpha\theta_1}{1 + \alpha\theta_2},$$

making α the subject.

SOLUTION

$$\frac{R_1}{R_2} = \frac{1 + \alpha\theta_1}{1 + \alpha\theta_2}.$$

Cross-multiplication gives

$$R_1(1 + \alpha\theta_2) = R_2(1 + \alpha\theta_1),$$
$$R_1 + R_1\alpha\theta_2 = R_2 + R_2\alpha\theta_1.$$

The terms containing α are now collected on one side so that

$$R_1\alpha\theta_2 - R_2\alpha\theta_1 = R_2 - R_1.$$

The common factor α is now extracted giving

$$\alpha(R_1\theta_2 - R_2\theta_1) = R_2 - R_1.$$

Dividing both sides by $(R_1\theta_2 - R_2\theta_1)$ produces the required formula which is

$$\alpha = \frac{R_2 - R_1}{R_1\theta_2 - R_2\theta_1}.$$

EXERCISES 10

1. The area of a circle is given by $A = \pi D^2/4$ and the circumference by $C = \pi D$, where D is the diameter. Write down a formula for A in terms of C.

2. A sphere has a volume $V = 4\pi R^3/3$ and a surface area $A = 4\pi R^2$, where R is the radius. Express V in terms of A and R.

3. Transpose the formula $A = \pi R^2$ making R the subject.

4. Transpose the formula $L = 2\pi R\theta/360$ making θ the subject.

5. Given that $A = \pi R^2\theta/360$, find a formula for R.

6. Transpose the formula $V = IR$ making (a) I and (b) R the subject.

7. If $V = \pi R^2 h/3$, find a formula for (a) h and (b) R.

8. Given that $v = u + at$, obtain a formula for (a) u and (b) a.

9. Transpose the formula $T = 2\pi\sqrt{(L/g)}$ making (a) L and (b) g the subject.

10. Use the formula $F = Gm_1m_2/L^2$ to obtain formulae for G and L.

11. Transpose the formula $L = L_0(1 + \alpha\theta)$ making (a) L_0 and (b) θ the subject.

12. Transpose the formula $\dfrac{1}{f} = \dfrac{1}{u} + \dfrac{1}{v}$ for u.

13. From the formula $\dfrac{1}{R} = \dfrac{1}{R_1} + \dfrac{1}{R_2}$ obtain a formula for R.

14. If $A = \dfrac{R^2}{2}(\theta - \sin\theta)$, find a formula for $\sin\theta$.

15. Transpose the formula $Q = mc(\theta_2 - \theta_1)$ making (a) c and (b) θ_2 the subject.

16. From the formula $I = \dfrac{nE}{R + nr}$ express n in terms of the other symbols.

17. Transpose the formula $V = \dfrac{2N}{N-n}$ making (a) N and (b) n the subject.

18. Transpose the formula $r = \sqrt{\dfrac{hR^2}{h+d}}$ to show that $h = \dfrac{dr^2}{R^2 - r^2}$ and calculate the value of h when $d = 0.4$, $r = 6.3$, and $R = 9.1$.

19. Calculate the value of T, if $T = \dfrac{n\mu W}{2}(R+r)^2$, when $n = 2$, $\mu = 0.32$, $W = 9400$, $R = 150$, and $r = 65$.

Transpose the given formula to show that $R = \sqrt{\dfrac{2T}{n\mu W}} - r$.

20. (a) The length of a cylindrical storage vessel is 1.75 times its diameter. Taking π as $\frac{22}{7}$, construct a formula for the capacity C in terms of the diameter d.
(b) Transpose the formula obtained in the answer to (a) to give a formula for the diameter d in terms of the capacity C.
(c) If the vessel has a capacity of one million litres (i.e. 1000 m^3), calculate
 (i) the diameter, in metres
 (ii) the length, in metres.
Give the answers to three significant figures.
(C.G.L.I.)

21. If a solid strut of diameter S is replaced by a tubular strut having an outside diameter of D and an inside diameter of d, the cross-sectional areas of the struts being equal, the ratio B of their stiffnesses can be obtained from the formula

$$B = \frac{D^4 - d^4}{DS^3}$$

(a) Find B, to two significant figures, when $D = 25$, $d = 15$, and $S = 20$.
(b) Transpose the formula to obtain an expression for d.
(C.G.L.I.)

22. (a) As a result of an experiment the following equation was deduced

$$\text{Log } T = 0.3010 + \log \pi + \left(\frac{\log L - \log g}{2}\right)$$

Obtain a formula for T, in terms of constants and the variables, which does not contain logarithms.
(b) When a projectile is discharged with a velocity V at an angle θ to the horizontal, the theoretical range R is given by the formula

$$R = \frac{2V^2 \sin \theta \cos \theta}{g}.$$

Calculate the value of R, in metres to three significant figures, when $V = 80$ m/s, $\theta = 40°$, and $g = 9.81$ m/s^2.
(C.G.L.I.)

23. The Brinell hardness number H of a material may be determined from the formula

$$H = \frac{W}{\dfrac{\pi D}{2}[D - \surd(D^2 - d^2)]}$$

where W is the dead load, in kilograms, applied to the ball, D is the diameter of the ball and d is the diameter of the indentation, both diameters being measured in millimetres.
(a) Use mathematical tables to calculate the Brinell hardness number H when $W = 3000$ kg, $D = 10$ mm, $d = 2.45$ mm, and $\pi = 3.142$.
(b) Transpose the formula to give an expression for d in terms of the other symbols.
(U.E.I.)

24. Given the formula:

$$C = \frac{NM(1 + G^{\frac{2}{3}})^{\frac{3}{2}}}{2}$$

(a) when $N = 24$, $M = 2$, and $G = 3$, calculate the value of C;
(b) transpose the formula to give an expression for G in terms of C, M, and N.
(U.E.I.)

25. The outside diameter C of a fully compressed close-coiled helical spring may be determined from the formula

$$C = \sqrt{\left(\frac{4D^2 - d^2 + p^2}{4}\right)} + d \text{ millimetres,}$$

where D is the nominal mean diameter of the spring, d is the diameter of the wire and p is the pitch of the coils.
(a) With the aid of mathematical tables, determine the value of C when $D = 24$ mm, $d = 4$ mm, and $p = 10$ mm.
(b) Transpose the formula to give an expression for p in terms of the other symbols.
(U.E.I.)

ANSWERS TO EXERCISES 10

1. $A = \dfrac{C^2}{4\pi}$.

2. $V = \dfrac{AR}{3}$.

3. $R = \sqrt{\dfrac{A}{\pi}}$.

4. $\theta = \dfrac{360L}{2\pi R}$.

5. $R = \sqrt{\dfrac{360A}{\pi\theta}}$.

6. (a) $I = V/R$,   (b) $R = V/I$.

7. (a) $h = \dfrac{3V}{\pi R^2}$,   (b) $R = \sqrt{\dfrac{3V}{\pi h}}$.

8. (a) $u = v - at$,   (b) $a = \dfrac{v - u}{t}$.

9. (a) $L = g(T/2\pi)^2$,   (b) $g = L(2\pi/T)^2$.

10. $G = \dfrac{FL^2}{m_1 m_2}$, $L = \sqrt{\dfrac{Gm_1 m_2}{F}}$

11. (a) $L_0 = \dfrac{L}{1 + \alpha\theta}$,   (b) $\theta = \dfrac{1}{\alpha}\left(\dfrac{L}{L_0} - 1\right)$.

12. $u = \dfrac{fv}{v-f}$

13. $R = \dfrac{R_1 R_2}{R_1 + R_2}$.

14. $\sin\theta = \theta - \dfrac{2A}{R^2}$.

15. (a) $c = \dfrac{Q}{m(\theta_2 - \theta_1)}$,   (b) $\theta_2 = \dfrac{Q}{mc} + \theta_1$

16. $n = \dfrac{IR}{E - Ir}$.

17. (a) $N = \dfrac{Vn}{V-2}$,   (b) $n = N\left(1 - \dfrac{2}{V}\right)$.

18. 0.3682.

19. 139 044 800.

20. (a) $C = \dfrac{11d^3}{8}$,   (b) $d = \sqrt[3]{\dfrac{8C}{11}}$,   (c) $d = 8.99$ m, $l = 15.7$ m.

21. (a) 1.7,   (b) $d = \sqrt[4]{(D^4 - BDS^3)}$.

22. (a) $T = 2\pi\sqrt{(L/g)}$,   (b) 630 m.

23. (a) 626.2,

(b) $d = \sqrt{\left[D^2 - \left(D - \dfrac{2W}{\pi DH}\right)^2\right]}$.

24. (a) 129.7,   (b) $G = \left[\left(\dfrac{2c}{NM}\right)^{2/3} - 1\right]^{3/2}$.

25. (a) 28.43 mm,
(b) $p = \sqrt{(4C^2 - 8Cd + 5d^2 - 4D^2)}$.

11 | Linear equations

11.1. EQUATIONS

An equation is simply a statement that two expressions are equal. The two types of equation dealt with in this chapter are collectively called linear equations, the term 'linear' indicating that such equations give rise to straight-line graphs.

11.2. SIMPLE EQUATIONS

A simple equation is an equation which contains only one unknown quantity and only the first power of that unknown quantity.

For example $2x = 4$ is a simple equation since it contains one unknown quantity x and the power of x is 1.

Referring again to the simple equation $2x = 4$, if twice the unknown quantity equals 4 then x itself equals half of that value; hence x equals 2.

The value of x found, i.e. 2, is called the solution or root of the equation $2x = 4$.

The process of finding the solution or root is termed solving the equation.

The root or solution is said to satisfy the equation.

11.2.1. Solution of simple equations. The methods of rearranging a simple equation in order to obtain the value of the unknown quantity may be more easily understood by reference to the analogy of a simple beam arrangement.

Consider a uniform beam pivoted at its centre and loaded as shown in Fig. 11.1. The beam is perfectly balanced and rests in a horizontal position.

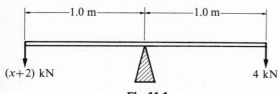

Fig. 11.1

From Fig. 11.1 it can be deduced that, since the beam is balanced, the forces on each side of the pivot are equal and therefore the following equation is true.

$$x + 2 = 4$$

Now providing the points of application of the forces are not changed the forces may be altered in any of the following ways without upsetting the balance of the beam.

(a) By reducing each of the forces by an equal amount $(x + 2) - 2 = 4 - 2$.
(b) By increasing each of the forces by an equal amount, $(x + 2) + 4 = 4 + 4$.
(c) By multiplying each of the forces by the same factor (number), $3(x + 2) = 3 \times 4$.
(d) By dividing each of the forces by an equal amount, $\dfrac{x + 2}{2} = \dfrac{4}{z}$.
(e) By interchanging the forces, $4 = x + 2$.

The resulting equations all remain satisfied by $x = 2$.

The five operations (a) to (e) carried out in the beam analogy serve to illustrate that provided both sides of an equation are treated in exactly the same manner, although the appearance of the equation may change, the sense of the equation remains the same.

Therefore when solving a simple equation it may be found necessary to:

(1) multiply or divide both sides of the equation by the same amount,
(2) add or subtract from equal quantities each side of the equation.

EXAMPLE 11.1. Solve the equation
$$4x + 3 = 2x + 9.$$

SOLUTION

Step 1: Where the unknown quantity occurs in more than one term, as in this equation, collect all such terms to one side of the equation and transfer all purely numerical terms to the other side.

Then $\qquad 4x - 2x = 9 - 3.$

Note that when terms are transferred across the equality sign ($=$) their sign is changed, i.e. $2x$ becomes $-2x$ and 3 becomes -3. This is another way of expressing the fact that $2x$ and 3 have been subtracted from each side.

Step 2: Simplify $4x - 2x = 9 - 3,$
then $\qquad\qquad 2x = 6,$
or $\qquad\qquad x = 3.$

$\therefore\ x = 3$ is the solution or root of the equation $4x + 3 = 2x + 9$.

Step 3: Check that $x = 3$ is the correct solution of the equation by substitution in that equation.

Substitute $\qquad x = 3$ in $4x + 3 = 2x + 9,$
then $\qquad\qquad 4 \times 3 + 3 = 2 \times 3 + 9,$
i.e. $\qquad\qquad\qquad 15 = 15.$

Hence $x = 3$ is the correct solution of the given equation.

EXAMPLE 11.2. Solve the following equation for t

$$3(t-2) = 2(t-1).$$

SOLUTION

Step 1: Multiply out the brackets.

$$3t - 6 = 2t - 2.$$

Step 2: Rearrange equation with terms containing unknown quantity t on one side and pure numbers on the other side of the equation.

$$3t - 2t = 6 - 2.$$

Step 3: Simplify equation $3t - 2t = 6 - 2$.

$$t = 4$$

$\therefore$ $t = 4$ is the solution or root of the equation $3(t-2) = 2(t-1)$.

Step 4: Check that $t = 4$ is the correct solution by substitution in the original equation.

$$3(4-2) = 2(4-1),$$

$$\text{or } 6 = 6$$

$\therefore$ $t = 4$ is the correct solution.

EXAMPLE 11.3. Find the value of P which satisfies the equation

$$\frac{P}{30} = \frac{20}{25}.$$

SOLUTION

Where a single fraction appears on each side of the equation the simplest method of solution is to remove fractions by cross multiplication, i.e. multiplying by both the denominators.

This gives

$$25P = 20 \times 30$$

$$= 600$$

$$\therefore P = \frac{600}{25} = 24.$$

Check by substitution of $P = 24$ in the original equation.

$$\frac{24}{30} = \frac{20}{25},$$

i.e.

$$\frac{4}{5} = \frac{4}{5}.$$

Hence $P = 24$ is the solution of the equation $\dfrac{P}{30} = \dfrac{20}{25}$.

EXAMPLE 11.4. Solve the equation

$$\frac{7R-3}{2} = \frac{3R+4}{5} - \frac{R-16}{4}.$$

SOLUTION

The most direct method of solving equations containing fractions is to obtain the L.C.M. of all the denominators and then multiply both sides of the equation by the L.C.M.

Note that this applies where more than one fractional term appears on either side of the equation; otherwise proceed as in example 11.3.

Step 1: L.C.M. $= 4 \times 5 = 20$

then

$$\frac{7R-3}{2} = \frac{3R+4}{5} - \frac{R-16}{4}$$

becomes

$$\frac{10(7R-3) = 4(3R+4) - 5(R-16)}{20}$$

Step 2: Multiply both sides of the equation by the L.C.M. 20. This is achieved by omitting the denominator.

Then

$$10(7R-3) = 4(3R+4) - 5(R-16)$$

Step 3: Multiply out the brackets.

$$70R - 30 = 12R + 16 - 5R + 80.$$

Step 4: Collect terms containing R and pure numerical terms on opposite sides of the equation.

$$70R - 12R + 5R = 16 + 80 + 30.$$

Step 5: Simplify equation.

$$63R = 126$$

Step 6: Divide through by the coefficient of R, i.e. 63

then

$$R = \frac{126}{63} = 2$$

i.e.

$$R = 2.$$

Step 7: Check solution by substitution in the original equation.

$$\frac{7 \times 2 - 3}{2} = \frac{3 \times 2 + 4}{5} - \frac{(2-16)}{4}$$

i.e.

$$\frac{11}{2} = \frac{10}{5} + \frac{14}{4}$$

or

$$5\tfrac{1}{2} = 2 + 3\tfrac{1}{2} = 5\tfrac{1}{2}$$

$\therefore$ $R = 2$ is the required solution to the equation.

EXAMPLE 11.5. Solve for R the equation

$$\frac{1}{R} = \frac{1}{30} + \frac{1}{5} + \frac{1}{10}.$$

SOLUTION

Note. A solution cannot be obtained by simply inverting the whole equation in the form given.

Step 1: Obtain the L.C.M. of the denominator of the right-hand side of the equation, i.e. 30.

Then
$$\frac{1}{R}=\frac{1+6+3}{30}.$$

Step 2: Simplify the right-hand side of the equation when
$$\frac{1}{R}=\frac{10}{30}.$$

Step 3: As each side of the equation is now reduced to a single fraction both sides of the equation may be inverted, giving
$$\frac{R}{1}=R=\frac{30}{10}.$$
$$\therefore R=3.$$

Step 4: Check solution by substituting $R=3$ in the original equation
$$\frac{1}{3}=\frac{1}{30}+\frac{1}{5}+\frac{1}{10},$$
i.e. $\frac{1}{3}=\frac{10}{30}=\frac{1}{3}.$

$\therefore R=3$ is the correct solution.

11.2.2. Formation of simple equations. In practice it often happens that a problem containing one unknown quantity is difficult or impossible to solve by an arithmetical method. The unknown quantity is then represented by a symbol and an equation is constructed which conforms with the data or facts of the problem. The solution of the equation will provide the value of the unknown quantity.

The following method is generally adopted in the formation of an equation from a given set of facts.
(a) Choose a suitable letter for the unknown number. Often the initial letter of the unknown quantity is taken. For example t for time, v for velocity, l for length, etc.
(b) Where units are involved the unknown quantity should be introduced in the following manner:

let the unknown velocity = v metres per second

let the unknown length = l centimetres or l metres

let the unknown time = t hours, etc.

EXAMPLE 11.6. The combined value of two resistors placed in series is 21 ohms. If the one resistor has twice the value of the other, calculate the individual values of the two resistors.

SOLUTION

Note. It should be appreciated that this particular problem could be solved by either an arithmetical or algebraic approach.

Let x ohms = resistance of smaller resistor. Then $2x$ ohms = resistance of larger resistor. An equation may now be formed as follows.

$$2x+x=21,$$
(ohms) (ohms)

i.e. $3x=21.$

$$\therefore x=\frac{21}{3}=7,$$
then
$$2x=2\times7=14.$$

The two resistors are therefore 7 ohms and 14 ohms.

EXAMPLE 11.7. A charge for a blast furnace consisted of iron ore together with $\frac{2}{3}$ of its mass of coke and 1/5 of its mass of limestone: if the mass of the ore used was 0.6 tonne more than that of the coke and limestone together, calculate the mass of the whole charge.

SOLUTION

In a problem of this type it is important to let the symbol represent the mass of the unknown quantity which will require the least amount of manipulation in determining the relative masses of the other quantities.

Let m tonne = mass of iron ore in the charge. Then $\frac{2}{3}m$ tonne = mass of coke in the charge and $\frac{1}{5}m$ tonne = mass of limestone in the charge.

Now problem states that:

Mass or iron ore = mass of coke + mass of
(tonne)　　limestone + 0.6
　　　　　　(tonne)
$$\therefore m=\tfrac{2}{3}m+\tfrac{1}{5}m+0.6$$

Collecting quantities containing m to the left hand side
$$m-\tfrac{2}{3}m-\tfrac{1}{5}m=0.6,$$
i.e.
$$m-\frac{10}{15}m-\frac{3}{15}m=0.6 \quad\text{(Note. L.C.M. of 3 and 5 is 15)}$$
$$\therefore m-\frac{13}{15}m=0.6,$$
hence
$$\frac{2}{15}m=0.6,$$
and
$$m=\frac{15}{2}\times0.6$$
when
$$m=4.5.$$

Mass of iron ore in charge = 4.5 tonnes.
To obtain mass of total charge:
Mass of coke = $\frac{2}{3}m$ tonne = $\frac{2}{3}\times4.5=3$ tonnes.
$$=1/5\times4.5=0.9 \text{ tonne.}$$
Mass of total charge = $4.5+3+0.9$ tonnes,
$$=8.4 \text{ tonnes.}$$

EXAMPLE 11.8. At its cruising speed a plane consumes 255 litres of fuel per hour and when travelling at its maximum speed its fuel consumption is increased by $33\frac{1}{3}$%. If it used 2380 litres of fuel on a 9 hour flight, find the period of time for which the plane was travelling at its maximum speed. Take-off and landing can be neglected.

SOLUTION

Let t hours = time plane was travelling at its cruising speed. Then $(9-t)$ hours = time plane was flying at its maximum speed. The equation will be constructed in the following manner:

Total fuel consumption (cruising speed) + total fuel consumption (maximum speed)
= Total fuel consumption for complete journey.

In symbols $255t + (255 + \frac{1}{3} \times 255)(9-t) = 2380$ (since $33\frac{1}{3}\% = \frac{1}{3}$)

$\therefore 255t + (255 + 85)(9-t) = 2380$ (Note: $\frac{1}{3} \times 255 = 85$)

$255t + 340(9-t) = 2380.$

Simplifying, $255t + 3060 - 340t = 2380$

$$-85t = -3060 + 2380$$
$$\therefore -85t = -680$$

or $85t = 680$ (multiplying each side by -1)

$$\therefore t = \frac{680}{85} = 8$$

i.e. plane was flying at cruising speed for 8 hours
$\therefore$ plane was flying at maximum speed for $(9-8)$ hours or 1 hour.

11.3. LINEAR SIMULTANEOUS EQUATIONS

The previous sections in this chapter were concerned with problems and equations having one unknown quantity. Frequently however problems arise in which two quantities are unknown. In such cases it is essential to have two independent equations in order to find the particular values of the unknown quantities.

Consider the following equation having two unknown numbers x and y:

$$x + y = 7.$$

It can be seen that such an equation standing by itself has numerous solutions. For example $x = 1$, $y = 6$; $x = 2$, $y = 5$; $x = 3$, $y = 4$, etc., all satisfy this equation.

However if a further equation is formed from another known relationship between x and y then it may be possible to find *particular values* for x and y which solve both equations.

Suppose the other relationship is $x - y = 3$ then the two equations are

$$x + y = 7 \quad \text{equation (1)}$$
$$x - y = 3 \quad \text{equation (2)}$$

It can be shown that the only values for x and y which satisfy equation (1) and equation (2) *at the same time* are $x = 5$ and $y = 2$.

Because $x = 5$ and $y = 2$ satisfy both equations *at the same time* they are said to be the roots of simultaneous equations.

Further, a graph drawn from either of the two equations would produce a straight line. Hence the term *linear* simultaneous equations.

Although this book is limited to the solution of simultaneous equations containing two unknowns it is worth noting that a problem containing three unknowns would require the formation of three equations, and in general 'n' unknowns require 'n' equations for solution.

11.3.1. Methods of solution. Two methods of calculation are adopted to solve a pair of simultaneous equations. Each method is dependent upon reducing the two given equations to a single simple equation.

The two methods of solution are:
1. substitution,
2. elimination.

The following example is solved by the two alternative methods.

EXAMPLE 11.9. Solve for i_1 and i_2 the simultaneous equations

$$6i_1 - 12i_2 = 0$$
$$10i_1 + 4i_2 = 24.$$

SOLUTION

(A) *Method of substitution*

Although specifically applied to this question the procedure is standard for all simultaneous equations.

(1) Choose one of the equations and express i_1 in terms of i_2, or i_2 in terms of i_1. The choice depends purely upon whichever operation is the easier. In this case i_1 will be expressed in terms of i_2.
(2) Substitute the expression for i_1 into the second equation. The equation is now reduced to a simple equation in i_2.
(3) Solve the simple equation for i_2.
(4) Substitute i_2 into one of the equations and hence find the value of i_1.
(5) Check that the values of i_1 and i_2 satisfy the two equations.

The above steps are now applied to the two equations:

$$6i_1 - 12i_2 = 0 \quad \text{equation (1)}$$
$$10i_1 + 4i_2 = 24 \quad \text{equation (2)}$$

Step 1: Expressing i_1 in terms of i_2

$$6i_1 - 12i_2 = 0 \quad \text{equation (1)}$$
$$\therefore 6i_1 = 12i_2$$
$$i_1 = \frac{12i_2}{6} = 2i_2$$
$$\therefore i_1 = 2i_2$$

Step 2: Substitute $2i_2$ for i_1 in equation (2)

then $10i_1 + 4i_2 = 24$ becomes

$$10(2i_2) + 4i_2 = 24$$

Step 3: Solve for i_2: $20i_2 + 4i_2 = 24$

$$24i_2 = 24$$

$$i_2 = \frac{24}{24} = 1$$

$$\therefore i_2 = 1$$

Step 4: Substitute $i_2 = 1$ into equation (1) and find value of i_1

$$6i_1 - 12i_2 = 0$$

when $i_2 = 1$, $\quad 6i_1 - 12 \times 1 = 0$

$$\therefore 6i_1 - 12 = 0$$

when $6i_1 = 12$

$$\therefore i_1 = \frac{12}{6} = 2$$

$$i_1 = 2$$

Step 5: Solutions are $i_1 = 2$ and $i_2 = 1$.
Check in equation (1) $6 \times 2 - 12 \times 1 = 12 - 12 = 0$.
$\therefore i_1 = 2$ and $i_2 = 1$ satisfy equation (1).
Check in equation (2). $10 \times 2 + 4 \times 1 = 20 + 4 = 24$.
$\therefore i_1 = 2$ and $i_2 = 1$ satisfy equation (2).
Solutions are therefore $i_1 = 2$ and $i_2 = 1$.

SOLUTION

(B) *Method of elimination.*

Again the general method of procedure will be applied specifically to the two equations

$$6i_1 - 12i_2 = 0 \quad \text{equation (1)}$$
$$10i_1 + 4i_2 = 24 \quad \text{equation (2)}$$

(1) Multiply one or both equations by a number or numbers in order to make the magnitude of the coefficients for either i_1 or i_2 equal in both equations.
In this particular case equation (2) will be multiplied by 3 making the coefficients of i_2 equal in both equations.
(2) Eliminate i_2 from the equations by addition of equation (1) and equation (2).
(3) Solve the simple equation formed for i_1.
(4) Substitute the value found for i_1 in equation (1) and find value of i_2.
(5) Check that the solutions found satisfy both equations.

The above steps are now applied to the two equations.

$$6i_1 - 12i_2 = 0 \quad \text{equation (1)}$$
$$10i_1 + 4i_2 = 24 \quad \text{equation (2)}$$

Step 1: Multiply equation (2) by 3 leaving equation (1) in its original form.

$$3(10i_1 + 4i_2) = 3 \times 24 \quad \text{equation (2) multiplied by 3}$$
i.e. $30i_1 + 12i_2 = 72 \quad \text{equation (3)}$

Step 2: Eliminate i_2 by adding equation (1) to equation (3).

$$6i_1 - 12i_2 = 0$$
$$30i_1 + 12i_2 = 72$$

Step 3: Solve for i_1: $\quad 36i_1 = 72$
(since $-12i_2 + 12i_2 = 0$).

$$\therefore i_1 = \frac{72}{36} = 2$$

$$i_1 = 2$$

Step 4: Substitute $i_1 = 2$ in equation (1) and obtain a value for i_2.

$$6 \times 2 - 12i_2 = 0$$
$$12 = 12i_2$$
$$i_2 = 1$$

Solutions of the equations are $i_1 = 2$ and $i_2 = 1$.
Step 5: Check the solutions as in previous method.
In general the second method of solution is more widely used for the solution of linear simultaneous equations having two unknowns.

EXAMPLE 11.10. Solve the equations

$$2a + 3b + 2 = 0$$
$$5a - 4b = 41$$

SOLUTION

Step 1: Arrange both equations in the same form, thus

$$2a + 3b = -2 \quad \text{equation (1)}$$
$$5a - 4b = 41 \quad \text{equation (2)}$$

Step 2: Using the method of elimination multiply equation (1) by 4 and equation (2) by 3.

$$4(2a + 3b) = 4 \times -2 \quad \text{equation (1)} \times 4$$
becomes
$$8a + 12b = -8 \quad \text{equation (3)}$$
$$3(5a - 4b) = 3 \times 41 \quad \text{equation (2)} \times 3$$
becomes
$$15a - 12b = 123 \quad \text{equation (4)}$$

Step 3: Add equations (3) and (4) in order to eliminate term containing 'b'.

$$8a + 12b = -8$$
$$15a - 12b = 123$$

Then
$$23a = 115$$

and
$$a = \frac{115}{23} = 5$$

Hence
$$a = 5.$$

Step 4: Substitute $a = 5$ into equation (1) and find the value for b

$$2a + 3b = -2$$

substituting $a = 5$: $2 \times 5 + 3b = -2$

$$10 + 3b = -2$$
$$3b = -10 - 2$$
$$3b = -12$$
$$\therefore b = \frac{-12}{3} = -4$$

Hence
$$b = -4$$

Step 5: Substitute the values $a = 5$ and $b = -4$ into the original equation (1) to determine that the correct solutions have been found.

Using
$$2a + 3b + 2 = 0$$

substitute
$$a = 5 \text{ and } b = -4$$

then
$$2 \times 5 + 3 \times -4 + 2 = 10 - 12 + 2 = 0$$

$\therefore a = 5$ and $b = -4$ are the required solutions.

EXAMPLE 11.11. Find the values of x and y which satisfy the equations

$$\frac{2}{x} - \frac{10}{y} = 2\tfrac{1}{2} \quad \text{equation (1)}$$

$$\frac{4}{x} + \frac{15}{y} = -2 \quad \text{equation (2)}$$

SOLUTION

Where reciprocals of letters are involved, i.e. $\frac{2}{x}, \frac{10}{y}$, etc. it is perhaps easier to convert them to a more conventional form by the following transformation.

Let
$$a = \frac{1}{x}, \text{ then } \frac{2}{x} = 2a \text{ and } \frac{4}{x} = 4a;$$

similarly,

let $b = \frac{1}{y}$, then $\frac{10}{y} = 10b$ and $\frac{15}{y} = 15b$

Equations (1) and (2) may now be rewritten as

$$2a - 10b = 2\tfrac{1}{2} \quad \text{equation (3)}$$

$$4a + 15b = -2 \quad \text{equation (4)}.$$

Using the method of elimination multiply equation (3) by 2 and subtract equation (4).

$$2(2a - 10b) = 2 \times 2\tfrac{1}{2} \quad \text{equation (3)} \times 2$$

thus
$$4a - 20b = 5 \quad \text{equation (5)}$$

$$4a + 15b = -2 \quad \text{equation (4)}$$

Subtract

$$-35b = 7 \text{ (note } -20b - 15b = -35b)$$

$$\therefore b = \frac{-7}{35} = \frac{-1}{5}$$

$$b = \frac{-1}{5}.$$

Substituting in equation (3) to find 'a'

$$2a - 10(-\tfrac{1}{5}) = 2\tfrac{1}{2}$$

$$\therefore 2a + 2 = 2\tfrac{1}{2}$$

$$2a = \tfrac{1}{2}.$$

Hence
$$a = \tfrac{1}{4}.$$

But
$$a = \frac{1}{x} \quad \text{and} \quad b = \frac{1}{y}.$$

$$\therefore \frac{1}{4} = \frac{1}{x} \quad \text{and} \quad x = 4 \quad \left(\text{because } \frac{4}{1} = \frac{x}{1}\right)$$

also

$$-\frac{1}{5} = \frac{1}{y} \quad \text{and} \quad y = -5 \quad \left(\text{since } \frac{-5}{1} = \frac{y}{1}\right)$$

Check. Substitute $x = 4$ and $y = -5$ in equations (1) and (2)

$$\frac{2}{x} - \frac{10}{y} = 2\tfrac{1}{2} \quad \text{equation (1)}$$

$$\frac{2}{4} - \frac{10}{-5} = \tfrac{1}{2} + 2 = 2\tfrac{1}{2}$$

$$\therefore x = 4, y = -5 \quad \text{satisfy equation (1)}$$

$$\frac{4}{x} + \frac{15}{y} = -2 \quad \text{equation (2)}$$

$$\frac{4}{4} + \frac{15}{-5} = 1 - 3 = -2$$

$$\therefore x = 4, y = -5 \text{ satisfy equation (2)}.$$

Hence $x = 4$, $y = -5$ are the required solutions.

11.3.2. Formation of simultaneous equations.
Simultaneous equations are used to solve problems where more than one unknown quantity is present.

The procedure is similar to that used in the formation of a simple equation except that in this case it is necessary to designate two letters to represent the unknown quantities.

EXAMPLE 11.12. Two types of machine are used in a certain factory. Machine A has an output of 250 units per week and occupies $450\,m^2$ of floor space; machine B has an output of 350 units per week and occupies $500\,m^2$ of floor space. The total floor space occupied by all the machines is $10\,500\,m^2$ and the total output is 6700 units per week.

How many machines of each kind are on the floor?

SOLUTION

Let x = number of machines of type A and y = number of machines of type B.

Two independent equations may now be constructed. Equation (1): total output of machines (A) + total output of machines (B) = total output

or in symbols $\quad 250x + 350y = 6700 \quad$ equation (1)

Equation (2): area occupied by machines (A) + area occupied by machines (B) = total floor space

or in symbols $\quad 450x + 500y = 10\,500 \quad$ equation (2)

Hence the two equations to be solved are

$$250x + 350y = 6700 \quad \text{equation (1)}$$
$$450x + 500y = 10\,500 \quad \text{equation (2)}$$

To ease the arithmetic involved in the problem equation (1) may be divided by 10 and equation (2) by 50 then

$$25x + 35y = 670 \quad \text{equation (3)}$$
$$9x + 10y = 210 \quad \text{equation (4)}$$

Eliminate y by multiplying equation (3) by 2 and equation (4) by 7

then $\quad 2(25x + 35y) = 2 \times 670 \quad$ equation (2)×2

or $\qquad 50x + 70y = 1340 \qquad$ equation (5)

and $\quad 7(9x + 10y) = 7 \times 210 \quad$ equation (4)×7

becomes $\quad 63x + 70y = 1470 \qquad$ equation (6)

Eliminate y between equations (5) and (6) by subtraction

$$63x + 70y = 1470 \qquad \text{equation (6)}$$
$$50x + 70y = 1340 \qquad \text{equation (5)}$$

Subtract, then $\qquad 13x = 130$

giving $\qquad\qquad x = 10$

To find y substitute $x = 10$ in equation (1),

Then $\qquad 250x + 350y = 6700$

becomes $\qquad\qquad 2500 + 350y = 6700$

$$\therefore \ 350y = 6700 - 2500$$
$$350y = 4200$$
$$\therefore \ y = \frac{4200}{350} = 12$$

The calculated values are $x = 10$ and $y = 12$.

Check. Substitute $x = 10$, $y = 12$ in equations (1) and (2)

$$250x + 350y = 6700 \quad \text{equation (1)}$$

$$250 \times 10 + 350 \times 12 = 2500 + 4200 = 6700$$

$$\therefore \ x = 10, \ y = 12 \text{ satisfy equation (1)}$$

$$450x + 500y = 10\,500 \quad \text{equation (2)}$$

$$450 \times 10 + 500 \times 12 = 4500 + 6000 = 10\,500$$

Hence $x = 10$, $y = 12$ satisfy equation (2)

$\therefore$ Number of machines $(A) = 10$

Number of machines $(B) = 12$

EXAMPLE 11.13. A certain component containing $100\,cm^3$ of steel and $60\,cm^3$ of copper has a mass of 1308 g. Another component containing $80\,cm^3$ of steel and $40\,cm^3$ of copper has a mass of 976 g. Find the densities of the steel and copper.

SOLUTION

Let the density of steel $= x(g/cm^3)$ and the density of copper $= y(g/cm^3)$.

Note. Mass = volume × density

$$\underset{\text{(steel)}}{\text{Volume} \times \text{density}} + \underset{\text{(copper)}}{\text{volume} \times \text{density}} = \text{total mass}$$

$$\therefore \ 100x + 60y = 1308 \quad \text{equation (1)}$$
$$80x + 40y = 976 \quad \text{equation (2)}$$

Multiply equation (1) by 4 and equation (2) by 6 and hence eliminate y.

$$400x + 240y = 5232 \quad \text{equation (1)×4}$$
$$480x + 240y = 5856 \quad \text{equation (2)×6}$$

By subtraction

$$-80x = -624$$

or $\qquad\qquad 80x = 624$

when $\qquad\qquad x = \dfrac{624}{80} = 7.8$

$$\therefore \ \text{density of steel} = 7.8 \text{ g/cm}^3.$$

Substituting $x = 7.8$ in equation (1) to find y

$$100x + 60y = 1308 \quad \text{equation (1)}$$

$$100 \times 7.8 + 60y = 1308$$

$$\therefore 780 + 60y = 1308$$

$$60y = 1308 - 780$$

$$60y = 528$$

when

$$y = \frac{528}{60} = 8.8$$

$$\therefore \text{density of copper} = 8.8 \text{ g/cm}^3.$$

Check: Substituting $x = 7.8$ and $y = 8.8$ in equations (1) and (2)

$$100x + 60y = 1308 \quad \text{equation (1)}$$

Then

$$100 \times 7.8 + 60 \times 8.8 = 780 + 528 = 1308$$

$\therefore$ equation (1) is satisfied by the two solutions.

$$80x + 40y = 976 \quad \text{equation (2)}$$

Then

$$80 \times 7.8 + 40 \times 8.8 = 624 + 352 = 976$$

$\therefore$ equation (2) is satisfied by the two solutions.
$\therefore$ Density of steel $= 7.8$ g/cm^3 and density of copper $= 8.8$ g/cm^3

EXAMPLE 11.14. $E = aW + b$, where a and b are constants.
Given $E = 19.5$ when $W = 130$, and $E = 39$ when $W = 520$, calculate the values of a and b and hence determine the value of W when $E = 63$.

SOLUTION

In this example the values of W and E are substituted into the expression $E = aW + b$ to form two simultaneous equations.

$$19.5 = 130a + b \quad \text{equation (1)}$$
$$39 = 520a + b \quad \text{equation (2)}$$

Eliminate 'b' by subtracting equation (1) from equation (2) when

$$19.5 = 390a$$

$$\therefore a = \frac{19.5}{390} = \frac{1}{20}$$

$$a = \frac{1}{20}$$

Substitution of $a = \frac{1}{20}$ into equation (1) provides the value for b. Thus

$$19.5 = 130 \times \frac{1}{20} + b$$

$$\therefore 19.5 = 6.5 + b$$

$$\therefore b = 19.5 - 6.5 = 13$$

$$b = 13$$

Check. Substitute $a = \frac{1}{20}$ and $b = 13$ into equations (1) and (2)

$$19.5 = 130a + b \quad \text{equation (1)}$$

Then

$$19.5 = 130 \times \frac{1}{20} + 13$$

$$\therefore 19.5 = 6.5 + 13 = 19.5$$

$$\therefore a = \frac{1}{20}, b = 13 \text{ satisfy equation (1)}$$

$$39 = 520a + b \quad \text{equation (2)}$$

$$39 = 520 \times \frac{1}{20} + 13 = 26 + 13 = 39$$

$$\therefore a = \frac{1}{20}, b = 13 \text{ satisfy equation (2)}$$

To find the value of W when $E = 63$ use is now made of the equation $E = aW + b$ where $a = \frac{1}{20}$ and $b = 13$

Hence

$$E = \frac{W}{20} + 13$$

becomes

$$63 = \frac{W}{20} + 13$$

Rearranging

$$63 - 13 = \frac{W}{20}$$

$$\therefore \frac{W}{20} = 50$$

and

$$W = 20 \times 50 = 1000$$

$$\therefore \text{when } E = 63, W = 1000$$

EXERCISES 11

1. Solve the following equations for x:
  (a) $5x + 3 = 2x + 7$.
  (b) $3.2x - 2.1 = 1.4x + 5.6$.
  (c) $6x + 11 = 25 - x$.
  (d) $5x + 13 - 8x = 41 - 7x$.
  (e) $15x - 11.5 - 2x - 3.2 = 11.4 - 0.05x$.
  (f) $3.1x - 0.25 - 1.3 = 0$.

2. Solve the following equations for y:
 (a) $3(y-2)=2(y-1)$.
 (b) $5(y+3)-8=3(4-2y)+6$.
 (c) $3y-2=0.8(y-8)$.
 (d) $2y(y-4)-3=y(2y-2)$.
 (e) $\frac{1}{2}(2y+3)=\frac{1}{2}-\frac{2}{3}(3y-6)$.
 (f) $3.2(3y-7)+8=8-5.4(3-4y)$.

3. Solve the following equations:
 (a) $\dfrac{2z}{5}-\dfrac{3z}{4}=\dfrac{3}{10}$.
 (b) $\dfrac{3x+1}{3x-1}=\dfrac{2}{3}$.
 (c) $\dfrac{3y-5}{5}-\dfrac{y-3}{4}=\dfrac{2y+4}{3}$.
 (d) $\dfrac{3}{x+1}+\dfrac{2}{x-1}=\dfrac{5}{x}$.
 (e) $\dfrac{3z-1}{4}-\dfrac{z}{2}=1+\dfrac{z+1}{6}$.
 (f) $\dfrac{2y-1}{2y+1}=\dfrac{3y-1}{3y+2}$.

4. Solve the following equations:
 (a) $\dfrac{x+1}{5}-2=\dfrac{3(x-1)}{10}$.
 (b) $3\left(\dfrac{1}{y}+2\right)-0.5\left(\dfrac{2}{y}-3\right)=3.5$
 (c) $\{z+3(z-1)\}=3.5z$.
 (d) $2\{2y-3(y-7)\}=3y+2$.
 (e) $\dfrac{2x\{3-2(1-x)\}}{x-2}=1+4x$.
 (f) $\{z-5(z-1)\}=\dfrac{1-40z^2}{10z}$.

5. Solve the following pairs of simultaneous equations for the two unknowns:
 (a) $4x+y=13,\qquad 6x-y=17$.
 (b) $3a+4b=7,\qquad 3a+1=4b$.
 (c) $7m+5n=-17,\qquad m-5n=13$.
 (d) $\dfrac{3x}{5}-\dfrac{y}{2}=4,\qquad \dfrac{3x}{4}+\dfrac{y}{2}=2.75$.

6. Solve the following pairs of simultaneous equations for the two unknowns:
 (a) $x+2y=35,\qquad 12x=11y$.
 (b) $3p-2q=22,\qquad 5p-4q=40$.
 (c) $14u+15v=57.5,\qquad 7u+30v=62.5$.
 (d) $1.5a+44=5.5b,\qquad 2.5a+11b=209$.

7. Solve the following pairs of simultaneous equations for the two unknowns:
 (a) $2c+4=3d,\qquad 3c+1=2d$.
 (b) $4x-3y=0,\qquad 16x-15y=12$.
 (c) $5m+9n=13.2,\qquad 2m+13n=12.8$.
 (d) $16x+8=4y,\qquad 5x+21y=42$.

8. Solve the following pairs of simultaneous equations for the two unknowns:
 (a) $\dfrac{1}{x}+\dfrac{1}{y}=0.75,\qquad \dfrac{2}{x}+\dfrac{3}{y}=1.75$.
 (b) $\dfrac{3}{u}+\dfrac{4}{v}=2,\qquad \dfrac{4}{u}-\dfrac{1}{v}=3$.
 (c) $\dfrac{2}{r}+\dfrac{1}{s}=8,\qquad \dfrac{7}{r}+\dfrac{1}{s}=23$.
 (d) $\dfrac{5}{x}+\dfrac{9}{y}=4.75,\qquad \dfrac{1}{x}-\dfrac{2}{y}=0$.

9. A certain alloy contains 25 per cent of zinc. How much of the alloy must be added to 10 kg of zinc in order to form another alloy containing 40 per cent of zinc? Assume no loss of metal on mixing.

10. A brass whose density is 8.5 g/cm³ is composed of copper and zinc whose densities are 8.8 g/cm³ and 7.1 g/cm³ respectively. How much of the copper will require to be mixed with 150 cm³ of the zinc in order to make a sample of the brass?

11. A workshop floor is rectangular, the perimeter being 140 m. If the length is 20 m more than the width, find these two distances.

12. A consignment of coal when loaded into 20-tonne trucks needs nine more trucks than if loaded into 30-tonne trucks. What is the amount of the consignment?

13. The relative density (specific gravity) of 120 cm³ of a dilute sulphuric acid is 1.10. What volume of sulphuric acid of relative density 1.36 must be added to produce an acid of relative density 1.25?

14. Two pipes are used to fill a water tank which has a capacity of 1500 litres. If it takes 8 minutes to fill the tank, and one pipe delivers water at twice the rate of the other, determine how many litres per minute each pipe delivers.

15. A steel oil-drum lying on a workshop floor is prevented from rolling by two blocks of wood, each 40 mm square, as shown by Fig. 11.2. If the blocks are 320 mm apart, calculate the diameter of the drum.

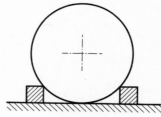

Fig. 11.2

16. A consignment of goods was sold at £20.00 per article. When the unit price was increased by £5.00, forty fewer articles were sold for the same total price. Find the number of articles in each consignment.

17. Two gear-wheels have their centres 300 mm apart. The smaller one turns eight times while the larger one turns seven times. Calculate the pitch circle diameter of each wheel.

18. The law of a simple lifting machine is $E = aW + b$, where a and b are constants. When $W = 120$ newtons, $E = 17$ newtons and when $W = 192$ newtons, $E = 23$ newtons. Calculate the values of the constants.

19. The mass of fuel oil, m kilograms, used in an engine test and the power, P kilowatts, developed were found to be connected by the relation $m = aP + b$. When m was 1.03 kg, P was 2.1 kW, and when m was 2.20 kg, P was 4.7 kW. Calculate:
(a) the values of the constants a and b,
(b) the value of m when P was 4.2 kW,
(c) the value of P when m was 2.47 kg.

20. (a) The cost of manufacturing a batch of pumps is made up of a fixed sum of £5000 plus £6.25 per pump. The pumps are sold at £8.75 each. How many must be sold to realize a profit of £1250?
(b) A manufacturer despatches goods to a wholesaler in boxes and in drums. For three boxes and nine drums the delivery cost is £41.40 and for six boxes and seven drums the cost is £41.00. Calculate the cost per box and per drum.

(U.E.I.)

ANSWERS TO EXERCISES 11

1. (a) $1\frac{1}{3}$, (b) 4.27, (c) 2, (d) 7, (e) 2, (f) 0.5.
2. (a) 4, (b) 1, (c) -2, (d) -0.5, (e) 1, (f) -0.516.
3. (a) $-\frac{6}{7}$, (b) $-1\frac{2}{3}$, (c) -5, (d) 5, (e) 17, (f) No solution.
4. (a) -15, (b) -0.5, (c) 6, (d) 8, (e) $-\frac{2}{9}$, (f) $\frac{1}{50}$.
5. (a) $x = 3, y = 1$.   (b) $a = 1, b = 1$.
(c) $m = -0.5, n = -2.7$.   (d) $x = 5, y = -2$.
6. (a) $x = 11, y = 12$.   (b) $p = 4, q = -5$.
(c) $u = 2.5, v = 1.5$.   (d) $a = 22, b = 14$.
7. (a) $c = 1, d = 2$.   (b) $x = -3, y = -4$.
(c) $m = 1.2, n = 0.8$.   (d) $x = 0, y = 2$.
8. (a) $x = 2, y = 4$.   (b) $u = \frac{19}{14}, v = -19$.
(c) $r = \frac{1}{3}, s = \frac{1}{2}$.   (d) $x = 2, y = 4$.
9. 40 kg.
10. 700 cm^3.
11. 45 m, 25 m.
12. 540 tonnes.
13. 163.6̇3 cm^3.
14. 125 l/min, 62.5 l/min.
15. 680 mm.
16. 200, 160.
17. 280 mm, 320 mm.
18. $a = \frac{1}{12}, b = 7$.
19. (a) $a = 0.45, b = 0.085$. (b) 1.975 kg. (c) 5.3 kW.
20. (a) 2500. (b) £2.40, £3.80.

12 | Graphs and diagrams

12.1. PICTORIAL PRESENTATION OF DATA

Data should always be presented in a clear and orderly manner. A commonly employed layout is a *table* in which the figures are arranged in columns and rows. Consider, for example, the sales figures, shown in the following table, of a company manufacturing pumps and compressors:

	1970	1971	1972	1973
Sales of pumps (*units*)	1441	1485	1534	1595
Sales of compressors (*units*)	217	328	437	546
	1974	1975	1976	1977
Sales of pumps (*units*)	1637	1684	1731	1826
Sales of compressors (*units*)	659	775	888	994

Only after a careful study of the figures is it seen that the sales of compressors increase each year by more units than sales of pumps. When the data are shown pictorially, in Fig. 12.1, the same conclusion is instantly arrived at.

Pictorial presentation of data can take various forms, but they can all be divided into two main groups, *graphs*

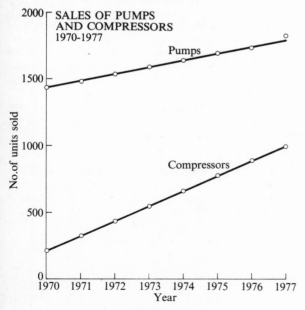

Fig. 12.1

and *diagrams*. The basic difference is that a graph is a picture illustrating, in the form of a *curve*, a definite mathematical relationship between two variable quantities, whilst a diagram is any other form of pictorial representation.

Note. The line on a graph is always referred to as a *curve*—even though it may be straight.

12.2. GRAPHS

The object of a graph is to present data visually and to show at a glance the magnitude of a variable quantity for any given value of another variable quantity on which the first depends. A graph may also be used in making predictions and estimates. Thus graphs can be divided into two main types, mathematical graphs and presentation graphs.

12.2.1. Construction of graphs. The basic principles to be observed in constructing graphs apply equally to mathematical graphs and presentation graphs. These basic principles are given below.

(a) The independent variable should be placed on the horizontal axis.
(b) The axes should be clearly labelled to explain what the numbers represent.
(c) The scales should be carefully chosen so as to avoid awkward fractions and so that a curve may occupy as large a space as possible on the graph.
(d) The curve of best fit should be drawn through the points plotted.
(e) The graph should have a title.

12.2.2. Cartesian co-ordinates. A useful method of illustrating algebraical relations graphically is due to the French mathematician Descartes (1596–1650). Two reference axes are arranged at right-angles as shown in Fig. 12.2, the axes forming the basis of Cartesian co-ordinates. The point where the axes intersect is known as the *origin* of the co-ordinates. Conventionally, values of x are measured horizontally, positive values to the right of the origin and negative values to the left: the x-value of a point is called its *abscissa*. Values of y are measured vertically, positive values above the origin and negative values below: the y-value of a point is called its *ordinate*.

It is seen from Fig. 12.2 that the axes divide two-dimensional space into four parts called *quadrants*. Consider, for example, the point $x = 4$, $y = 3$, which is represented by the cartesian co-ordinates (4, 3). Such a

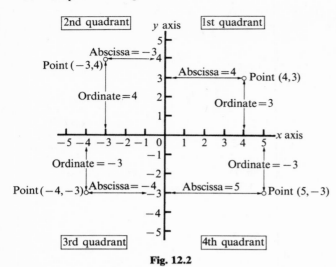

Fig. 12.2

point, whose abscissa and ordinate are both positive, is seen to lie in the first quadrant. The second quadrant is seen to contain points with negative abscissae and positive ordinates, the third those points whose abscissae and ordinates are both negative, and the fourth those points having positive abscissae and negative ordinates.

12.2.3. The linear law. It is a well known fact that the shortest distance between two points is a straight line. Consider the straight line that passes through the points $(2, 5)$ and $(-2, -3)$ shown in Fig. 12.3. The ordinate in

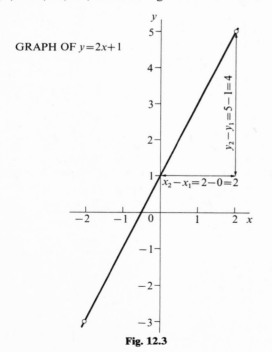

GRAPH OF $y = 2x + 1$

Fig. 12.3

both cases is twice the abscissa plus 1 which is also true for any and every other point on the line. Thus the equation $y = 2x + 1$ is satisfied by all points on the line.

The constant gradient of a straight line (linear) graph is given by:

$$m = \frac{\text{the difference in the } y\text{-values of two points}}{\text{the difference in the corresponding } x\text{-values}},$$

or, using symbols,

$$m = \frac{y_2 - y_1}{x_2 - x_1}.$$

An inspection of the straight line in Fig. 12.3 shows that between the points $(0, 1)$ and $(2, 5)$ the difference in the y-values is 4, while the corresponding difference in the x-values is 2. Thus, the gradient of the line is

$$m = \frac{5 - 1}{2 - 0} = \frac{4}{2} = 2.$$

A further inspection of Fig. 12.3 shows that the line passes through the y-axis at $+1$. Now, the equation $y = 2x + 1$ was seen to satisfy all points on the line. It, therefore, follows that the coefficient of x represents the gradient of the line and the absolute term represents the y-axis intercept. Thus, in general:

(i) Any equation of the form $y = mx + c$ (where m and c are constants) represents a straight line.
(ii) The coefficient of x, that is, m, is the constant gradient of the line.
Note. The gradient is positive $(+)$ if the line runs up from left to right and negative $(-)$ if the line runs down from left to right. (See examples 12.1 and 12.2 in particular.)
(iii) The number which stands alone, that is, c, is the distance from the origin at which the line intersects the y-axis.

EXAMPLE 12.1. Draw the straight line joining the points $(3, 3)$ and $(-3, -2)$. Calculate the gradient of the line and hence write its equation.

SOLUTION

The points are plotted and the curve drawn as shown in Fig. 12.4.
The equation of a straight line is of the form $y = mx + c$. The gradient of the line,

$$m = \frac{y_2 - y_1}{x_2 - x_1},$$

$$= \frac{3 - 0.5}{3 - 0}$$

$$= \frac{2.5}{3} = \frac{5}{6} \quad \text{or} \quad 0.8\dot{3}.$$

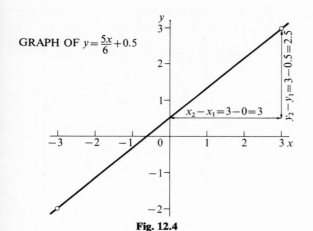

GRAPH OF $y = \dfrac{5x}{6} + 0.5$

Fig. 12.4

Note that the line runs up from left to right and that the gradient is positive $(+\frac{5}{6})$.

The line passes through the y-axis at the point where $y = 0.5$.

$\therefore$ the constant $c = 0.5$.

The equation of the line passing through the points $(3, 3)$ and $(-3, -2)$ is thus

$$y = \frac{5x}{6} + 0.5,$$

in standard form, or

$$6y = 5x + 3.$$

EXAMPLE 12.2. Plot the points $(-10, 5)$ and $(10, -15)$ and join them with a straight line. Determine the gradient of the line and hence write its equation.

SOLUTION

The points are plotted and the curve drawn as shown in Fig. 12.5.

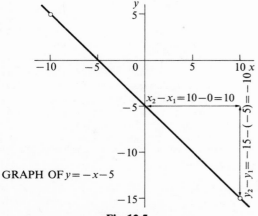

GRAPH OF $y = -x - 5$

Fig. 12.5

The equation of a straight line is of the form $y = mx + c$. The gradient of the line,

$$m = \frac{y_2 - y_1}{x_2 - x_1},$$

$$= \frac{-15 - (-5)}{10 - 0}$$

$$= \frac{-10}{10} = -1.$$

Note that the line runs down from left to right and that the gradient is negative (-1). The line passes through the y-axis at the point where $y = -5$.

$\therefore$ the constant $c = -5$.

The equation of the line passing through the points $(-10, 5)$ and $(10, -15)$ is thus

$$y = -1x - 5,$$

which can be written as

$$y = -x - 5, \quad \text{or} \quad x + y + 5 = 0.$$

12.3. INTERPOLATION AND EXTRAPOLATION

The curve of a graph is often used to estimate and predict other values by processes known as:

(i) *interpolation*, which means reading a value on that part of the curve which lies between the two extreme points plotted, and

(ii) *extrapolation*, which means finding a value on that part of the curve that lies outside the two extreme points plotted.

It will be seen from Fig. 12.6 that, while interpolation is possible from the known curve, extrapolation should be treated with caution outside the two extreme points plotted where the pattern may be unknown.

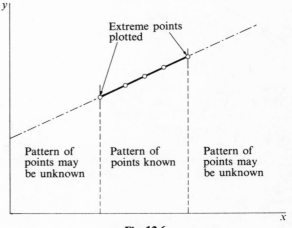

Fig. 12.6

EXAMPLE 12.3. Draw the graph of $y = 3x - 2$ for values of x from 5 to -5 and from it read off:

(i) the value of y when x is -3.5,
(ii) the value of x when y is 7.

SOLUTION

The equation $y = 3x - 2$ is of the form $y = mx + c$ so that a straight-line graph will be drawn.

The cartesian co-ordinates of three points are now calculated and tabulated as follows:

when $x = 5$, $y = 3 \times 5 - 2 = 13$

when $x = 0$, $y = 3 \times 0 - 2 = -2$

(Note that this is the value of the constant c.)

when $x = -5$, $y = 3 \times -5 - 2 = -17$.

x	5	0	-5
y	13	-2	-17

It should be noted that, while only two points are necessary to obtain the straight line, the co-ordinates of a third point are calculated to serve as a check on the other two.

The points are plotted and the curve drawn as shown in Fig. 12.7.

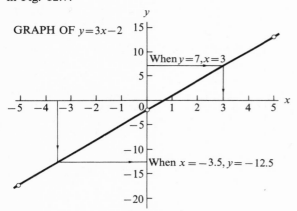

GRAPH OF $y = 3x - 2$

When $y = 7, x = 3$

When $x = -3.5, y = -12.5$

Fig. 12.7

The three points lie on the line which must be correct.

From the graph, by interpolation, it is seen that when x is -3.5, y is -12.5, and when y is 7, x is 3.

These values may be checked by calculation using the given equation $y = 3x - 2$.

EXAMPLE 12.4. The following results were obtained from a tensile test on a steel specimen:

Load, F (kN)	5	10	15
Extension, x (mm)	0.019	0.038	0.057
Load, F (kN)	20	25	30
Extension, x (mm)	0.076	0.095	0.114

(a) Plot the load–extension graph and find its gradient.
(b) What conclusion can be made from the shape of the graph?
(c) Use the graph to estimate the load when the extension was 0.05 mm.

SOLUTION

The points are plotted and the curve drawn as shown in Fig. 12.8.

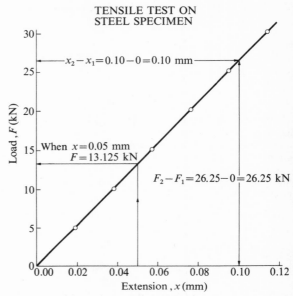

TENSILE TEST ON STEEL SPECIMEN

$x_2 - x_1 = 0.10 - 0 = 0.10$ mm

When $x = 0.05$ mm $F = 13.125$ kN

$F_2 - F_1 = 26.25 - 0 = 26.25$ kN

Fig. 12.8

(a) The gradient of the line,

$$m = \frac{F_2 - F_1}{x_2 - x_1}$$

$$= \frac{26.25 - 0 \text{ kN}}{0.10 - 0 \text{ mm}}$$

$$= \frac{26.25 \text{ kN}}{0.10 \text{ mm}} = 262.5 \text{ kN/mm}.$$

(b) The curve (straight line) passes through the origin. It can, therefore, be concluded that the extension is directly proportional to the load producing it.

Note. This important relationship for an elastic material is known as Hooke's law.

(c) From the curve, by interpolation, it is found that when the extension was 0.05 mm the applied load was 13.125 kN.

EXAMPLE 12.5. For workpieces to be turned at a particular surface cutting speed the relationship between the rotational speed of a workpiece and its diameter is given by the formula:

$$N = \frac{10\,500}{D} \text{ where}$$

N = rotational speed (rev/min) and

D = diameter of workpiece (mm).

Plot a graph that illustrates this relationship for values of D from 40 mm to 140 mm in steps of 20 mm.

(a) Show how the graph may be used to find the correct rotational speed for a workpiece of diameter 70 mm.
(b) Calculate the value of the surface cutting speed using a point on the graph.

(U.E.I.)

SOLUTION

The first step is to calculate suitable values of N and hence plot the graph shown in Fig. 12.9.

When D = 40 mm, $\quad N = \dfrac{10\,500}{40} = 262.5$ rev/min;

When D = 60 mm, $\quad N = \dfrac{10\,500}{60} = 175$ rev/min;

When D = 80 mm, $\quad N = \dfrac{10\,500}{80} = 131.25$ rev/min;

When D = 100 mm, $\quad N = \dfrac{10\,500}{100} = 105$ rev/min;

When D = 120 mm, $\quad N = \dfrac{10\,500}{120} = 87.5$ rev/min;

When D = 140 mm, $\quad N = \dfrac{10\,500}{140} = 75$ rev/min.

N (rev/min)	262.5	175	131.25	105	87.5	75
D (mm)	40	60	80	100	120	140

(a) By interpolation, it is found that the rotational speed for a workpiece of diameter 70 mm is 150 rev/min.

Note. The curve may be used to find a suitable value of N for all values of D up to 140 mm, thus eliminating separate calculations and possible errors.
(b) Using the point from (a) above:

Surface cutting speed, $v = \pi D N$,

$$= \pi \times 70 \times 150$$
$$= 33\,000 \text{ mm/min}$$
$$= 33 \text{ m/min.}$$

Note. The surface cutting speed of 33 m/min would be obtained using any corresponding values of N and D from the curve.

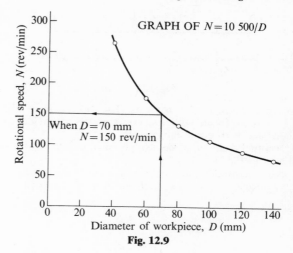

Fig. 12.9

12.4. RELATED PARALLEL SCALES

It is often convenient to relate a set of values on one scale to a corresponding set of values on a parallel scale. Consider, for example, Boyle's law for gases. This important law states that the absolute pressure p of a given mass of any gas varies inversely as the volume V, provided that the temperature remains constant. A graph of the change of pressure with volume has the form shown by curve (i) in Fig. 12.10, which cannot readily be interpreted. By plotting p against $1/V$ (i.e. the reciprocal of V), curve (ii) is obtained which shows clearly that pressure is inversely proportional to volume.

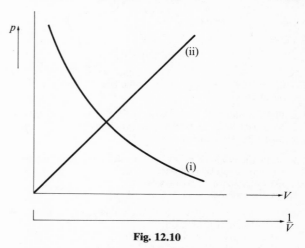

Fig. 12.10

The relationship between the horizontal scales used in Fig. 12.10 is shown in Fig. 12.11 from which it should be noted that, while values of V (numbers) increase in equal increments from left to right, corresponding values of $1/V$ (reciprocals of numbers) decrease from left

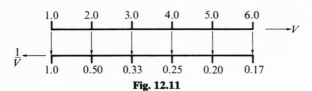

Fig. 12.11

to right in unequal increments. The $1/V$ scale in Fig. 12.10 is arranged with ascending values from left to right, and with equal increments.

Another example of the usefulness of parallel scales is shown in Fig. 12.12.

All electromagnetic radiation travels at a velocity of very nearly 3×10^8 m/s in a vacuum (this velocity is almost unchanged in air). For all waves,

$$v = f\lambda, \quad \text{where} \quad v = \text{velocity (metres per second, m/s)}$$
$$f = \text{frequency (hertz, Hz)}$$
$$\lambda = \text{wavelength (metres, m).}$$

By transposition, it will be seen that

$$f = v/\lambda \quad \text{and} \quad \lambda = v/f.$$

A growing number of radios now have dials marked with kilohertz (kHz) rather than the familiar metres. Fig. 12.12 shows the relationship between the scales used for medium wave radio communication.

MEDIUM WAVE

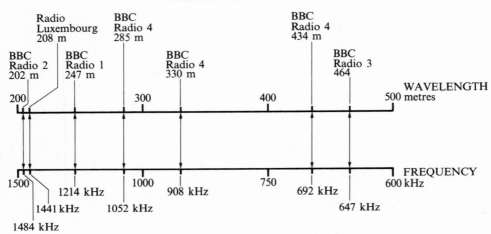

Fig. 12.12

EXERCISES 12

1. Draw the straight line joining the points $(-1, -7)$ and $(1, 1)$. Calculate the gradient of the line and hence state its equation.

2. Plot the points $(-1, 3.5)$ and $(1, -1.5)$ and join them with a straight line. Determine the gradient of the line and hence write its equation.

3. Draw the graph of $y = \frac{1}{2}x - 3$ for values of x from -5 to 5. Use the graph to estimate:
(a) the value of y when x is 3.5,
(b) the value of x when y is -3.5.

4. Draw the graph of $y = 3 - 0.25x$ for values of x from -4 to 4 and from it read off:
(a) the value of y when x is 2.8,
(b) the value of x when y is 3.4.

5. Draw the straight line joining the points $(-1, -4)$ and $(1, 2)$. Find the ordinates of points on this line which have abscissae -0.5 and 0.75. Calculate the gradient of the line and hence write its equation. Write the equation of a line parallel to this one, but passing through the origin.

6. Draw, on the same axes, the lines:
(i) $y = -1$, (ii) $y = 3$, (iii) $x = -2$, (iv) $x = 2$.
For the figure enclosed by these lines, find the equation of the diagonal with a positive gradient.

7. Draw, using the same axes, the curves of $y = 3x - 1$ and $y = (5x + 1)/3$ for values of x from 0 to 2. Write down the cartesian co-ordinates for the point of intersection of the two lines.

8. A helical spring extends when an axial load is applied, as shown in the following table:

Load, F(N)	7.2	21.6	37.8	59.4	77.4	90.0	117.0
Extension, x (mm)	4	12	21	33	43	50	65

Draw the load-extension graph and find its gradient. What does the gradient represent?
Does the spring obey Hooke's Law? Given a reason for your answer.

9. A steel slider was pulled at constant speed along a horizontal cast-iron surface during an experiment. Weights W were placed on the slider and the corresponding horizontal forces F required to maintain motion were recorded as follows:

F (N)	0.35	0.46	0.54	0.65	0.74	0.85
W (N)	0.5	1.0	1.5	2.0	2.5	3.0

Plot a graph of F against W (i.e. F vertically, W horizontally). Determine the gradient of the curve and state what this gradient represents.

10. A machine part is being accelerated and its velocity v at a given time t is shown in the table below:

Velocity, v (m/s)	0.36	0.62	0.88	1.14	1.40	1.66
Time, t (second)	0.2	0.4	0.6	0.8	1.0	1.2

Draw the velocity-time graph. Find the gradient of the curve and hence state the acceleration of the machine part.

11. A closed-coiled helical spring was loaded in compression and the length of the spring L was measured when various forces F were applied. The following results were obtained:

Length, L (mm)	63.5	61.0	58.5	56.0	53.5	51.0
Force, F (N)	50	60	70	80	90	100

(a) Plot these values and from the graph find:
   (i) the value of L when $F = 64$ N,
   (ii) the value of F when $L = 55$ mm.
(b) Estimate the nominal unloaded length of the spring.

12. The clearance c between a shaft and a journal bearing is found to change with the temperature t as shown in the following table:

c (mm)	0.104	0.095	0.086	0.080	0.072	0.059	0.050
t (°C)	20	50	80	100	125	170	200

(a) Plot these values, c vertically and t horizontally.
(b) From the graph find the clearance when the temperature is (i) 35 °C, (ii) 135 °C.
(c) Estimate the temperature of bearing seizure.

13. The following relationships exist between the nominal outside diameter D and the number of teeth T of a set of spur gears of a particular metric module.

D (mm)	88	104	128	152	208	248
T	20	24	30	36	50	60

Plot these values and from the graph find:
(a) the value of D when $T = 68$
(b) the value of T when $D = 108$ mm.

14. The following information has been extracted from a manufacturer's recommendation for the clearance between a

shaft and an oil-impregnated self-aligning bearing.

Shaft diameter D (mm)	10	20	30	40	50	60
Clearance C (μm)	10	14	18	22	26	30

(a) Plot these values:
   D horizontally, scale 20 mm = 10 mm;
   C vertically, scale 20 mm = 5 μm.
(b) Determine:
   (i) the value of C when $D = 25$ mm.
   (ii) the value of D when $C = 20$ μm.

15. If workpieces are to be turned with a cutting speed of 33 m/min, the relationship between the diameter D mm and the rotational speed N rev/min can be obtained from the relationship

$$ND = 10\,500.$$

Plot a graph that illustrates this relationship for values of D between 20 mm and 160 mm

   D horizontally, scale 20 mm = 20 mm (i.e. full size)
   N vertically, scale 20 mm = 50 rev/min.

Using the graph, and showing the answers on the graph, determine
(a) the value of D when $N = 250$ rev/min
(b) the value of N when $D = 140$ mm.

(C.G.L.I.)

16. The mass per unit length of circular bars of deoxidized copper varies with the diameter as shown in the following table:

Diameter (mm)	10	20	30	40	50	60
Mass (kg/m)	0.7	2.8	6.3	11.2	17.5	25.2

Illustrate these values on a graph, and use the graph to estimate the mass of a tube of copper of outside diameter 45 mm, inside diameter 35 mm, and length 200 mm.

(U.E.I.)

17. For a particular cutting speed the relationship between the rotational speed of a drill and its diameter is given by

$$N = \frac{9450}{d}$$

where $N =$ rotational speed of drill in revolutions per minute
   $d =$ drill diameter in millimetres.
Determine the value of N for drill sizes from 10 to 40 millimetres diameter, in steps of 5 millimetres, and plot a graph of speed against diameter.
From your graph determine the required speeds for a 12 mm and a 32 mm diameter drill.
Suggested scales 20 mm : 100 rev/min (vertical axis)
                20 mm : 5 mm diameter (horizontal axis).

(U.E.I.)

1. 4, $y = 4x - 3$.

2. -2.5, $y = 1 - 2.5x$.

3. (a) -1.25,   (b) -1.

4. (a) 2.3,   (b) −1.6.

5. −2.5,   1.25,   3, $y = 3x - 1$, $y = 3x$.

6. $y = x + 1$.

7. (1, 2).

8. 1.8 N/mm (spring stiffness).   Yes, $x \propto F$.

9. 0.2 (coefficient of friction).

10. 1.3,   1.3 m/s².

11. (a) 60 mm, 84 N.   (b) 76 mm.

12. (b) 0.0995 mm,   0.0695 mm,   (c) 367 °C.

13. (a) 280 mm,   (b) 25.

14. (b) 16 μm,   35 mm.

15. (a) 42 mm,   (b) 75 rev/min.

16. 1.1 kg.

17. 788 rev/min,   295 rev/min.

13 | The geometry of rectilinear figures

13.1. INTRODUCTION

The geometry dealt with in the next two chapters concerns the mathematical study of and relationship between points, lines, and plane angles.

13.2. MEASUREMENT OF PLANE ANGLES

A plane angle may be defined as the difference in direction of two intersecting lines or planes. The SI unit of plane angle is the radian (rad) which is dealt with in Chapter 14. The degree (°), minute ('), and second (″) are units outside the SI which, because of their practical importance, are in general use and which are, therefore, used throughout the present chapter.

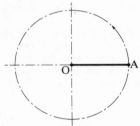

Fig. 13.1

A plane angle may also be described as the measurement of an amount of turning. In Fig. 13.1 the line *OA* is said to have moved through one complete revolution if it turns about the point *O* and returns to its original position.

One complete revolution = 360 degrees.
A degree is a unit of angle measurement.

A degree may be defined as $\frac{1}{360}$ part of a complete revolution.
Symbolically 1 degree is written as 1°.
A minute is a subdivision of a degree and is equal to $\frac{1}{60}$ of a degree.
In symbols 1 minute is written as 1'.
A second is a subdivision of a minute and is equal to $\frac{1}{60}$ of a minute.
Symbolically 1 second is written as 1″.
Summarising: 1 revolution = 360°

$$1° = 60' = 3600''$$

$$1' = 60''$$

Relationships between parts of a revolution and their corresponding value in degrees are of some significance particularly in later work.

Note. The angle formed by the intersection of the lines *OA* and *OB* (Fig. 13.2(a)) is called angle *AOB* or *BOA*. The symbol ∠ usually replaces the word angle.

Referring to Figs 13.2(a), (b), and (c)

$$\angle AOB = \tfrac{1}{4} \text{ revolution} = 90° \quad \text{(a right angle)}$$

$$\angle AOC = \tfrac{1}{2} \text{ revolution} = 180° \quad \text{(often described as a straight angle)}$$

$$\angle AOD = \tfrac{3}{4} \text{ revolution} = 270°$$

13.2.1. Positive and Negative Angles.
Angles formed by an anticlockwise rotation are called positive angles. Angles formed by a clockwise rotation are termed negative angles.

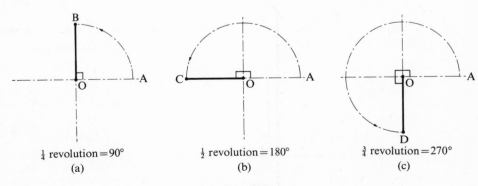

$\frac{1}{4}$ revolution = 90°
(a)

$\frac{1}{2}$ revolution = 180°
(b)

$\frac{3}{4}$ revolution = 270°
(c)

Fig. 13.2

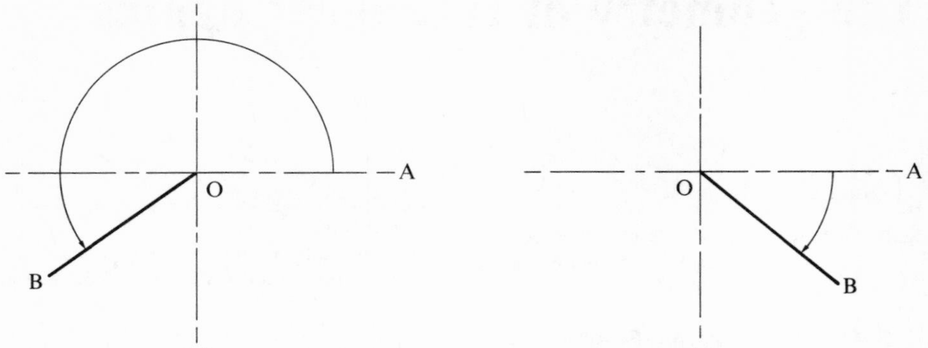

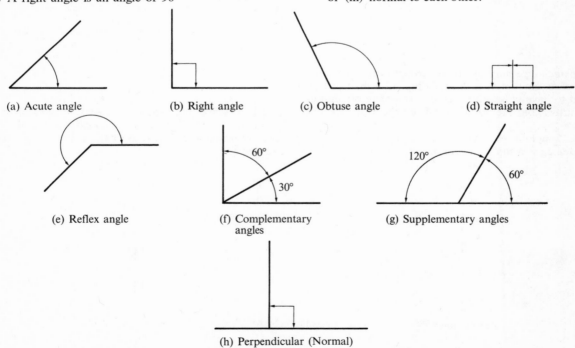

(a)
Positive angle

(b)
Negative angle

Fig. 13.3

In Fig. 13.3(a) ∠*AOB* is considered to be a positive angle since it is measured in an anticlockwise direction from the line *OA*.

Conversely ∠*AOB*, Fig. 13.3(b), measured from *OA* in a clockwise direction is considered to be a negative angle.

13.2.2. Angle definitions. The angles shown in Fig. 13.4(a to h) are defined as follows.
(a) An acute angle has a value less than 90°
(b) A right angle is an angle of 90°

(c) An obtuse angle is between 90° and 180°
(d) A straight angle is 180° or two right angles
(e) A reflex angle is between 180° and 360°
(f) Complementary angles are two angles whose sum is 90°
(g) Supplementary angles are two angles whose sum is 180°
(h) When two lines include an angle of 90° between them the two lines are said to be:
      (i) at right angles to each other,
  or (ii) perpendicular to each other,
  or (iii) normal to each other.

(a) Acute angle   (b) Right angle   (c) Obtuse angle   (d) Straight angle

(e) Reflex angle   (f) Complementary angles   (g) Supplementary angles

(h) Perpendicular (Normal)

Fig. 13.4

EXAMPLE 13.1. Find the sum of the angles 36° 22′ 33″ and 25° 14′ 32″.

SOLUTION

$$36° 22′ 30″$$
$$\underline{25° 14′ 32″} \quad \text{(Note. } 30″ + 32″ = 62″ = 1′ 2″)$$
$$61° 37′ 2″$$

EXAMPLE 13.2. Express 40° 15′ in degrees and decimal fractions of a degree.

SOLUTION

$$60′ = 1°$$

$$\therefore \ 1′ = \frac{1°}{60}$$

Hence

$$15′ = 15 \times \frac{1°}{60} = \frac{15°}{60}$$

$$\frac{15°}{60} = \frac{1°}{4} = 0.25°$$

$$\therefore \ 40° 15′ = 40.25°$$

13.3. PROPERTIES OF ANGLES AND STRAIGHT LINES

13.3.1. Intersection of two straight lines.

Referring to Fig. 13.5

$\angle AOB + \angle AOD = 180°$ (since $\angle BOD$ is a straight angle)

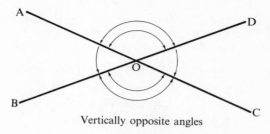

Vertically opposite angles

Fig. 13.5

also

$\angle DOC + \angle AOD = 180°$ (since $\angle AOC$ is a straight angle)

$\therefore \ \angle AOB + \angle AOD = \angle DOC + \angle AOD$ (since sum of each pair $= 180°$)

$\therefore \ \angle AOB = \angle DOC$ (subtracting $\angle AOD$ from each side)

In a similar manner $\angle AOD = \angle BOC$.

$\angle AOB$ and $\angle DOC$ are called vertically opposite angles.

$\angle AOD$ and $\angle BOC$ are also vertically opposite.

When two lines intersect the vertically opposite angles formed are equal.

13.3.2. Intersection of two parallel lines by a straight line.

(a) Corresponding angles. In Fig. 13.6(a) AB and CD are a pair of parallel lines. XY is a line intersecting the parallel lines and is called a transversal.

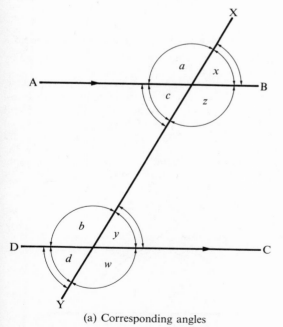

(a) Corresponding angles

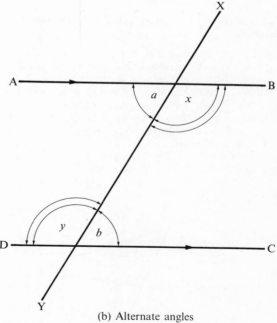

(b) Alternate angles

Fig. 13.6

The following pairs of angles are equal since they occupy corresponding positions with respect to the parallel lines and the transversal.

$$\angle a = \angle b \quad \text{(corresponding angles)}$$
$$\angle c = \angle d \quad \text{(corresponding angles)}$$
$$\angle x = \angle y \quad \text{(corresponding angles)}$$
$$\angle w = \angle z \quad \text{(corresponding angles)}$$

When parallel lines are cut by a transversal the corresponding angles formed are equal.

(b) Alternate angles. Referring to Fig. 13.6(b)

$$\angle a = \angle b \quad \text{(alternate angles)}$$
$$\angle x = \angle y \quad \text{(alternate angles)}$$

When parallel lines are cut by a transversal the alternate angles formed are equal.

(c) Interior angles. In Fig. 13.6(a) the angles b, c, y, and z are called interior angles.

Similarly in Fig. 13.6(b) the angles a, b, x, and y are also interior angles.

The following relationship exists between these pairs of angles:

$$\text{in Fig. 13.6(a)} \quad \angle c + \angle b = 180°$$
$$\angle z + \angle y = 180°$$
$$\text{and in Fig. 13.6(b)} \quad \angle a + \angle y = 180°$$
$$\angle x + \angle b = 180°$$

13.3.3. Intersection of non-parallel straight lines by a transversal.

In Fig. 13.7 the angles a and w, c and y, b and x, and d and z are pairs of corresponding angles and angles c and x, and d and w are pairs of alternate angles.

It must be emphasised that in the case of non-parallel straight lines these pairs of angles are not equal.

If therefore a problem arises in which it is necessary to prove that two straight lines are parallel, this may be achieved by showing that either:
(1) a pair of corresponding angles are equal, or
(2) a pair of alternate angles are equal.

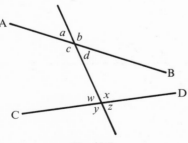

Fig. 13.7

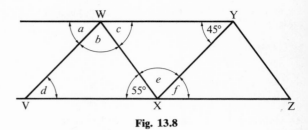

Fig. 13.8

EXAMPLE 13.3. Fig. 13.8 represents part of a framework. If WY is parallel to VZ, WX parallel to YZ, and WV parallel to YX, find the values of the angles a, b, c, d, e, and f.

SOLUTION

$\angle a = 45°$ (corresponding angles since $WV \parallel YX$)
$\angle c = 55°$ (alternate angles since $WY \parallel VZ$)
$\angle b = 180° - (a + c)$ (since $\angle a + \angle b + \angle c = $ straight angle)
But
$\angle a = 45°$ and $\angle c = 55°$
$\therefore \ \angle b = 180° - (45° + 55°)$
$\qquad = 180° - 100°$
$\therefore \ \angle b = 80°$
$\angle a = \angle b = 80°$ (alternate angles since $WV \parallel YX$)
$\angle d = \angle a$ (alternate angles since $WY \parallel YZ$)
But
$\angle a = 45°$
$\therefore \ \angle d = 45°$
$\angle f = \angle d$ (corresponding angles since $WV \parallel YX$)
$\therefore \ \angle f = 45°$

13.4. TRIANGLES AND QUADRILATERALS

A triangle may be defined as a plane figure bounded by three straight lines.

Referring to Fig. 13.9, the three points A, B, and C are called the vertices of the triangle. In the position drawn the line BC or 'a' is the base of the triangle and the point A is the vertex of the triangle. The usual convention in both trigonometry (Chapter 15) and geometry is to denote the sides AB, BC, and AC by the lower case letters, c, a, and b where side c is opposite angle C, side b is opposite angle B and side a is opposite angle A.

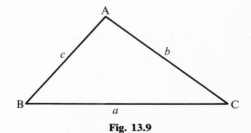

Fig. 13.9

 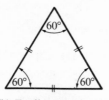

(a) Isosceles triangle   (b) Equilateral triangle

Fig. 13.10

13.4.1. Classification of Triangles. Triangles may be grouped in the following broad categories.

1. A scalene triangle is one in which all sides are unequal.
2. An acute-angled triangle is one in which all the angles are acute angles.
3. An obtuse-angled triangle is one in which one of the angles is an obtuse angle.
4. A right-angled triangle is one which contains an angle of 90°.
5. An isosceles triangle is a triangle having two equal sides. The angles opposite to the equal sides are also equal (see Fig. 13.10a).
6. An equilateral triangle is a triangle having three equal sides. Each angle in an equilateral triangle is equal to 60° (see Fig. 13.10b).

13.4.2. Angle Properties of a triangle.

1. *Sum of the interior angles of a triangle equals* **180°**.

Proof. Let *ABC* be any triangle

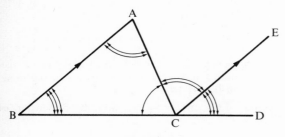

Fig. 13.11

Extend line *BC* to *D* and draw a line *CE* through *C* parallel to *AB*. Then since *AB* is parallel to *CE*

$\angle ACE = \angle BAC$ (alternate angles)
$\angle ABC = \angle ECD$ (corresponding angles)

But

$\angle ACB + \angle ACE + \angle ECD = 180°$ (straight angle)
$\therefore \angle ABC + \angle BAC + \angle ACB = 180°$ ($\angle ACD$ is common to straight line angle and the triangle).

$\therefore$ Sum of three interior angles of a triangle = 180°.

2. *The exterior angle of a triangle equals the sum of the opposite interior angles.*

Proof. Referring to Fig. 13.11
$\angle ABC + \angle BAC + \angle ACB = 180°$ (sum of interior angles of a triangle)

Also

$\angle ACE + \angle ECD + \angle ACB = 180°$ (straight angle)
$\therefore \angle ABC + \angle BAC + \angle ACB$
$\qquad\qquad\qquad\qquad = \angle ACE + \angle ECD + \angle ACB$

If $\angle ACB$ is subtracted from each side of the equation then

$\angle ABC + \angle BAC = \angle ACE + \angle ECD$

but

$\angle ACE + \angle ECD = \angle ACD$
$\therefore \angle ABC + \angle BAC = \angle ACD$

i.e. sum of opposite interior angles = exterior angle.

3. *In every triangle the greatest angle is opposite to the longest side.*

Conversely the longest side is opposite the greatest angle. Again in any triangle the sum of the lengths of two sides is greater than the length of the third side.

4. *Angles of a quadrilateral.*

A quadrilaterial is any four-sided figure. Since a quadrilateral can always be subdivided into two triangles the sum of its internal angles is 360°, i.e. referring to Fig. 13.12:

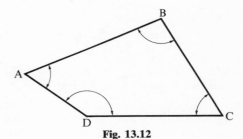

Fig. 13.12

13.5. POLYGONS

A polygon is a plane figure bounded by straight lines. In practice it is usual to refer to figures having five or more sides as a polygon. A regular polygon is one in which all sides and angles are equal. Polygons are accorded different names dependent upon the number of sides they contain. The following list gives the names of six common polygons:

Pentagon:	5 sides
Hexagon:	6 sides
Heptagon:	7 sides
Octagon:	8 sides
Nonagon:	9 sides
Decagon:	10 sides

13.5.1. Angles of a polygon. If none of the interior angles of a polygon are reflex angles (greater than 180°), the polygon is known as a convex polygon. In a convex polygon the sum of an interior angle and an exterior angle equals 180° as shown in Fig. 13.13.

The sum of the interior angles of a convex polygon having n sides is given by $(2n-4)\times 90°$.

The sum of the exterior angles of any polygon equals 360°.

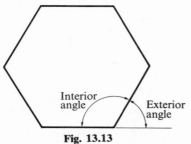

Fig. 13.13

EXAMPLE 13.4. The angles of a triangle measured in degrees are x, $3x$, and $5x$. Find the value of x and the angles of the triangle.

SOLUTION

Since the sum of the interior angles of a triangle $= 180°$

$$x+3x+5x = 180$$
$$9x = 180$$
$$\therefore x = \frac{180}{9} = 20$$
$$x = 20.$$

The angles of the triangle $= 20°$; $3\times 20°$; $5\times 20°$; i.e. 20°, 60°, and 100°.

EXAMPLE 13.5. An isosceles triangle contains an angle of 110°. Find the value of the other two angles.

SOLUTION

In an isosceles triangle two of the angles are equal.

$$\therefore \text{ sum of two equal angles} = 180° - 110° = 70°.$$

$$\text{Value of required angles} = \frac{70°}{2} = 35°.$$

EXAMPLE 13.6. A template is in the form of a regular polygon having twelve sides. Calculate the number of degrees in each interior angle of the template.

SOLUTION

The word 'regular' indicates that all sides and angles of the polygon are equal.

Sum of the interior angles of a polygon $= (2n-4)\times 90°$

In this case $n = 12$ (twelve sides).

Then $(2n-4)\times 90°$ becomes $(2\times 12-4)\times 90°$

and $(2\times 12-4)\times 90° = (24-4)\times 90°$

$$= 20\times 90° = 1800°.$$

Sum of interior angles $= 1800°$

A polygon with 12 sides has 12 angles and since the polygon is regular all angles are equal.

$$\therefore \text{ one interior angle} = \frac{1800}{12} = 150°.$$

13.6. SIMILAR TRIANGLES

Two triangles are said to be similar when three angles of one triangle are equal to three angles of the other in corresponding positions.

In Fig. 13.14, if $\angle X = \angle A$, $\angle Y = \angle B$, and $\angle Z = \angle C$ then the triangles ABC and XYZ are said to be similar.

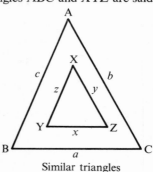

Similar triangles
Fig. 13.14

13.6.1. Properties of similar triangles.
1. Similar triangles are equiangular.
2. If two triangles have two angles of the one equal to the two corresponding angles of the other, then the two triangles must be similar since the remaining angles must be equal to each other.
3. In Fig. 13.14 $\triangle XYZ$ is a scaled-down version of $\triangle ABC$.
4. In similar triangles the ratios of corresponding sides are equal. Thus, referring to Fig. 13.14, since $\triangle ABC$ is similar to $\triangle XYZ$,

$$\frac{a}{x} = \frac{b}{y} = \frac{c}{z}$$

5. The converse of (4) above is also true, i.e. if the corresponding sides of two triangles are in the same ratio then the triangles are similar.

EXAMPLE 13.7. In Fig. 13.15 find the dimension of side a.

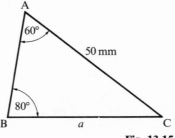
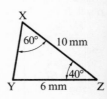

Fig. 13.15

SOLUTION

Using the principle of similar triangles it is first of all necessary to show that corresponding angles are equal.
In $\triangle ABC$, $\angle C = 180° - 80° - 60° = 40°$
In $\triangle XYZ$, $\angle Y = 180° - 60° - 40° = 80°$
∴ since the corresponding angles in $\triangle ABC$ and $\triangle XYZ$ are equal the two triangles are similar.
Corresponding sides are therefore proportional,

i.e.
$$\frac{XZ}{AC} = \frac{YZ}{a}$$

$$\therefore \frac{10}{50} = \frac{6}{a}$$

then $\qquad 10a = 300 \qquad$ (by cross multiplication)

and $\qquad a = \dfrac{300}{10} = 30$ mm.

Length of $a = 30$ mm.

EXAMPLE 13.8. In $\triangle ABC$ (see Fig. 13.16) a line DE is drawn parallel to the base BC. If $AD = 60$ mm, $DB = 20$ mm, $BC = 90$ mm and $AC = 70$ mm, calculate the lengths of DE and AE.

SOLUTION

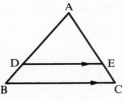

Fig. 13.16

Since DE is parallel to BC

$\qquad \angle ADE = \angle ABC \qquad$ (corresponding angles)

and $\quad \angle AED = \angle ACB \qquad$ (corresponding angles)

The third $\angle BAC$ is common to $\triangle ADE$ and $\triangle ABC$

$\qquad \therefore$ triangles ABC and ADE are equiangular.

Since the triangles are equiangular they are similar and corresponding sides are therefore proportional.
To find DE:

$$\frac{DE}{BC} = \frac{AD}{AB}$$

or
$$\frac{DE}{90} = \frac{60}{80}$$

$$\therefore DE = \frac{90 \times 60}{80} = 67.5$$

Length of $DE = 67.5$ mm.

To find AE:
In a similar manner, $\dfrac{AE}{70} = \dfrac{60}{80}$,

$$\therefore AE = \frac{70 \times 60}{80} = 52.5$$

Length of $AE = 52.5$ mm
   Note. A useful fact arising from this question is that a straight line drawn parallel to one side of a triangle cuts the other two sides proportionally.

13.7. CONGRUENT TRIANGLES

Two triangles are said to be congruent to each other if the sides and angles of one triangle are equal to the corresponding sides and angles of the other triangle.

13.7.1. Conditions for congruent triangles. Two triangles are said to be congruent when:

1. three sides of one triangle are equal to three sides of the other;
2. two angles and a side of one triangle are equal to two angles and the corresponding side of the other;
3. two sides and the included angle of one triangle are equal to two sides and the included angle of the other;
4. a right angle, hypotenuse, and side of one triangle are equal to the right angle, hypotenuse, and side of the other.

The conditions for congruency may be more easily memorised by the following abbreviations:
$\qquad$ SSS—three sides
$\qquad$ AAS—two angles and one side
$\qquad$ SAS—two sides and the included angle
$\qquad$ RHS—right angle, hypotenuse, and side.

EXAMPLE 13.9. In the parallelogram $ABCD$, Fig. 13.17, find the value of the angle at D.

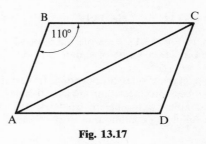

Fig. 13.17

SOLUTION

A parallelogram is a four-sided figure having opposite sides equal and parallel.
Consider the two triangles ADC and ABC.

From the definition of a parallelogram,

$$AD = BC \quad \text{(opposite sides equal)},$$

$$DC = AB \quad \text{(opposite sides equal), and}$$

$$AC \text{ is common to both triangles.}$$

Hence since three sides of triangle ADC equal the three sides of the triangle ABC the two triangles are congruent.

As the triangles are congruent the corresponding angles are equal.

$$\therefore \angle ADC = \angle ABC = 110°$$

$$\therefore \angle D = 110°.$$

13.8. THEOREM OF PYTHAGORAS

This theorem states that in any right-angled triangle the square on the hypotenuse is equal to the sum of the squares on the other two sides. The hypotenuse is the side opposite the right angle.

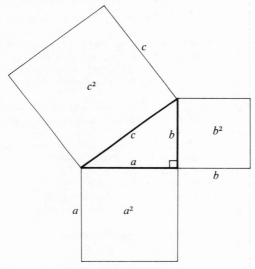

Fig. 13.18

Referring to Fig. 13.18, area of square on side c = area of square on side a + area of square on side b, or more simply, $a^2 + b^2 = c^2$.

Triangles having sides proportional to certain sets of whole numbers produce right angled triangles.

For example, right-angled triangles are produced from the following combination of numbers.

Sides containing right angle	Hypotenuse	Application of Theorem of Pythagoras
3:4:	5	$3^2 + 4^2 = 5^2$
5:12:	13	$5^2 + 12^2 = 13^2$
8:15:	17	$8^2 + 15^2 = 17^2$
9:40:	41	$9^2 + 40^2 = 41^2$

EXAMPLE 13.10. Two forces act at right angles to each other as shown in Fig. 13.19. Calculate the magnitude of the resultant.

SOLUTION

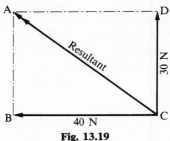

Fig. 13.19

Applying the Theorem of Pythagoras to $\triangle ABC$:

$$R^2 = 40^2 + 30^2 \text{ (since } AB = DC = 30 \text{ newtons)}$$

then

$$R^2 = 1600 + 900 = 2500$$

$$R^2 = 2500$$

$$\therefore R = 50$$

$$\text{Resultant} = 50 \text{ N.}$$

EXAMPLE 13.11. A piece of 60 mm diameter round steel bar has flats milled on it to form the largest possible square section.

Find the length of the side of the square section.

SOLUTION

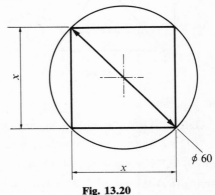

Fig. 13.20

In this case the diameter of the circle is also the diagonal of the required square as shown in Fig. 13.20. Applying the Theorem of Pythagoras

$$60^2 = x^2 + x^2$$

or

$$60^2 = 2x^2$$

i.e.

$$3600 = 2x^2$$

$$\therefore x^2 = \frac{3600}{2} = 1800$$

Hence $x = \sqrt{1800} = 42.4$

Length of side of required square = 42.4 mm.

EXAMPLE 13.12. A framework is constructed as shown in Fig. 13.21. The vertical members *BF* and *CE* trisect *AD* and *GD*. Find the lengths of the members; (a) *AD*, (b) *BF*, and (c) *CE*.

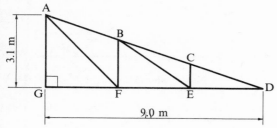

Fig. 13.21

SOLUTION

(a) To find *AD*:
Applying the Theorem of Pythagoras to △*ADG*
$$AD^2 = AG^2 + GD^2$$
or
$$AD^2 = 3.1^2 + 9^2$$
$$\therefore\ AD^2 = 10.21 + 81 = 91.21$$
Hence
$$AD = \sqrt{91.21} = 9.6$$

Length of *AD* = 9.6 m.

(b) To find *BF*:
Triangles *BDF* and *ADG* are similar since
∠*BFD* = ∠*AGD* = 90°
∠*DBF* = ∠*DAG* (corresponding angles as *AG* and *BF* are parallel)
and ∠*CDE* is common to both triangles.
As the triangles are similar corresponding sides are proportional
$$\therefore\ \frac{FD}{GD} = \frac{BF}{AG}$$
but $FD = \frac{2}{3} \times 9 = 6$ (since *DG* trisected)
$$\therefore\ \frac{6}{9} = \frac{BF}{3.1}$$
Hence
$$9BF = 18.6$$
and
$$BF = \frac{18.6}{9} = 2.07\ \text{m}$$

Length of member *BF* = 2.07 m.

(c) To find *CE*:
CE is found in a similar manner to *BF*
Triangles *AGD* and *CED* are similar
$$\therefore\ \frac{DE}{DG} = \frac{CE}{AG}$$
Hence
$$\frac{3}{9} = \frac{CE}{3.1}$$
$$\therefore\ CE = \frac{3 \times 3.1}{9} = \frac{9.3}{9}$$

Hence
$$CE = 1.03$$
Length of member *CE* = 1.03 m.

EXERCISES 13

1. Find the sum of the following angles:
   (a) 26° 30′ and 70° 32′
   (b) 43° 16′ 10″ and 53° 17′ 52″
   (c) 41° 40′ 50″ and 48° 19′ 10″
   (d) 120° 0′ 10″ and 30° 40′ 50″
   (e) 19° 10′, 31° 42′ and 52° 40′ 18″

2. What angles are complementary to:
   (a) 76° (b) 61° (c) 46° 31′ (d) 84° 20′ 10″?

3. What angles are supplementary to:
   (a) 108° (b) 92° (c) 67° 36′ (d) 121° 30′ 40″?

4. How many degrees are there in the following angles:
   (a) $\frac{2}{3}$ revolution (b) $\frac{1}{2}$ revolution (c) $\frac{3}{4}$ revolution
   (d) $\frac{3}{2}$ right angles (e) 2 right angles (f) $\frac{1}{3}$ straight angle.

5. Express the following angles in degrees, minutes and seconds:
   (a) 30.61° (b) 71.422° (c) 23.711° (d) 84.924°.

6. If the sum of the three angles $2x°$, $4x°$ and $3x°$ equals one right angle, find the value of x.

7. Members of part of the framework shown in Fig. 13.22 meet at the point *O*. Find the values of the angles *a*, *b*, *c*, and *d*.

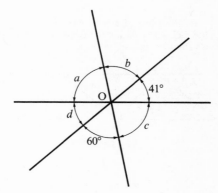

Fig. 13.22

8. Fig. 13.23 represents one edge of a template. Find the value of the angle *x*.

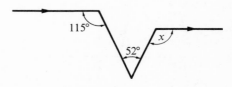

Fig. 13.23

9. Find the values of the angles *x*, *y*, and *z* in Fig. 13.24.

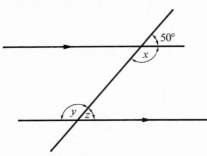

Fig. 13.24

10. In Fig. 13.25 prove that *AB* is parallel to *CD*.

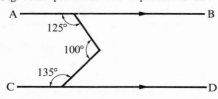

Fig. 13.25

11. Fig. 13.26 represents part of a framework. If *AB* is parallel to *EC*, *AD* parallel to *BC* and *AE* parallel to *BD*, find the values of the angles, *x*, *y*, *z*, *w*, *v*, and *t*.

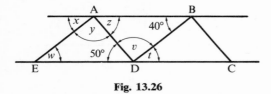

Fig. 13.26

12. In Fig. 13.27 *AB* is parallel to *CD* and *EC* is parallel to *AD*. From the information given in the figure, calculate the values of *x* and *y*.

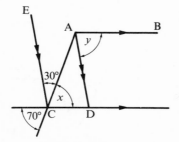

Fig. 13.27

13. In Fig. 13.28 *AX* and *DC* are parallel, $\angle DAB = 65°$ and $\angle CBX = 146°$. Calculate the sizes of the angles *ADC* and *BCD*.

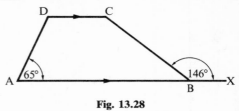

Fig. 13.28

14. Find the value of the angle θ in the isosceles triangles shown in Figs. 13.29(a), (b), and (c).

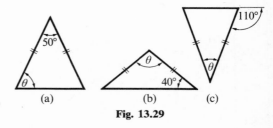

Fig. 13.29

15. Find the values of the angles *x* and *y* shown in Fig. 13.30.

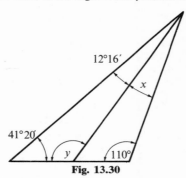

Fig. 13.30

16. Prove that in a rectangle *ABCD* the diagonals *AC* and *BD* are equal.

17. An isosceles triangle *ABC* (Fig. 13.31) has each base angle equal to 50°. The bisectors of the angles *ABC* and *ACB* meet at *D*. Calculate the angle *BDC*.

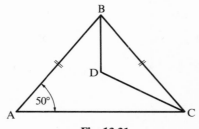

Fig. 13.31

18. The angles of a triangle are given as $3x$ degrees, $x+60$ degrees and $2x-30$ degrees. Find the value of x and the size of each angle of the triangle in degrees.

(N.C.T.E.C.)

19. Find the value of the angle θ shown in Fig. 13.32 when $AB = AC = CD$ and angle $BAC = 72°$.

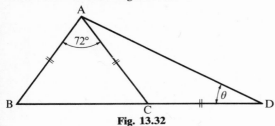

Fig. 13.32

20. In Fig. 13.33 $ABCD$ is a sketch of part of a regular hexagon and $EBCF$, part of a regular octagon. Calculate the size of the angle ABE.

(N.C.T.E.C.)

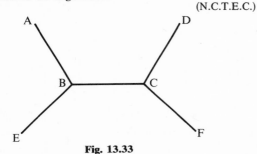

Fig. 13.33

21. Find the number of sides in a regular polygon in which each interior angle is $165°$.

22. Find the value of the angle θ in Fig. 13.34.

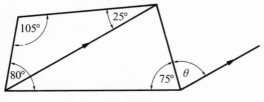

Fig. 13.34

23. In a quadrilateral $ABCD$ the angles A, B, and C are respectively $60°$, $103°$, and $135°$. The bisector of the angle D meets AB at E. Calculate angle AED.

24. The sides of a triangle are 18 cm, 14 cm, and 12 cm long. If the longest side of a similar triangle is 12 cm find the dimensions of the other two sides.

25. In a triangle ABC, angle A is a right angle and AD is drawn perpendicular to BC.
(a) What angle in the figure is equal to (i) angle DAC· (ii) angle DAB? Give reasons.
(b) If $AB = 30$ cm, $AC = 40$ cm and $DB = 18$ cm, calculate the length of AD.

26. A thin sheet of metal in the form of a triangle, Fig. 13.35, is used as a gauge to find the internal diameters of tubes. If in a particular case the gauge slots in the tube as far as the line marked DE, find the diameter of the tube.

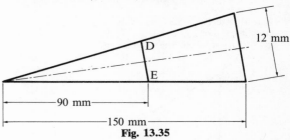

Fig. 13.35

27. In a triangle of forces experiment the diagrams obtained are shown in Fig. 13.36. If $AB = 30$ cm, $BC = 50$ cm and $CA = 40$ cm use the theory of similar triangles to obtain values for T_1 and T_2 the tensions in AB and AC.

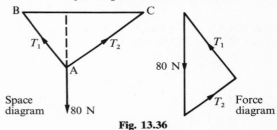

Fig. 13.36

28. In Fig. 13.37 prove that the triangles ABC and CDE are similar to each other. If $AB = 15$ cm, $BC = 10$ cm, and $CE = 6$ cm, find the length of DE.

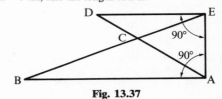

Fig. 13.37

29. In Fig. 13.38 ST is drawn so that the angle PTS is equal to the angle PQR.
Prove that PST and PQR are similar triangles.
Express the ratio $\dfrac{ST}{PT}$ in terms of the sides of triangle PQR.

(C.G.L.I.)

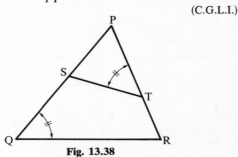

Fig. 13.38

30. The adjacent sides of a rectangle are 70 mm and 240 mm. Calculate the length of the diagonal of a similar rectangle whose longer side is 600 mm.

(N.C.T.E.C.)

31. Referring to Fig. 13.39, calculate:
(a) c if $a = 4$ m and $b = 6$ m
(b) b if $a = 11.6$ cm and $c = 14.3$ cm.

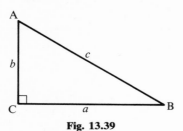

Fig. 13.39

32. Two forces act at right angles to each other as shown in Fig. 13.40. Calculate the magnitude of the resultant.

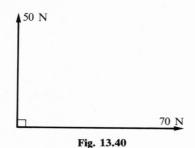

Fig. 13.40

33. A length of 40 mm diameter round steel bar has flats milled on it to form the largest possible square section. Find the length of the side of the square section.

34. Three North Sea oil rigs form an isosceles triangle ABC as in Fig. 13.41. If $AB = AC = 50$ km and $AD = 24$ km find the distance between the rigs at B and C.

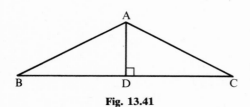

Fig. 13.41

35. A round bar 25 mm diameter is shown in Fig. 13.42. A flat surface 20 mm wide is machined on the bar. Calculate the dimension x.

(E.M.E.U.)

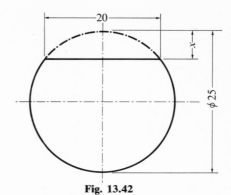

Fig. 13.42

ANSWERS TO EXERCISES 13

1. (a) 97° 2′ (b) 96° 34′ 2″ (c) 90° (d) 150° 41′ (e) 103° 3
2. (a) 14° (b) 29° (c) 43° 29′ (d) 5° 39′ 50″.
3. (a) 72° (b) 88° (c) 112° 24′ (d) 58° 29′ 20″.
4. (a) 240° (b) 180° (c) 270° (d) 135° (e) 180° (f) 60°.
5. (a) 30° 36′ 36″ (b) 71° 25′ 19″ (c) 23° 42′ 40″ (d) 84° 55′
6. 10°.
7. 80°, 59°, 80°, 40°.
8. 117°.
9. 130°, 130°, 50°.
10. *AB* parallel to *CD*.
11. 40°, 90°, 50°, 90°, 40°, 40°.
12. 70°, 80°.
13. 115°, 146°.
14. (a) 65° (b) 100° (c) 40°.
15. 16° 24′, 126° 24′.
16. $AC = BD$.
17. 115°.
18. 25, 75°, 85°, 20°.
19. 54°.
20. 255°.
21. 24.
22. 75°
23. 89°.
24. 9.33 cm, 8 cm.
25. (a) *ABD, ACD* (b) 12 cm.
26. 7.2 mm.
27. 48 N, 64 N.
28. 9 cm.
29. *QR/PQ*.
30. 625 mm.
31. (a) 7.2 m (b) 8.3 cm.
32. 8.6 N.
33. 28.29 mm.
34. 87.7 km.
35. 5 mm.

14 | The geometry of the circle

14.1. DEFINITIONS

A point which moves in a plane so that its distance from a fixed point in that plane is constant lies on the *circumference* of a circle.

The fixed point is called the *centre* of the circle.

The constant distance from the centre to any point on the circle is called the *radius*.

The *diameter* of a circle is twice the radius.

A *chord* is a straight line joining two points on the circumference of a circle.

Any chord divides a circle into two parts called *segments*. The part which includes the centre of the circle is termed the major segment, the other part is called the minor segment.

An *arc* of a circle is part of its circumference.

An area enclosed by an arc of a circle and two radii is called a *sector* of a circle.

Any straight line cutting a circle is called a *secant*.

A *tangent* is a line which meets a circle at a single point without intersecting it even if further extended.

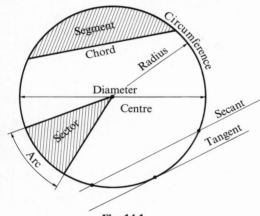

Fig. 14.1

14.2. ANGLE PROPERTIES OF A CIRCLE

(I) An angle at the centre of a circle is twice the angle at the circumference standing on the same arc.

In Fig. 14.2, if O is the centre of the circle then

$$\angle AOC = \text{twice } \angle ABC$$

Note. Both angles stand on the common arc AC.

EXAMPLE 14.1. A, B, C are points on the circumference of a circle of which O is the centre. If angle $OAB = 30°$, find the angle ACB.

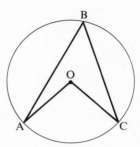

Fig. 14.2

SOLUTION

Referring to Fig. 14.3, in the triangle AOB,
$\angle OAB = \angle OBA$ (triangle AOB is isosceles since $AO = OB$; radii of circle).
$\therefore \angle OBA = 30°$.
Hence $\angle AOB = 180° - (30° + 30°)$ (angle sum of triangle equals $180°$)
$\therefore \angle AOB = 120°$.
But $\angle AOB = 2 \times \angle ACB$ (angle at centre equals twice angle at the circumference)
$\therefore \angle ACB = \dfrac{120°}{2} = 60°$
Angle $ACB = 60°$.

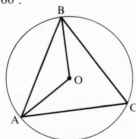

Fig. 14.3

(II) Angles in the same segment of a circle are equal.

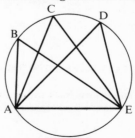

Fig. 14.4

Referring to Fig. 14.4 the angles *ABE*, *ACE*, and *ADE* all stand on the same chord *AE* and are in the same segment *ABCDE*, therefore

$$\angle ABE = \angle ACE = \angle ADE.$$

(III) The angle in a semicircle is a right angle.

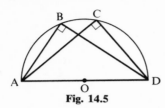

Fig. 14.5

In Fig. 14.5, *O* is the centre and *AD* the diameter of the semicircle.

Then $\angle ABD = \angle ACD = 90°.$

EXAMPLE 14.2. The three holes *X*, *Y*, and *Z* are to be marked off as shown in Fig. 14.6. Calculate the diameter of the pitch circle.

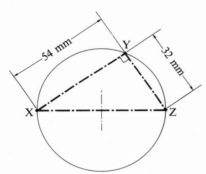

Fig. 14.6

SOLUTION

Since $\angle XYZ$ is a right angle (given) then the chord *XZ* on which it stands is a diameter of the circle. *XZ* is therefore the pitch circle diameter required.
Applying the theorem of Pythagoras to triangle *XYZ*,
$XZ^2 = 32^2 + 54^2$
$\therefore XZ^2 = 1024 + 2916 = 3940$
Hence $XZ = \sqrt{3940} = 62.76$ mm.
Pitch circle diameter $(XZ) = 62.76$ mm.

14.3. PROPERTIES OF CHORDS

(I) A straight line drawn from the centre of a circle to the mid-point of a chord is at right angles to the chord.

In Fig. 14.7 the line *OP* bisects the chord *AB* at *P*. Hence *OP* is at right angles to *AB*.

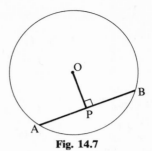

Fig. 14.7

(II) If two chords of a circle intersect either inside or outside the circle the product of the parts of one is equal to the product of the parts of the other.

(a) *Internal intersection.*
    Referring to Fig. 14.8 (a):

$$AO \times OB = CO \times OD.$$

(b) *External intersection.*
    Referring to Fig. 14.8 (b):

$$AO \times OB = CO \times OD.$$

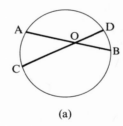
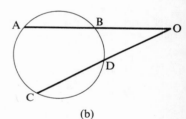

(a)   (b)

Note that if the corresponding letters are used in the two diagrams then one statement satisfies both cases, the letter 'O' being the point of intersection in each case.

EXAMPLE 14.3. *AB* and *CD* are two chords which intersect inside a circle at *O*. If $CO = 60$ mm, $AO = 90$ mm, and $DO = 120$ mm, calculate *OB*.

SOLUTION

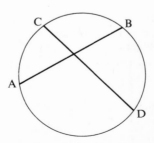

Fig. 14.9

Referring to Fig. 14.9 and applying the intersecting chord theorem,

$$AO \times OB = CO \times OD.$$

Substituting values for AO, CO, and OD the equation becomes

$$90 \times OB = 60 \times 120.$$

Hence $OB = \dfrac{60 \times 120}{90} = 80.$

∴ length of $OB = 80$ mm.

EXAMPLE 14.4. AB and CD are two chords which when produced meet outside the circle at O.
 If $AB = 7$ cm, $OB = 5$ cm, and $OD = 4$ cm, calculate CD.

SOLUTION

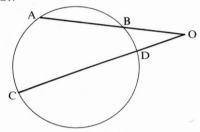

Fig. 14.10

Referring to Fig. 14.10 and applying the intersecting chord theorem,

$$AO \times OB = CO \times OD.$$

Now $\quad AO = AB + OB = 7 + 5 = 12.$

and $\quad\quad\quad\quad CO = CD + 4.$

Then $\quad AO \times OB = CO \times OD$ becomes

$$12 \times 5 = (CD + 4) \times 4.$$

Hence $\quad\quad\quad 60 = 4CD + 16$

or $\quad\quad\quad\quad 4CD = 60 - 16$

$$\therefore 4CD = 44$$

and $\quad\quad\quad CD = \dfrac{44}{4} = 11.$

∴ length of $CD = 11$ cm.

EXAMPLE 14.5. The arch of a bridge has the form of a minor segment of a circle, the maximum height of the segment being 9 m. Calculate the radius of the arch given that the bridge span is 30 m.

SOLUTION

Fig. 14.11 shows the circle of which the arch forms part. The bridge span is represented by the chord AB.

The geometry of the circle 101

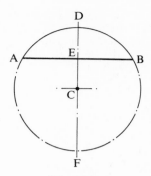

Fig. 14.11

The line drawn from the centre of the circle, C, through the mid-point of the chord AB to meet the circumference at D, is the radius of the arch. Applying the theorem of intersecting chords,

$$AE \times EB = DE \times EF.$$

On substitution, $15 \times 15 = 9 \times EF$ (E is mid-point of span AB)

$$\therefore 225 = 9\,EF$$

Hence $\quad\quad\quad EF = \dfrac{225}{9} = 25.$

∴ length of $EF = 25$ m.

Diameter of circle $= EF + DE = 25 + 9 = 34$ m.

$$\therefore \text{radius of arch} = \dfrac{34}{2} = 17 \text{ m}.$$

14.4. TANGENTS

A tangent may be defined as a line which meets a circle or curve at a single point without intersecting it even if further extended. The application of tangents to circles occurs frequently in engineering in the form of belt and chain drives, etc. A number of the more important relationships between tangents and chords are now given.

14.4.1. Properties of tangents to circles.

(I) **A tangent drawn to a circle is at right angles to a radius drawn to the point of contact: Fig. 14.12.**

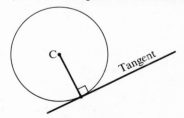

Fig. 14.12

(II) If from a point outside a circle two tangents are drawn to a circle, Fig. 14.13, then the two tangents are equal in length.

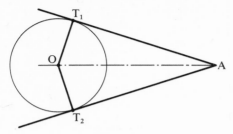

Fig. 14.13

Referring to Fig. 14.13:

$$\text{length of tangent } AT_1 = \text{length of tangent } AT_2.$$
$$\text{Also } \angle OAT_1 = \angle OAT_2.$$

(III) If two circles touch either internally or externally then the line through their centres also passes through the point of tangency: Fig. 14.14.

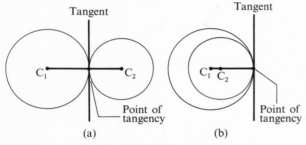

Fig. 14.14

(IV) If from a point outside a circle a tangent and a secant are drawn to the circle, then the square on the tangent is equal to the product of the whole secant and that part of it outside the circle.

In Fig. 14.15 $OT^2 = AO \times OB$.

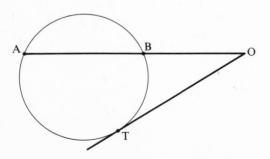

Fig. 14.15

14.4.2. Length of a direct common tangent. Fig. 14.16 shows two circles whose centres are A and B. AD and BC are the radii of the larger and smaller circles respectively.
A line from B drawn parallel to tangent DC meets AD at E.
Then length of tangent $DC = EB$.
Applying the theorem of Pythagoras to triangle EAB.

$$AB^2 - AE^2 = EB^2.$$
$$\text{But} \qquad EB = DC.$$
$$\therefore DC^2 = AB^2 - AE^2.$$
$$\text{Hence} \qquad DC = \sqrt{(AB^2 - AE^2)}.$$

Note. AB is the distance between the centres of the circles and AE is the difference in length of the radii of the two circles.

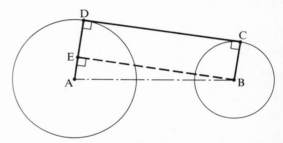

Fig. 14.16

14.4.3. Length of a transverse common tangent. Fig. 14.17 shows two circles with centres A and B having radii AD and BC respectively. DC is a transverse tangent to two circles.
The line BE is drawn parallel to DC to meet AD produced at E.
Then, length of tangent $DC = BE$.
Applying the theorem of Pythagoras to triangle AEB:

$$BE^2 = AB^2 - AE^2.$$
$$\text{But} \qquad BE = DC$$
$$\therefore DC^2 = AB^2 - AE^2.$$

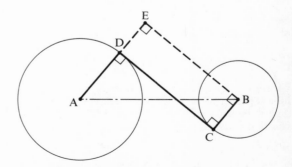

Fig. 14.17

Hence $$DC = \sqrt{(AB^2 - AE^2)}.$$

∴ length of transverse tangent $DC = \sqrt{(AB^2 - AE^2)}.$

Note. AB is the distance between the centres of the circles and AE the sum of the radii of the circles.

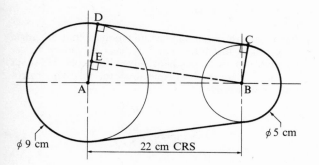

Fig. 14.18

EXAMPLE 14.6. Fig. 14.18 shows a belt passing over two pulleys. Find the length of a straight portion of the belt.

SOLUTION

Draw EB parallel to DC.
Then length of a straight portion of belt $DC = EB$.
Applying the theorem of Pythagoras to triangle EAB,

$$EB^2 = AB^2 - EA^2.$$

But $EB = DC$.

∴ $DC^2 = AB^2 - EA^2$

Now $EA = AD - BC$, i.e. the difference in the radii.

∴ $EA = \dfrac{9}{2} - \dfrac{5}{2} = 2$ cm (Diameters are 9 cm and 5 cm).

Substituting values for AB and EA in the equation

$$DC^2 = AB^2 - EA^2$$

$$DC^2 = 22^2 - 2^2$$

$$\therefore DC^2 = 480.$$

Hence $DC = \sqrt{480} = 21.9$ cm.

∴ length of one straight section of the belt equals 21.9 cm.

14.5. RADIAN MEASURE

Many problems in engineering are concerned with rotating masses, such as flywheels and pulleys. It is therefore necessary to be able to express angular motion in a convenient form. For this and other reasons use is made of a fundamental unit called the radian.

A radian is the angle subtended at the centre of a circle by an arc equal in length to the radius (see Fig. 14.19).

The relationship between arc length, radius, and angle in radians is illustrated in Fig. 14.20.

Let s = length of arc,

θ = angle in radians,

r = radius of the circle.

From the definition of a radian $\dfrac{s}{r} = \theta.$

$$\therefore s = r\theta,$$

i.e. length of an arc = radius $\times \theta$ (in radians).

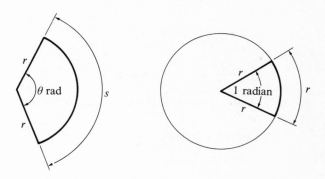

Fig. 14.19   **Fig. 14.20**

14.5.1. Relationship between radians and degrees. In the equation $s = r\theta$, if the length of the arc s is equal to the circumference,
then $2\pi r = r\theta$ (circumference of circle = $2\pi r$)
or, cancelling each side of the equation by r,

$$2\pi = \theta.$$

That is, 1 revolution = $360° = 2\pi$ radians.
Given that π is approximately equal to 3.142, then

$$2\pi \text{ radians} = 2 \times 3.142 = 6.284 \text{ radians}.$$

Hence 6.284 radians = 360°.

$$1 \text{ radian} = \frac{360°}{6.284} = 57.3° \text{ approximately},$$

or 1 radian = 57.3° = 57° 18'.

Most books of mathematical tables provide a table for conversion from degrees to radians and vice versa. However in practice an angle in radians is often left as a multiple or submultiple of π.

For example, since 2π radians $= 360°$ then,

$$\pi \text{ radians} = 180°$$
$$\pi/2 \text{ radians} = 90°$$
$$\pi/4 \text{ radians} = 45°$$
$$\pi/3 \text{ radians} = 60°$$
$$\pi/6 \text{ radians} = 30°, \text{ etc.}$$

EXAMPLE 14.7. Express the following angles in radians, giving the angles in terms of π: (a) 72°, (b) 220°.

SOLUTION

(a) Starting from the basic relationship:

$$360° = 2\pi \text{ radians}$$

then $$1° = \frac{2\pi}{360} \text{ radians}$$

and $$72° = \frac{2\pi}{360} \times 72 \text{ radians}$$

$$\therefore 72° = \frac{2\pi}{5} \text{ after cancellation.}$$

(b) In a similar manner 220° may be converted into radians:

$$360° = 2\pi \text{ radians}$$

$$1° = \frac{2\pi}{360} \text{ radians}$$

$$\therefore 220° = \frac{2\pi}{360} \times 220 \text{ radians,}$$

when $$220° = \frac{11\pi}{9} \text{ radians after cancellation.}$$

EXAMPLE 14.8. Express the following angles in degrees and minutes:

(i) $\frac{3\pi}{4}$ rad   (ii) $\frac{2\pi}{3}$ rad   (iii) 3 rad.

SOLUTION

(i) $$2\pi \text{ radians} = 360°$$

$$\therefore \pi \text{ radians} = \frac{360°}{2} = 180°.$$

Hence $$\frac{3\pi}{4} \text{ radians} = \frac{3}{4} \times 180° = 135°.$$

$$\therefore \frac{3\pi}{4} \text{ radians} = 135°.$$

(ii) $$2\pi \text{ radians} = 360°$$

$$\therefore \pi \text{ radians} = \frac{360°}{2} = 180°.$$

Hence $$\frac{2\pi}{3} \text{ radians} = \frac{2}{3} \times 180° = 120°.$$

$$\therefore \frac{2\pi}{3} \text{ radians} = 120°.$$

(iii) In general it should be understood that an angle given in this form, i.e. 3 radians, would be better obtained from a radian conversion table. However to illustrate the basic reasoning the following calculation is made.

$$2\pi \text{ radians} = 360°.$$

$$1 \text{ radian} = \frac{360°}{2\pi}.$$

$$\therefore 3 \text{ radians} = \frac{360°}{2\pi} \times 3.$$

If π is given the value 3.142 then:

$$3 \text{ radians} = \frac{360°}{6.284} \times 3 = \frac{1080°}{6.284}$$

or 3 radians $= 171.86°$ approx.

Converting 0.86° to minutes:

$$0.86° \times 60 = 52'.$$

$$\therefore 3 \text{ radians} = 171° 52'.$$

EXAMPLE 14.9. The braking surface of a brake lining is in the form of an arc of a circle of radius 12 cm and the angle subtended by the arc is 120°. Calculate the length of the braking surface, in centimetres, giving the answer correct to one place of decimals. (Take π as 3.142.)

(Y.H.C.F.E.)

SOLUTION

Referring to Fig. 14.21, the required length of arc l is given by the equation $l = r\theta$, where θ is the angle at the centre in radians. It is first of all necessary to convert 120° to radians.

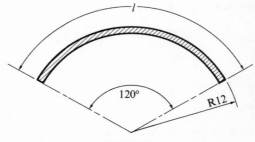

120°   R12

Fig. 14.21

Applying the relationship $360° = 2\pi$ radians,

$$120° = \frac{2\pi}{360} \times 120 \text{ radians.}$$

$$\therefore 120° = \frac{2\pi}{3} \text{ radians.}$$

Substituting in the expression $l = r\theta$,

$$l = 12 \times \frac{2\pi}{3}$$

$$\therefore l = \frac{24\pi}{3} = 8\pi.$$

However, since $\pi = 3.142$ (given)

$$l = 8 \times 3.142 = 25.1 \text{ cm.}$$

Length of braking surface $= 25.1$ cm.

EXAMPLE 14.10. Fig. 14.22 shows a direct belt drive system consisting of two pulleys. Calculate the total length of the belt assuming it to be perfectly taut. Take $\pi = 3.14$.

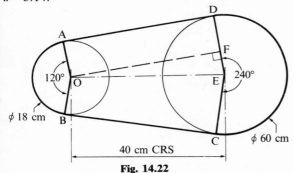

Fig. 14.22

SOLUTION

Referring to Fig. 14.22:

total length of belt
  = angle of lap of smaller pulley (arc AB)
  + angle of lap of larger pulley (arc DC)
  + length of two equal straight portions AD and BC.

Before the arc lengths AB and DC can be obtained the angles 120° and 240° must be expressed in radians.

Since $360° = 2\pi$ radians

$$120° = \frac{2\pi}{3} \text{ radians} \quad (120° = \tfrac{1}{3} \times 360°)$$

and $240° = \dfrac{4\pi}{3}$ radians.

Length of arc $AB = 9 \times \dfrac{2\pi}{3}$ (Using $l = r\theta$)

$$= 6\pi \text{ cm.}$$

Length of arc $DC = 30 \times \dfrac{4\pi}{3}$

$$= 40\pi \text{ cm.}$$

To calculate one straight length of the belt, lines OF and OE are introduced, where OF is parallel to AD. Applying the theorem of Pythagoras to triangle OFE:

$$OF^2 = OE^2 - EF^2,$$

but $\qquad OF = AD,$

$$\therefore AD^2 = OE^2 - EF^2.$$

Substituting values for OE and EF:

$$AD^2 = 40^2 - 21^2 \text{ (since } EF \text{ equals difference in radii).}$$

Hence $AD^2 = 1600 - 441 = 1159$
and $AD = \sqrt{1159} = 34$ cm approximately.
Hence total length of belt $= 6\pi$ cm $+ 40\pi$ cm $+ 2 \times 34$ cm.
Given $\pi = 3.14$,
$$6\pi + 40\pi + 2 \times 34 = 18.84 + 125.6 + 68$$
$$= 212.44 \text{ cm.}$$
Total belt length $= 212.44$ cm.

14.6. ANGULAR DISPLACEMENT

In linear motion the symbol s represents the distance travelled or linear displacement.

The Greek letter θ is the corresponding symbol for displacement in angular motion.

The displacement θ is measured in radians.

14.6.1. Angular velocity. Angular velocity may be defined as the rate of increase in the angle θ (in radians) with respect to time.

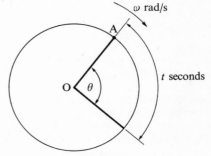

Fig. 14.23

In Fig. 14.23 the line OA is rotating about the point O and has moved through an angle θ radians in t seconds.

$$\text{Average angular velocity} = \frac{\text{angle moved through}}{\text{time taken}},$$

$$= \frac{\theta \text{ (rad)}}{t \text{ (s)}}$$

$$= \frac{\theta}{t} \text{ (rad/s).}$$

Angular velocity $\dfrac{\theta}{t}$ is given the symbol ω (ω—'omega' is a Greek letter), where ω is measured in rad/s.

14.6.2. Relationship between angular and linear velocity. Consider the point A on the outer rim of the flywheel in Fig. 14.24.

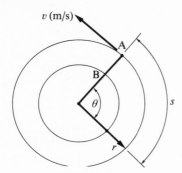

Fig. 14.24

Suppose the wheel rotates through θ (rad) in t (s). Using length of arc = radius × angle in radians,

$$s = r\theta.$$

To obtain the average velocity divide both sides of the equation by t, then

$$\frac{s}{t} = \frac{r\theta}{t}.$$

But $\dfrac{s}{t}$ = linear velocity v, and $\dfrac{\theta}{t} = \omega$.

$$\therefore v = r\omega$$

or linear velocity = angular velocity × radius.

Note. A point such as B on the inner rim of the flywheel has the same angular velocity as A but a smaller linear velocity.

If the radius r is in metres and the angular velocity ω in rad/s then the linear velocity v is expressed in m/s. In many problems the angular velocity is expressed in rev/min, and before substituting into the formula $v = r\omega$ the angular velocity must be converted to rad/min or rad/s.

Since 1 revolution = 2π radians,

$$N \text{ revolutions} = 2\pi N \text{ radians}.$$

Hence N rev/min = $2\pi N$ rad/min,

$$= \frac{2\pi N}{60} \text{ rad/s}.$$

EXAMPLE 14.11. Convert (a) 40 rev/min to rad/s, (b) 10 rad/s to rev/min.

SOLUTION

(a)   1 rev/min = 2π rad/min,

$$\therefore 40 \text{ rev/min} = 40 \times 2\pi \text{ rad/min},$$

$$= 80\pi \text{ rad/min},$$

$$= \frac{80\pi}{60} \text{ rad/s},$$

$$= \frac{4\pi}{3} \text{ rad/s}.$$

$$\therefore 40 \text{ rev/min} = \frac{4\pi}{3} \text{ rad/s} = 4.19 \text{ rad/s (taking}$$

$\pi = 3.142$).

(b) 2π rad/s = 1 rev/s.

$$\therefore 1 \text{ rad/s} = \frac{1}{2\pi} \text{ rev/s}.$$

$$10 \text{ rad/s} = \frac{10}{2\pi} \text{ rev/s}$$

$$= \frac{60 \times 10}{2\pi} \text{ rev/min}.$$

Taking $\pi = 3.142$,

$$\frac{60 \times 10}{2\pi} = \frac{600}{6.284} = 95.4 \text{ rev/min}.$$

$$\therefore 10 \text{ rad/s} = 95.4 \text{ rev/min}.$$

EXAMPLE 14.12. The wheels of a vehicle are 0.5 m diameter. What is the angular velocity of the wheels in radians per second when the vehicle travels at 48 km/h?
(C.G.L.I.)

SOLUTION

Using the formula $v = r\omega$,

i.e. linear velocity = radius of wheel × angular velocity.

Since the angular velocity is required in rad/s and the wheel diameter is given in metres, then 48 km/h must be expressed in metres per second.

Now $48 \text{ km/h} = \dfrac{48 \times 1000}{60 \times 60} \text{ m/s} = \dfrac{40}{3} \text{ m/s}.$

Substituting in $v = r\omega$, $v = \dfrac{40}{3}$ m/s, $r = \dfrac{0.5}{2}$ m, and ω is required.

$$\therefore \frac{40}{3} = \frac{0.5}{2} \times \omega$$

$$\text{and } \omega = \frac{40 \times 2}{3 \times 0.5} \text{ rad/s}$$

$$= 53\tfrac{1}{3} \text{ rad/s}.$$

Angular velocity of wheel = 53.3 rad/s.

EXERCISES 14

1. Find the angle subtended at the circumference of a circle by the side of a regular hexagon inscribed in the circle.

2. *ABC* is a triangle inscribed in a circle of centre *O*. If $\angle CBA = 58°$ and $\angle CAB = 41°$, find $\angle BCA$, $\angle AOB$, and $\angle OBA$.

3. *XYZ* is a triangle inscribed in a circle having centre *C*. If $\angle XCZ = 132°$ and $\angle YCZ = 118°$ calculate the internal angles of the triangle *XYZ*.

4. *ABC* is a triangle inscribed in a circle centre *O*. If $AB = AC$ and $\angle BOC = 84°$ find the angles *ABC*, *ACB*, *OBA*, and *OCA*.

5. *X* is a point on the circumference of a semicircle, *YZ* being the diameter. If $\angle XZY = 42°$ find the value of the $\angle XYZ$.

6. A circle has a diameter *AB*. If *P* is a point on the circumference of one semicircle and *Q* is a point on the circumference of the other semicircle show that $\angle PBA + \angle PQB = 90°$.

7. In Fig. 14.25, $AB = 3$ m, $BX = 5$ m, and $DX = 4$ m. Find the length *CD*.

(N.C.T.E.C.)

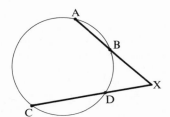

Fig. 14.25

8. *AB* and *CD* are two chords which meet outside the circle at *X*. If $AB = 7$ cm, $BX = 5$ cm, and $DX = 4$ cm, calculate *CD*.

(Y.H.C.F.E.)

9. A steel ball rests in a circular hole of diameter 50 mm in a horizontal plate with its lowest point 10 mm below the top surface of the plate. Calculate the diameter of the sphere.

(Y.H.C.F.E.)

10. A cylindrical bar is to have a flat surface machined on to it, such that the width *CD* across the flat is 8 cm and *AX* is 8 cm, as in Fig. 14.26. Find the diameter of the bar.

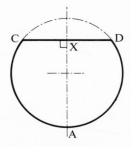

Fig. 14.26

11. A hole of 160 mm diameter is cut in a horizontal plate of negligible thickness. A sphere which has a diameter larger than that of the hole, is placed so that it rests in the hole. If the lowest point of the sphere is 40 mm below the level of the plate, calculate the radius of the sphere.

(E.M.E.U.)

12. The diameter *AB* of a circle cuts a chord *CD* at right angles at a point *X*. If $AX = 100$ mm and $XB = 50$ mm, calculate the radius of the circle and the length of *CX* correct to two significant figures.

(N.C.T.E.C.)

13. A motor pole-piece has a cross-sectional shape shown in Fig. 14.27. Find the radius of the circle of which the arc is part.

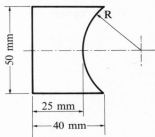

Fig. 14.27

14. Calculate the length of a tangent to a circle of diameter 160 mm from a point 170 mm from its centre.

15. *TX* and *TY* are tangents from *T* to a circle centre *O*. If the angle $TXY = 70°$, find the angle *XOY*.

16. Find the angle θ marked in Fig. 14.28, where *O* is the centre of the circle and *TA* and *TB* are tangents to the circle.

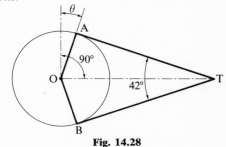

Fig. 14.28

17. Two plugs are placed in a surface table as shown in Fig. 14.29. Calculate the dimension '*a*'.

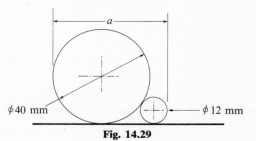

Fig. 14.29

18. Fig. 14.30 shows a belt passing over two pulleys. Calculate the length of a straight portion of the belt assumed to be taut.

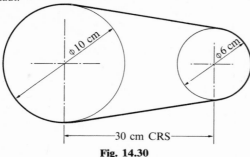

Fig. 14.30

19. Fig. 14.31 shows a crossed belt passing over two pulleys. Calculate the length of a straight portion of the belt assumed to be taut.

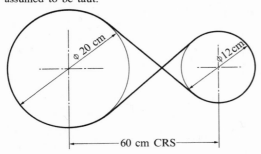

Fig. 14.31

20. Express the following angles in radians, giving the answer in terms of π: (i) 90°; (ii) 45°; (iii) 270°; (iv) 180°; (v) 30°; (vi) 300°; (vii) 60°; (viii) 210°; (ix) 330°; (x) 240°.

21. Express the following angles in degrees:

(i) π rad;   (ii) $\dfrac{\pi}{2}$ rad;   (iii) $\dfrac{\pi}{6}$ rad;   (iv) $\dfrac{2\pi}{3}$ rad;   (v) $\dfrac{3\pi}{2}$ rad;

(vi) $\dfrac{3\pi}{4}$ rad;   (vii) $\dfrac{\pi}{4}$ rad;   (viii) $\dfrac{3\pi}{16}$ rad;   (ix) $\dfrac{5\pi}{12}$ rad;

(x) $\dfrac{3\pi}{8}$ rad.

22. What angle is subtended at the centre of a circle, radius 70 mm, by an arc of length 200 mm? Give the answer in radians to four places of decimals.

(N.C.T.E.C.)

23. An arc AB of a circle centre O and radius 1.25 metres subtends an angle of 2.4 radians at the centre. Calculate the length of the arc AB.

24. An electric fan blade is formed from a sector of a circle of radius 250 mm. If the angle of the sector is 22°, calculate the perimeter of the blade.

25. A belt passes over a small pulley of radius 10 cm. If 20 cm of the belt is in contact with the pulley, calculate the angle at the centre of the pulley subtended by this portion of the belt in (a) radians, (b) degrees.

(U.E.I.)

26. The braking surface of a brake lining is in the form of an arc of a circle of radius 14 cm and the angle subtended by the arc is 120°. Calculate the length of this braking surface, giving the answer correct to one place of decimals.

(Y.H.C.F.E.)

27. In Fig. 14.32 TA is a tangent at A to the circle centre O, radius 10 cm, and angle TAD is 54°. State the value of angle TAO and angle DAB and calculate: (i) angle DAO, (ii) angle ADB, (iii) angle AOB, (iv) the length of the minor arc AD.

(N.C.T.E.C.)

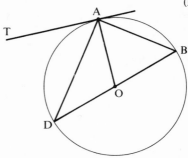

Fig. 14.32

28. An arc of length 3.6 cm subtends an angle of 0.9 radians at the centre of a circle. Calculate the radius of the circle.

29. Find the distance travelled by the point on a rim of a wheel of radius 25 cm if the wheel turns through 2.2 radians.

30. Two pulleys 0.3 m and 0.9 m diameter respectively are connected by an open belt. If the distance between the centres of the pulleys is 1.5 m, calculate the length of belting (Fig. 14.33).

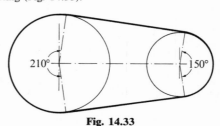

Fig. 14.33

31. Calculate the length of a driving chain which couples a wheel of 1.3 m effective diameter to a sprocket 0.26 m effective diameter, the distance between the centres of the wheels being 1 m (Fig. 14.34).

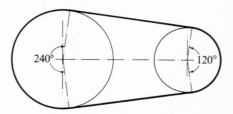

Fig. 14.34

32. Convert the following to rad/s:
(a) 50 rev/min,   (b) 20 rev/min,   (c) 191 rev/min,
(d) 160 rev/min.

33. A planer block revolves at 3500 rev/min. Find its angular velocity in rad/s.

34. A lathe spindle revolves at 300 rev/min. What is its angular velocity in rad/s?

35. A driving belt moving at 6 m/s is required to turn a pulley at 8 rev/s. What is the diameter of the pulley?

36. A car travels at 72 km/h. If the wheel diameter is 460 mm what is the angular velocity of the wheels in rev/s?

37. In a belt drive a 130 mm diameter pulley rotates at 8 rev/s and drives another pulley 300 mm diameter. Calculate (a) the belt speed in m/s, (b) the speed of the 300 mm diameter pulley.

38. The wheels of a vehicle are 0.5 m diameter. What is the angular velocity of the wheels in radians per second when the vehicle travels at 48 km/h?

39. A conveyor belt roller rotates with an angular velocity of 6 rad/s. Calculate the linear velocity of the belt (assuming no slipping between belt and roller) if the diameter of the roller is 25 cm.

40. A crankshaft rotates at 200 rev/min. Express this speed in rad/s.

ANSWERS TO EXERCISES 14

1. 30°.

2. 81°, 162°, 9°.

3. 66°, 59°, 55°.

4. 69°, 69°, 21°, 21°.

5. 48°.

6. Proof.

7. 6 metres.

8. 11 cm.

9. 72.5 mm.

10. 10 cm.

11. 100 mm.

12. 75 mm, 71 mm.

13. 28.3 mm.

14. 150 mm.

15. 140°.

16. 21°.

17. 47.9 mm.

18. 29.93 cm.

19. 57.9 cm.

20. (i) $\dfrac{\pi}{2}$,   (ii) $\dfrac{\pi}{4}$,   (iii) $\dfrac{3\pi}{4}$,   (iv) π,
(v) $\dfrac{\pi}{6}$,   (vi) $\dfrac{5\pi}{3}$,   (vii) $\dfrac{\pi}{3}$,   (viii) $\dfrac{7\pi}{6}$,
(ix) $\dfrac{11\pi}{6}$,   (x) $\dfrac{4\pi}{3}$.

21. (i) 180°,   (ii) 90°.   (iii) 30°,   (iv) 120°,
(v) 270°,   (vi) 135°,   (vii) 45°,   (viii) 33° 45′,
(ix) 75°,   (x) 67° 30′.

22. 2.8571 rad.

23. 3 metres.

24. 594.9 mm.

25. (a) 2 rad,   (b) 114.6°.

26. 29.3 cm.

27. 90°,   90°,   (i) 36°,   (ii) 36°,   (iii) 72°,   (iv) 6π cm.

28. 4 cm.

29. 55 cm.

30. 4.981 m.

31. 4.703 m.

32. (a) 5.23 rad/s,   (b) 2.09 rad/s,   (c) 20 rad/s,
(d) 16.75 rad/s.

33. 366.56 rad/s.

34. 31.42 rad/s.

35. 0.24 m.

36. 13.8 rev/s.

37. (a) 3.27 m/s,   (b) 3.5 rev/s.

38. 53.3 rad/s.

39. 75 cm/s.

40. 20.95 rad/s.

15 | Trigonometry

15.1. FUNDAMENTAL TRIGONOMETRICAL RATIOS

Trigonometry is the study of the relations between the sides and the angles of triangles. It has applications in many branches of mathematics and science.

Fig. 15.1 shows a line rotating from AB in an anti-clockwise direction about A. When the line reaches the position AB', the angle formed between AB and AB' is θ. Perpendicular lines erected from AB to meet AB' are seen to form right-angled triangles each of which possesses the angle θ. These triangles are all similar.

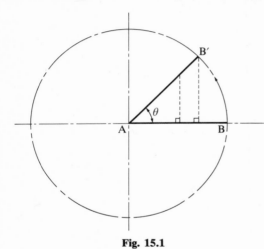

Fig. 15.1

15.1.1. The sine ratio.
Consider the series of right-angled triangles $AB'C'$, $AB''C''$, etc., shown in Fig. 15.2. For the angle A, if any side opposite the angle is divided by the hypotenuse of the respective triangle a ratio is obtained which will always be constant, because the triangles are similar.

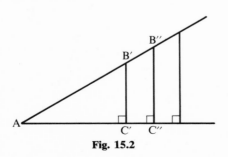

Fig. 15.2

It can be seen that

$$\frac{\text{the side opposite angle } A}{\text{hypotenuse of the appropriate right-angled triangle}} = \frac{B'C'}{AB'} = \frac{B''C''}{AB''}, \text{ etc.}$$

This constant ratio for the angle A is termed the **sine** of the angle, and is denoted by sin A.

For any angle θ, $\sin\theta = \dfrac{\text{opposite side}}{\text{hypotenuse}}$.

From a table of natural sines it is seen that $\sin 30° = 0.5000$. This means that in any right-angled triangle containing an angle of $30°$, the ratio of

$$\frac{\text{opposite side}}{\text{hypotenuse}} = 0.5000 = 1/2 \text{ or } 1:2.$$

Thus the length of the side opposite the angle of $30°$ is always one-half of the length of the hypotenuse of the triangle.

EXAMPLE 15.1. In a triangle ABC, the angle $A = 50° 32'$, angle $B = 90°$ and the side $a = 40$ mm. Calculate the length of the hypotenuse.

SOLUTION
The triangle is shown in Fig. 15.3.

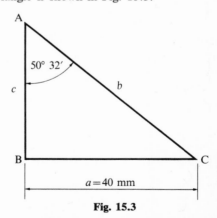

Fig. 15.3

The hypotenuse b and the known quantities angle A and side a are connected by the ratio,

$$\sin 50° 32' = 40/b$$
$$\therefore \ b \sin 50° 32' = 40$$

and
$$b = 40/\sin 50° 32'$$

The value of sin 50° 32′ is now obtained from sine tables, the appropriate extract being given below.

	Natural Sines										Mean Differences				
Degrees	0′	6′	12′	18′	24′	30′	36′	42′	48′	54′	1′	2′	3′	4′	5′
50						.7716								4	

Note. The '4' shown in the mean difference column represents 0.0004.

$$\sin 50° 32′ = \sin(50° 30′ + 2′)$$
$$\therefore \ \sin 50° 32′ = 0.7716 + 0.0004$$
$$= 0.7720$$

The hypotenuse, $b = 40/0.7720 = 5.181$ mm.

EXAMPLE 15.2. The jib of a crane is 8 m long and the tie rod, which is horizontal, is 5 m long. Calculate the angle which the jib makes with the vertical.

SOLUTION

Fig. 15.4 shows the arrangement of the crane.

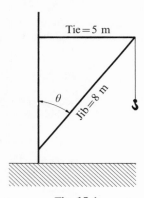

Tie = 5 m

θ

Jib = 8 m

Fig. 15.4

Let the jib make an angle θ with the vertical.
The ratio connecting the unknown angle θ and the two known sides is given by

$$\sin \theta = \text{opposite side/hypotenuse}$$
$$= 5/8$$
$$= 0.6250$$

Note. It is required to 'find the angle θ whose sine is 0.6250' which may be written as 'find arcsin 0.6250'.

An extract from the sine tables is given below.

	Natural Sines										Mean Differences				
Degrees	0′	6′	12′	18′	24′	30′	36′	42′	48′	54′	1′	2′	3′	4′	5′
38							.6239								11

The largest value less than 0.6250 in the tables is 0.6239, which thus requires an addition of 0.0011 from the mean difference column.

$$0.6250 = \sin 38° 36′ + 5′$$
$$= \sin 38° 41′$$
$$\therefore \ \theta = 38° 41′$$

15.1.2. The cosine ratio. Consider again the right-angled triangles shown in Fig. 15.2. When the length of the hypotenuse is divided into the appropriate side adjacent to the angle A a constant ratio is again the result. It will be seen that

$$\frac{\text{the side adjacent to angle } A}{\substack{\text{hypotenuse of the approp-}\\ \text{riate right-angled triangle}}} = \frac{AC'}{AB'} = \frac{AC''}{AB''}, \text{etc.}$$

This constant ratio for the angle A is known as the **cosine** of the angle, and is written cos A.
For any angle θ,

$$\cos \theta = \frac{\text{adjacent side}}{\text{hypotenuse}}.$$

EXAMPLE 15.3. In a right-angled triangle ABC, angle $A = 40° 38′$, angle $B = 90°$, and the side $c = 66$ mm. Calculate the length of the side b.

SOLUTION

The triangle is shown in Fig. 15.5.

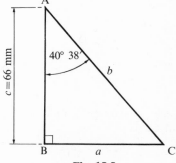

A

$c = 66$ mm

40° 38′

b

B a C

Fig. 15.5

The relationship between the angle A and the sides b and c is given by

$$c/b = \cos 40° 38'$$
$$\therefore c = b \cos 40° 38'$$

and
$$b = c/\cos 40° 38'$$

Substituting for c, $b = 66/\cos 40° 38'$.

The value of $\cos 40° 38'$ is now obtained from the cosine tables, the appropriate line of which is given below.

	Natural Cosines										Subtract Mean Differences				
Degrees	0′	6′	12′	18′	24′	30′	36′	42′	48′	54′	1′	2′	3′	4′	5′
40							.7593							4	

Note. Since the cosine of an angle decreases as the angle increases from 0° to 90° the mean difference column is subtracted,

i.e. $\cos 40° 38'$ is smaller than $\cos 40° 36'$

$$\cos 40° 38' = 0.7593 - 0.0004$$
$$= 0.7589$$
$$\therefore b = 66/0.7589 \text{ mm}$$

or
$$b = 86.9 \text{ mm}$$

EXAMPLE 15.4. In the mechanism shown in Fig. 15.6, calculate the value of the angle θ, given that $AB = 175$ mm, $BC = 375$ mm, and the crank AB is vertical.

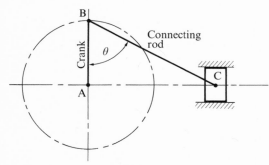

Fig. 15.6

SOLUTION

The relationship between the unknown angle θ and the sides AB and BC is given by,

$$\cos \theta = AB/BC$$
$$\therefore \cos \theta = 175/375 = 0.4667$$

Note. It is required to 'find the angle θ whose cosine is 0.4667' which may be written as 'find arccos 0.4667'.

From the cosine tables, the appropriate extract of which is given below, the nearest lower value to 0.4667 is 0.4664.

	Natural Cosines										Subtract Mean Differences				
Degrees	0′	6′	12′	18′	24′	30′	36′	42′	48′	54′	1′	2′	3′	4′	5′
62			.4664										3		

In the mean difference column 1′ is subtracted from the angle 62° 12′,

hence
$$\theta = 62° 12' - 1' = 62° 11'$$
$$\theta = 62° 11'.$$

15.1.3. The tangent ratio. Consider once more the right-angled triangles shown in Fig. 15.2. For the angle A, if any side opposite the angle is divided by the respective side adjacent to the angle another ratio is obtained which will always be constant. It can be seen that

$$\frac{\text{the side opposite angle } A}{\text{the side adjacent to angle } A} = \frac{B'C'}{AC'} = \frac{B''C''}{AC''}, \text{ etc.}$$

This constant ratio for the angle A is called the **tangent** of the angle and is denoted by $\tan A$.

For any angle θ, $\tan \theta = \dfrac{\text{opposite side}}{\text{adjacent side}}$.

EXAMPLE 15.5. In a right-angled triangle XYZ, $XY = 100$ mm, $YZ = 150$ mm, and the angle at $Y = 90°$. Calculate the value of the angle Z.

SOLUTION

The triangle is shown in Fig. 15.7.

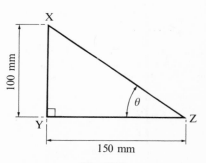

Fig. 15.7

Let the required angle be θ, then the ratio involving the angle θ and the known sides XY and YZ is

$$\tan \theta = XY/YZ = 100/150$$

$$\therefore \ \tan \theta = 0.6667$$

Note. It is required to 'find the angle θ whose tangent is 0.6667' which may be written as 'find arctan 0.6667'. An inspection of the complete table of natural tangents will show that the exact value of 0.6667 is not available. The nearest value (0.6665) is, therefore, taken.

The appropriate extract from the tangent tables is given below.

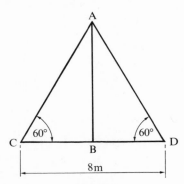

Note. Utmost care must be taken when reading the tangent tables to include any whole number appearing before the decimal, since the values of tangents of angles from 0° to 90° range from 0 to infinity.

$$\theta = 33° \ 36' + 5'$$

$$\therefore \ \theta = 33° \ 41'$$

EXAMPLE 15.6. A simple framework is shown in Fig. 15.8. Find the length of the member AB.

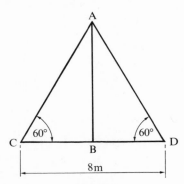

Fig. 15.8

SOLUTION

In this case the side AB is required and the known quantities are the angle C and the side CB.

The ratio connecting these quantities is

$$\tan 60° = AB/CB$$

or

$$\tan 60° = AB/4$$

$$\therefore \ AB = 4 \tan 60°.$$

The appropriate extract from the tangent tables is given below.

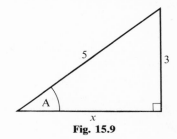

From the tables given, $\tan 60° = 1.7321$

$$\therefore \ AB = 4 \times 1.7321$$

$$AB = 6.9284 \text{ m}.$$

EXAMPLE 15.7. If $\sin A = 3/5$, find, without using tables, $\cos A$ and $\tan A$.

SOLUTION

The fact that $\sin A = 3/5$ may also be expressed as,

$$\frac{\text{the side opposite angle } A}{\text{hypotenuse}} = \frac{3}{5};$$

i.e. the sides are in the ratio of 3 to 5.

Therefore a right-angled triangle may be drawn having one side and the hypotenuse proportional to 3 units and 5 units respectively.

The third side, which is required, may be found by applying Pythagoras' theorem to the triangle.

Fig. 15.9

Using Pythagoras' theorem, $x^2 = 5^2 - 3^2$

$$x^2 = 25 - 9$$

$$x^2 = 16$$

$$\therefore \ x = 4$$

The third side is therefore proportional to 4.

Hence $\cos A = 4/5$

and $\tan A = 3/4$

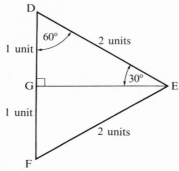

Fig. 15.10

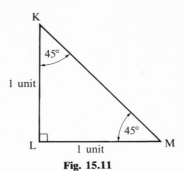

Fig. 15.11

15.2. RATIOS FOR ANGLES OF 30°, 60°, AND 45°.

The fundamental trigonometrical ratios for angles of 30°, 60°, and 45° can be found simply, and without the use of tables, by applying the theorem of Pythagoras to the right-angled triangles shown above.

In Fig. 15.10, *DEF* is an equilateral triangle and *GE* is at right-angles to *DF*. Let the length of each side of the triangle *DEF* be 2 units.
Then $DG = GF = 1$ unit. For the triangle *DEG*, length of side $EG = \sqrt{(2^2 - 1^2)} = \sqrt{3}$ units. Then,

$\sin 30° = DG/DE = 1/2$
  ($= 0.5000$ as given by a table of natural sines).
$\cos 30° = EG/DE = \sqrt{3}/2$
  ($= 0.8660$ as given by a table of natural cosines).
$\tan 30° = DG/EG = 1/\sqrt{3}$
  ($= 0.5774$ as given by a table of natural tangents).
$\sin 60° = EG/DE = \sqrt{3}/2$
  ($= 0.8660$ as given by a table of natural sines).
$\cos 60° = DG/DE = 1/2$
  ($= 0.5000$ as given by a table of natural cosines).
$\tan 60° = EG/DG = \sqrt{3}/1$
  ($= 1.7321$ as given by a table of natural tangents).

In Fig. 15.11, *KLM* is a triangle in which the angle $L = 90°$ and the sides *KL* and *LM* are each 1 unit long. Then, length of side $KM = \sqrt{(1^2 + 1^2)} = \sqrt{2}$ units. Hence,
$\sin 45° = KL/KM = 1/\sqrt{2}$
  ($= 0.7071$ as given by a table of natural sines).
$\cos 45° = LM/KM = 1/\sqrt{2}$
  ($= 0.7071$ as given by a table of natural cosines).
$\tan 45° = KL/LM = 1/1$
  ($= 1.0000$ as given by a table of natural tangents).

It will be seen from the foregoing that as the angle decreases, both the sine and tangent also decrease while the cosine increases.

When the angle becomes zero:
  $\sin 0° = 0$, $\cos 0° = 1$ and $\tan 0° = 0$.

As the angle increases the sine and tangent both increase but the cosine decreases.
When the angle becomes 90°:

$\sin 90° = 1$, $\cos 90° = 0$ and $\tan 90° = \infty$ (infinity)

The ratios of these several special angles are tabulated below and should be carefully noted.

θ	0°	30°	45°	60°	90°
$\sin \theta$	0	1/2	$1/\sqrt{2}$	$\sqrt{3}/2$	1
$\cos \theta$	1	$\sqrt{3}/2$	$1/\sqrt{2}$	1/2	0
$\tan \theta$	0	$1/\sqrt{3}$	1	$\sqrt{3}$	∞

15.3. COMPLEMENTARY ANGLES

Two angles are **complementary** when their sum is 90°. Thus θ and $(90° - \theta)$ are complementary, and each of the angles is said to be the complement of the other. It has been seen that
  $\sin 30° = \cos 60° = 0.5000$
and $\sin 60° = \cos 30° = 0.8660$.

The angles 30° and 60° are complementary because their sum is 90°. Then if θ is any acute angle,
  $\sin \theta = \cos(90° - \theta)$
and $\cos \theta = \sin(90° - \theta)$.

15.4. THE RECIPROCAL RATIOS

Fig. 15.12 shows a right-angled triangle *ABC*.

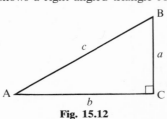

Fig. 15.12

It will be seen that

$$\sin A = \frac{a}{c}, \ \cos A = \frac{b}{c} \ \text{and} \ \tan A = \frac{a}{b}.$$

Thus $\quad \dfrac{1}{\sin A} = \dfrac{c}{a}, \quad \dfrac{1}{\cos A} = \dfrac{c}{b}, \ \text{and} \ \dfrac{1}{\tan A} = \dfrac{b}{a}.$

These reciprocal ratios are known as **cosecant, secant,** and **cotangent** respectively. For any angle θ,

$$\text{cosecant } \theta \ (\text{written cosec } \theta) = \frac{1}{\sin \theta}$$

$$= \frac{\text{hypotenuse}}{\text{opposite side}},$$

$$\text{secant } \theta \ (\text{written sec } \theta) = \frac{1}{\cos \theta}$$

$$= \frac{\text{hypotenuse}}{\text{adjacent side}},$$

$$\text{cotangent } \theta \ (\text{written cot } \theta) = \frac{1}{\tan \theta}$$

$$= \frac{\text{adjacent side}}{\text{opposite side}}.$$

15.5. RELATIONS BETWEEN THE RATIOS

From Fig. 15.13,

$$\sin \theta = \frac{a}{c}, \quad \cos \theta = \frac{b}{c}, \quad \text{and} \quad \tan \theta = \frac{a}{b}.$$

Then $\quad \dfrac{\sin \theta}{\cos \theta} = \dfrac{a/c}{b/c} = \dfrac{a}{b} = \tan \theta.$

The statement $\sin \theta / \cos \theta = \tan \theta$ is true for all values of θ and is therefore termed an **identity**.

$$\frac{\sin \theta}{\cos \theta} \equiv \tan \theta \tag{1}$$

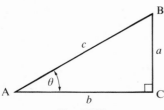

Fig. 15.13

Applying the theorem of Pythagoras to the triangle ABC in Fig. 15.13,

$$a^2 + b^2 = c^2.$$

Dividing through by a^2 gives

$$\frac{a^2}{a^2} + \frac{b^2}{a^2} = \frac{c^2}{a^2}.$$

But $b/a = 1/\tan \theta = \cot \theta$, so that $b^2/a^2 = \cot^2 \theta$, and $c/a = 1/\sin \theta = \text{cosec } \theta$, so that $c^2/a^2 = \text{cosec}^2 \theta$.

$$\therefore \ 1 + \cot^2 \theta \equiv \text{cosec}^2 \theta \tag{2}$$

Dividing $a^2 + b^2 = c^2$ throughout by b^2 gives

$$\frac{a^2}{b^2} + \frac{b^2}{b^2} = \frac{c^2}{b^2}.$$

But $a/b = \tan \theta$ so that $a^2/b^2 = \tan^2 \theta$ and $c/b = 1/\cos \theta = \sec \theta$ so that $c^2/b^2 = \sec^2 \theta$.

$$\therefore \ \tan^2 \theta + 1 \equiv \sec^2 \theta. \tag{3}$$

Dividing the equation $a^2 + b^2 = c^2$ by c^2 gives

$$\frac{a^2}{c^2} + \frac{b^2}{c^2} = \frac{c^2}{c^2}.$$

But $a/c = \sin \theta$ so that $a^2/c^2 = \sin^2 \theta$ and $b/c = \cos \theta$ so that $b^2/c^2 = \cos^2 \theta$.

$$\therefore \ \sin^2 \theta + \cos^2 \theta \equiv 1. \tag{4}$$

EXAMPLE 15.8. Referring to a right-angled triangle ABC, the angle B being the right angle, derive the relations between

(a) $\sin^2 A$ and $\cos^2 A$
(b) $\sin A, \cos A,$ and $\tan A$.

Using the relations obtained in parts (a) and (b), show that the expression

$$\frac{\cos A}{\tan A} \left(\frac{1 - \cos^2 A}{1 - \sin^2 A} \right) \text{ simplifies to } \sin A.$$

(C.G.L.I.)

SOLUTION

For the solutions to parts (a) and (b) refer to section 15.5.

To prove $\dfrac{\cos A}{\tan A} \left(\dfrac{1 - \cos^2 A}{1 - \sin^2 A} \right) = \sin A$

$$\frac{\cos A}{\tan A} \left(\frac{1 - \cos^2 A}{1 - \sin^2 A} \right) = \frac{\cos A}{\tan A} \left(\frac{\sin^2 A}{\cos^2 A} \right)$$

since $\sin^2 A + \cos^2 A = 1$, $1 - \cos^2 A = \sin^2 A$ and similarly $1 - \sin^2 A = \cos^2 A$.

Again $\dfrac{\cos A}{\tan A} \left(\dfrac{\sin^2 A}{\cos^2 A} \right) = \dfrac{\cos A}{\tan A} \cdot \tan^2 A,$

since $\dfrac{\sin A}{\cos A} = \tan A, \ \dfrac{\sin^2 A}{\cos^2 A}$

$$= \tan^2 A \cdot \frac{\cos A}{\tan A} \cdot \tan^2 A$$

$$= \cos A \cdot \tan A = \cos A \cdot \frac{\sin A}{\cos A}$$

which reduces to $\sin A$.

EXAMPLE 15.9. Prove that $\tan \theta = \dfrac{\sin \theta}{\sqrt{(1 - \sin^2 \theta)}}$

SOLUTION

$$\frac{\sin\theta}{\sqrt{(1-\sin^2\theta)}} = \frac{\sin\theta}{\sqrt{\cos^2\theta}} \text{ since } 1-\sin^2\theta = \cos^2\theta.$$

$$\therefore \frac{\sin\theta}{\sqrt{\cos^2\theta}} = \frac{\sin\theta}{\cos\theta} = \tan\theta.$$

15.6. ANGLES OF ELEVATION AND DEPRESSION

15.6.1. Elevation and depression. When an observer views an object which is placed above the level of his eye, then the line of sight is turned through an angle called the angle of elevation. Fig. 15.14 shows the angle of elevation which is measured from the horizontal. When the line of sight is depressed through an angle, the angle between the horizontal and the line of sight is termed the angle of depression, and is also shown in Fig. 15.14.

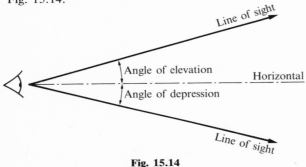

Fig. 15.14

15.6.2. Slope and gradient. Much confusion exists over the use of the terms 'slope' and 'gradient' in mathematics and allied subjects. For the purpose of uniformity in this book, the word slope will be employed when $\sin\theta$ is involved and the word gradient will be used when $\tan\theta$ is involved. Thus, a slope of 1 in 100 is represented by Fig. 15.15, since $\sin\theta = 1/100$. This shows that there is

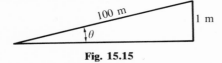

Fig. 15.15

a vertical rise of 1 m for each 100 m measured along the incline. A gradient of 1 in 100 is shown by Fig. 15.16 because $\tan\theta = 1/100$. In this case there is a vertical rise of 1 m for each 100 m measured horizontally. It is obvious that, for small angles, the difference is negligible.

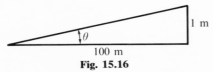

Fig. 15.16

15.7. SINE AND COSINE CURVES

In Fig. 15.17 a line AB, having unit length, is inclined at an angle θ to the horizontal. A projection on the horizontal plane (i.e. the plan) is represented by a line of length $\cos\theta$, while a projection on the vertical plane (i.e. the side view) is represented by a line of length $\sin\theta$.

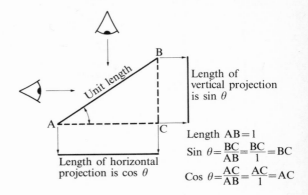

Fig. 15.17

Now if the line AB is rotated through 1 revolution (2π rad or 360°) about A, the locus of B is a circle as shown in Fig. 15.18. The projection of AB on the vertical plane is related to the angle turned through as shown by the curve $y = \sin\theta$. The relationship between the projection of AB on the horizontal plane and the angle turned through is shown by the curve $y = \cos\theta$. For the purpose of simplicity, construction lines are shown for some angles in the first quadrant only.

The sin and cosine curves are similar waves differing only in that they start at different places as shown in Fig. 15.19.

The curve of $y = \sin\theta$ lies between the values $+1$ and -1 of y and its value is zero at 0 rad, or 0°, and multiples of π rad, or 180°, (π rad, or 180°; 2π rad, or 360°; 3π rad, or 540°; etc.).

The curve of $y = \cos\theta$ also lies between the values $+1$ and -1 of y but leads the sine wave by $\pi/2$ rad, or 90°. Its value is zero at odd multiples of $\pi/2$ rad, or 90°, ($\pi/2$ rad, or 90°; $3\pi/2$ rad, or 270°; etc.).

15.8. TANGENT CURVE

The tangent curve, shown in Fig. 15.20, is very different from the sine and cosine curves. It consists of a number of parts having the same shape. Like the sine curve, the tangent is zero at 0 rad, or 0°, and multiples of π rad, or 180°. The curve approaches the lines passing through odd multiples of $\pi/2$ rad, or 90°, asymptotically. (An asymptote is a line which continually approaches a given curve, but does not meet it within a finite distance).

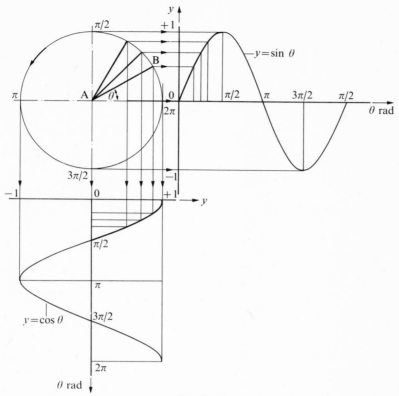

Fig. 15.18

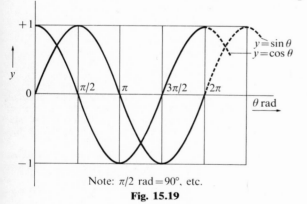

Note: $\pi/2$ rad$=90°$, etc.
Fig. 15.19

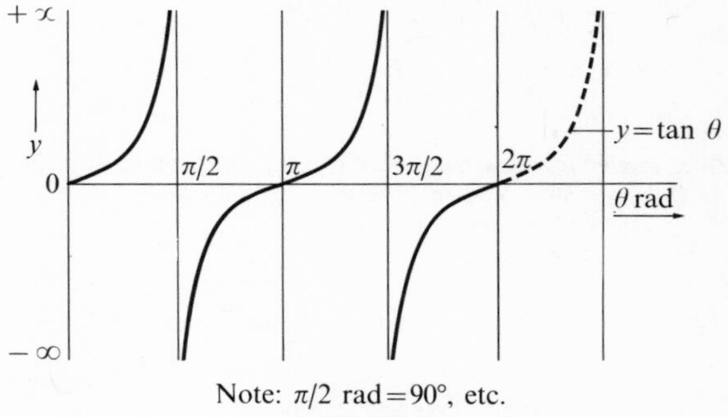

Note: $\pi/2$ rad$=90°$, etc.
Fig. 15.20

EXERCISES 15

1. Find the values of:
 (a) $\sin 18° 32'$ (b) $\sin 34° 19'$
 (c) $\sin 59.7°$ (d) $\sin 82.2°$

2. Find the values, where the angle is acute, of:
 (a) arcsin 0.3513   (b) arcsin 0.9071
 (c) arcsin 0.7581   (d) arcsin 0.2198

3. Find the values of:
 (a) $\cos 19° 45'$ (b) $\cos 40° 33'$
 (c) $\cos 57.6°$ (d) $\cos 72.4°$

4. Find the values, where the angle is acute, of:
 (a) arccos 0.3344   (b) arccos 0.9688
 (c) arccos 0.8406   (d) arccos 0.5534.

5. Find the values of:
(a) tan 34° 27'   (b) tan 54° 31'
(c) tan 80.7°   (d) tan 86.3°

6. Find the values, where the angle is acute, of:
(a) arctan 0.5221   (b) arctan 1.9008
(c) arctan 2.5517   (d) arctan 7.3962

7. Find the values of:
(a) cosec 10.9°   (b) cosec 72° 4'
(c) sec 34.4°   (d) sec 82° 14'
(e) cot 18° 10'   (f) cot 58.7°

8. Find the value of θ from each of the following equations:
(a) $\sin \theta = \cos 71°$
(b) $\cot \theta = 1/\tan 12°$
(c) $\operatorname{cosec} \theta = 1/\cos 14°$
(d) $\operatorname{cosec} \theta = \sec 27°$

9. Given that $\sin \theta = 12/13$ find, without using tables, the values of $\cos \theta$, $\tan \theta$, $\operatorname{cosec} \theta$, $\sec \theta$ and $\cot \theta$.

10. In a triangle ABC, the angle $B = 90°$, the angle $C = 67° 43'$ and the side $AB = 141$ mm. Calculate the angle A and the sides AC and BC.

11. Fig. 15.21 shows a quadrilateral in which $AB = 30$ mm, $AD = 100$ mm, $CD = 40$ mm, $A = 78°$ and $D = 65°$. Calculate the length of BC and the angles B and C.

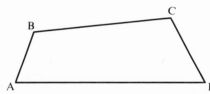

Fig. 15.21

12. Using any known trigonometrical identities, or with the aid of a right-angled triangle, show that:

$$\tan A + \frac{1}{\tan A} \equiv \frac{1}{\sin A \cos A}$$

(U.E.I.)

13. Using common axes, sketch in good proportion the curves of (i) $y = \sin x$ and (ii) $y = \cos x$ for values of x from zero to 2π radians. Mark on each curve the value of y when x is $3\pi/2$ radians.

(U.E.I.)

14. An arrangement for checking the dimensions of a dovetail slide is shown in the Fig. 15.22 below. Calculate the dimension x, to four significant figures, for the conditions shown. All dimensions are in millimetres.

(U.E.I.)

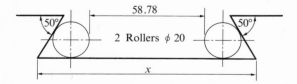

Fig. 15.22

15. Two holes are to be located as shown at A and B in Fig. 15.23. Calculate the dimensions x and y from the two datum faces. All dimensions are in millimetres.

(U.E.I.)

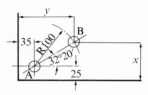

Fig. 15.23

16. Fig. 15.24 below shows a theoretical metric thread cut in a nut.
(a) The M5 metric thread has a major diameter of 5 mm and a pitch of 0.8 mm. Calculate the theoretical minor diameter.
(b) A useful way of selecting tapping drills for metric threads is to use a drill of diameter equal to the major diameter minus the pitch. If this method is used for the M5 thread calculate
  (i) the actual depth of thread in the nut
  (ii) the percentage ratio of the actual depth to the theoretical depth.

(C.G.L.I.)

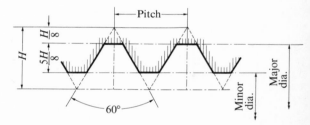

Fig. 15.24

17. Fig. 15.25 shows two pulleys A and B, of diameter 100 mm and 70 mm respectively, connected by an open belt. The centre distance between the pulleys is 140 mm.
(a) Calculate the length of the belt assuming that it does not sag.
(b) If pulley A rotates at 210 rev/min, find the rotational speed of pulley B assuming that no slip or creep occurs between the belt and the pulleys.

(U.E.I.)

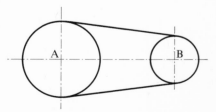

Fig. 15.25

18. In the diagram, Fig. 15.26 below, *AB* represents the path of articles on a conveyor belt. *OP* represents the maximum lift radius of the arm of a crane, pivoted at *O*, so that articles can be lifted from the conveyor belt between points P_1 and P_2. Articles move along the conveyor at a speed of 2 m/min.
Calculate
(a) the distance *AC*
(b) the distance *CO*
(c) the distance CP_1
(d) the time available during which articles can be lifted from the conveyor belt.

(C.G.L.I.)

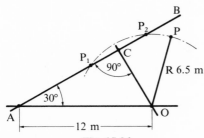

Fig. 15.26

19. Referring to the template shown in Fig. 15.27 below, *calculate*, giving your answers to the nearest millimetre
(a) the co-ordinates of point E (i.e. the distances indicated by *x* and *y*)
(b) the distance *CD*
(c) the distance *ED*.
All dimensions are in millimetres.

(C.G.L.I.)

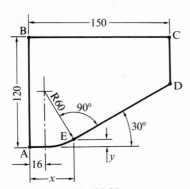

Fig. 15.27

20. Fig. 15.28 below shows a tight cable *AB*, running from the top of a building to ground level, and passing over a wall *D*. Sag in the cable can be neglected.
(a) Calculate
    (i) the length of the cable *AB*
    (ii) the angle of inclination θ.

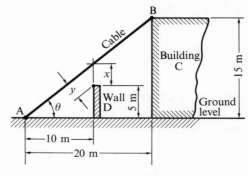

Fig. 15.28

(b) Using the properties of similar triangles, or otherwise, calculate
    (i) the vertical clearance *x*
    (ii) the minimum clearance *y*
    between the cable and the wall *D*.

(C.G.L.I.)

ANSWERS TO EXERCISES 15

1. (a) 0.3179 (b) 0.5637 (c) 0.8634 (d) 0.9907.
2. (a) 20° 34′ (b) 65° 7′ (c) 49.3° (49° 18′)
  (d) 12.7° (12° 42′).
3. (a) 0.9412 (b) 0.7598 (c) 0.5358 (d) 0.3024.
4. (a) 70° 28′ (b) 14° 21′ (c) 32.8° (32° 48′)
  (d) 56.4° (56° 24′).
5. (a) 0.6860 (b) 1.4028 (c) 6.1066 (d) 15.46.
6. (a) 27° 34′ (b) 62° 15′ (c) 68.6° (68° 36′)
  (d) 82.3° (82° 18′).
7. (a) 5.2883   (b) 1.0511   (c) 1.2120
  (d) 7.3680   (e) 3.0479   (f) 0.6080.
8. (a) 19° (b) 12° (c) 76° (d) 63°.
9. 5/13, 12/5, 13/12, 13/5, 5/12.
10. 22° 17′, 152.4 mm, 57.77 mm.
11. 77.17 mm, 107° 8′, 109° 52′.
13. (i) −1 (ii) 0.
14. 121.7 mm.
15. 78.49 mm,   119.5 mm.
16. (a) 4.128 mm   (bi) 0.4 mm   (bii) 91.5 %.
17. (a) 548.6 mm   (b) 300 rev/min.
18. (a) 10.392 m (b) 6 m (c) 2.5 m (d) 2.566 min.
19. (a) 46 mm, 8.04 mm   (b) 51.91 mm   (c) 120.1 mm.
20. (a)(i) 25 m (ii) 36.87° (b)(i) 2.5 m (ii) 2 m.

16 | Mensuration

16.1. MENSURATION

Mensuration is the branch of mathematics concerned with the measurement of lengths, areas, and volumes. For definitions of these quantities and an explanation of their units see section 1.2.

16.2. AREAS AND PERIMETERS OF PLANE FIGURES

A plane figure is a definite form constituted by a line or lines enclosing two-dimensional space. Thus the straight line joining any two points in the figure lies wholly in it. Circles and triangles are examples of plane figures.

It is often convenient to divide a given plane figure (e.g. a polygon) into two or more simpler shapes. It should then be remembered that all quadrilaterals (i.e. figures bounded by four straight lines) can be split into two triangles.

Formulae for calculating the areas and perimeters of various plane figures are given below. Some of these formulae will be readily understood by referring to the appropriate diagrams; others, however, cannot be proved within the scope of the present book.

16.2.1. Triangle. A triangle is a plane rectilinear figure with three angles and three sides. Fig. 16.1 shows a triangle having sides a, b, and c, and perpendicular height (i.e. altitude) h. The distance h is measured at right angles to the base.

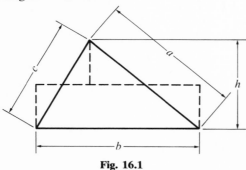

Fig. 16.1

$$\text{Area} = \frac{bh}{2}.$$

$$\text{Area} = \sqrt{[s(s-a)(s-b)(s-c)]},$$

$$\text{where } s = \frac{a+b+c}{2}.$$

$$\text{Perimeter} = a+b+c.$$

16.2.2. Rectangle. A plane rectilinear four-sided figure with four right angles, especially one with adjacent sides of unequal length, is known as a rectangle. A rectangle of length L and breadth B is shown in Fig. 16.2.

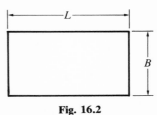

Fig. 16.2

$$\text{Area} = LB$$

$$\text{Perimeter} = 2L + 2B = 2(L+B).$$

16.2.3. Square. A square is a plane rectilinear rectangular figure with four equal sides. Fig. 16.3 shows a square having length of side L.

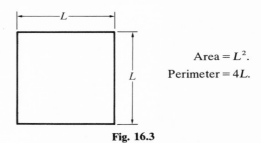

$$\text{Area} = L^2.$$

$$\text{Perimeter} = 4L.$$

Fig. 16.3

16.2.4. Parallelogram. A four-sided rectilinear figure whose opposite sides are parallel, as shown in Fig. 16.4, is known as a parallelogram. Opposite angles are equal, two being acute and two obtuse.

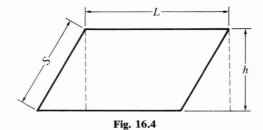

Fig. 16.4

$$\text{Area} = Lh$$

$$\text{Perimeter} = 2L + 2S = 2(L+S).$$

16.2.5. Rhombus. A rhombus is a plane equilateral figure with opposite angles equal, two being acute and two obtuse. Fig. 16.5 shows a rhombus having length of side L.

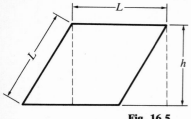

$$\text{Area} = Lh.$$
$$\text{Perimeter} = 4L.$$

Fig. 16.5

16.2.6. Trapezium. A quadrilateral with two of its sides, thought of as base and opposite side, parallel is called a trapezium. Fig. 16.6 shows a trapezium in which sides a and b are parallel, the perpendicular distance between them being h.

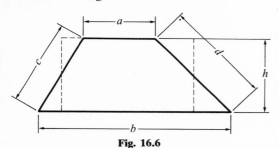

Fig. 16.6

$$\text{Area} = h\left(\frac{a+b}{2}\right).$$

$$\text{Perimeter} = a + b + c + d.$$

16.2.7. Regular polygon. A plane rectilinear figure with many (usually taken as being more than four) angles and sides is called a polygon. Any polygon having n sides can be divided into n triangles.

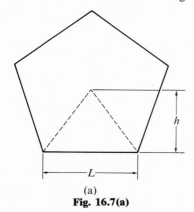

(a)
Fig. 16.7(a)

A regular polygon has all of its sides and all of its angles equal. Fig. 16.7(a) shows a regular pentagon (five-sided polygon) with length of side L. The perpendicular distance measured from any of the sides to the centre of the polygon is h.

For any regular polygon having n sides of length L:

$$\text{Area} = n\left(\frac{Lh}{2}\right).$$

$$\text{Perimeter} = nL.$$

The regular hexagon (six-sided polygon), shown in Fig. 16.7(b), is well known for its many uses in engineering. The distance F is generally called 'the distance across the flats'.

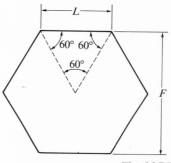

$$\text{Area} = 1.5LF.$$
$$\text{Area} = 0.866F^2.$$
$$\text{Area} = 2.598L^2.$$
$$\text{Perimeter} = 6L.$$

Fig. 16.7(b)

16.2.8. Circle. A circle is a plane figure with its circumference (perimeter) everywhere equidistant from its centre. A chord passing through the centre is known as the diameter of the circle. The ratio of the circumference of a circle to its diameter is a constant, represented by the Greek letter π (pi), its approximate value being 3.142 to three decimal places or 22/7 when expressed as an improper fraction. The value of π cannot be stated exactly either as a decimal or as a vulgar fraction. Fig. 16.8(a) shows a circle of diameter D and radius R.

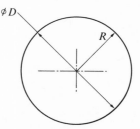

Fig. 16.8(a)

$$\text{Area} = \frac{\pi D^2}{4}.$$

$\text{Area} = \pi R^2$, where $R\left(=\frac{D}{2}\right)$ is the radius of the circle.

$\text{Circumference} = \pi D.$

$\text{Circumference} = 2\pi R.$

A semicircle is half of a circle, the dividing line being its diameter, as shown in Fig. 16.8(b).

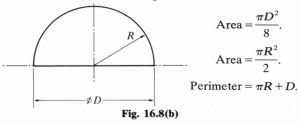

$$\text{Area} = \frac{\pi D^2}{8}.$$

$$\text{Area} = \frac{\pi R^2}{2}.$$

$$\text{Perimeter} = \pi R + D.$$

Fig. 16.8(b)

16.2.9. Sector of a circle. A plane figure contained by two radii and the arc of a circle is known as a sector of a circle. A sector, having length of arc L and radius R, is shown in Fig. 16.9.

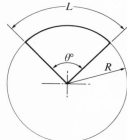

Fig. 16.9

$$\text{Area} = \frac{\pi R^2 \theta}{360}.$$

$$\text{Area} = \frac{RL}{2}.$$

$$\text{Perimeter} = L + 2R.$$

$$\text{Perimeter} = \frac{2\pi R\theta}{360} + 2R = 2R\left(\frac{\pi\theta}{360} + 1\right).$$

16.2.10. Segment of a circle. A plane figure contained by a chord and the arc of a circle is called a segment of a circle. Fig. 16.10 shows a segment having length of arc L and length of chord W.

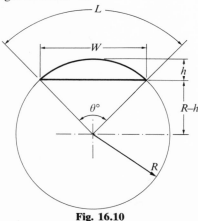

Fig. 16.10

$$\begin{matrix}\text{Area of} \\ \text{segment}\end{matrix} = \begin{matrix}\text{Area of} \\ \text{sector}\end{matrix} - \begin{matrix}\text{Area of} \\ \text{triangle}\end{matrix}.$$

$$\text{Area} = \frac{\pi R^2 \theta}{360} - \frac{W(R-h)}{2}.$$

$$\text{Area} = \frac{RL}{2} - \frac{W(R-h)}{2}.$$

$$\text{Perimeter} = L + W.$$

$$\text{Perimeter} = \frac{2\pi R\theta}{360} + W.$$

16.3. AREAS OF SIMILAR PLANE FIGURES

Figures are said to be similar when their corresponding sides are proportional and their corresponding angles are equal. Thus all squares must be similar and all circles similar.

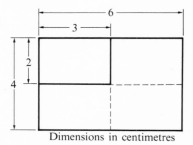

Dimensions in centimetres

Fig. 16.11

Now consider Fig. 16.11 which shows one rectangle, of length 3 cm and breadth 2 cm, in a corner of another rectangle, of length 6 cm and breadth 4 cm.

$$\frac{\text{Length of large rectangle}}{\text{Length of small rectangle}} = \frac{6 \text{ cm}}{3 \text{ cm}} = 2.$$

$$\frac{\text{Breadth of large rectangle}}{\text{Breadth of small rectangle}} = \frac{4 \text{ cm}}{2 \text{ cm}} = 2.$$

The length and breadth of the large rectangle are respectively twice the length and breadth of the small rectangle, and the rectangles are, therefore, similar. Area of large rectangle $= 6 \text{ cm} \times 4 \text{ cm} = 24 \text{ cm}^2$, and

Area of small rectangle $= 3 \text{ cm} \times 2 \text{ cm} = 6 \text{ cm}^2$.

$$\therefore \frac{\text{Area of large rectangle}}{\text{Area of small rectangle}} = \frac{24 \text{ cm}^2}{6 \text{ cm}^2} = 4,$$

which is 2^2.

Thus, the areas of the similar rectangles are in the ratio of the squares of their corresponding linear dimensions.

In the same way, for all plane figures, if a figure A has its linear dimensions n times the corresponding linear dimensions of another figure B, then:

$$\frac{\text{Area of figure } A}{\text{Area of figure } B} = n^2.$$

EXAMPLE 16.1. The washer in Fig. 16.12 has the dimensions given. Find the area of the surface shown.

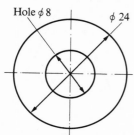

Dimensions in millimetres

Fig. 16.12

SOLUTION

Let $D = 24$ mm, and $A =$ corresponding area; $d = 8$ mm, and $a =$ corresponding area.

The problem will now be solved by two methods as follows.

Method (i)

Area of $\phi 8$ hole $= \dfrac{\pi d^2}{4}$,

$$= \frac{\pi \times 8^2}{4} = \frac{64\pi}{4} = 16\pi \text{ mm}^2.$$

Now, $\dfrac{D}{d} = \dfrac{24 \text{ mm}}{8 \text{ mm}} = 3,$

and all circles are similar, so that

$$\frac{A}{a} = 3^2 = 9.$$

The area of a $\phi 24$ circle is nine times the area of a $\phi 8$ circle.

$\therefore$ area of $\phi 24$ disc $= 9 \times 16\pi = 144\pi$ mm^2.
Area of washer $= 144\pi - 16\pi$,
$\qquad = 128\pi,$
$\qquad = 402.1$ mm^2.

Method (ii)

Area of $\phi 8$ hole $= \dfrac{\pi d^2}{4}$,

$$= \frac{\pi \times 8^2}{4} = \frac{64\pi}{4} = 16\pi \text{ mm}^2.$$

Area of $\phi 24$ disc $= \dfrac{\pi D^2}{4}$,

$$= \frac{\pi \times 24^2}{4} = \frac{576\pi}{4} = 144\pi \text{ mm}^2.$$

Area of washer $= 144\pi - 16\pi$,
$\qquad = 128\pi,$
$\qquad = 402.1$ mm^2.

The relative merits of the methods used are left for the readers to judge.

A further method is as indicated below:

$$A - a = \frac{\pi D^2}{4} - \frac{\pi d^2}{4},$$

$$= \frac{\pi}{4}(D^2 - d^2),$$

$$= \frac{\pi}{4}(D + d)(D - d).$$

16.4. VOLUMES AND SURFACE AREAS OF SOLID FIGURES

A solid figure is a definite form constituted by a surface or surfaces enclosing three-dimensional space. The word 'solid' refers to the three-dimensional shape of the figure, and not necessarily to the state of the substance of which it is composed. Spheres, prisms, and cylinders are examples of solid figures.

In addition to possessing volume and surface area, a solid figure of any matter also has mass (see section 1.2).

Formulae for determining the volumes and surface areas of several solid figures are given below. Some of the formulae will be easily understood by referring to the relevant diagrams; others cannot be proved within the scope of this book.

16.4.1. Right prism. A right prism is a solid figure whose two ends are similar, equal, and parallel rectilinear figures and whose sides are rectangles. Examples of some prisms are shown in Fig. 16.13.

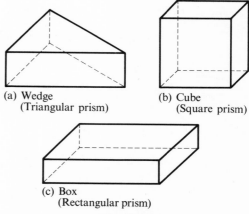

(a) Wedge
(Triangular prism)

(b) Cube
(Square prism)

(c) Box
(Rectangular prism)

Fig. 16.13

For any right prism:
Volume $=$ cross-sectional area $\times$ length.
Lateral surface area $=$ perimeter of cross-section $\times$ length.
Total surface area $=$ lateral surface area $+$ area of ends.

16.4.2. Right cylinder. A right cylinder is a solid figure whose two ends are circular, equal, and parallel. Its lateral surface, of length L, is curved as shown in Fig. 16.14.

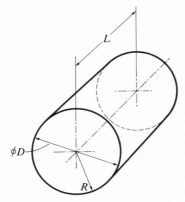

Fig. 16.14

$$\text{Volume} = \frac{\pi D^2 L}{4}.$$

$$\text{Volume} = \pi R^2 L.$$

Lateral surface area $= \pi DL$.

Lateral surface area $= 2\pi RL$.

$$\text{Total surface area} = \pi DL + \frac{\pi D^2}{2} = \pi D\left(L + \frac{D}{2}\right).$$

$$\text{Total surface area} = 2\pi RL + 2\pi R^2 = 2\pi R(L + R).$$

16.4.3. Sphere. A sphere is a body bounded by surface every point of which is equidistant from a point within called the centre. A sphere, of radius R, is shown in Fig. 16.15.

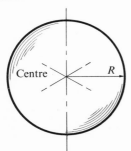

$$\text{Volume} = \frac{4\pi R^3}{3}.$$

$$\text{Surface area} = 4\pi R^2.$$

Fig. 16.15

16.4.4. Right circular cone. A circular cone is a body of which the base is a circle and the summit a point, and every point in the intervening surface is in a straight line between the vertex and the circumference of the base.

A right circular cone is one in which the base lies at right-angles to the axis joining the vertex and the centre of the base. Fig. 16.16 shows a right circular cone having perpendicular height H, and slant height S.

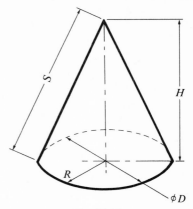

Fig. 16.16

$$\text{Volume} = \frac{\pi D^2 H}{12}.$$

$$\text{Volume} = \frac{\pi R^2 H}{3}.$$

Total surface area $= \pi R^2 + \pi RS = \pi R(R + S)$.

16.4.5. Right pyramid. A pyramid is a solid body with a polygonal base and sloping sides meeting at its apex.

When the base lies at right-angles to the axis joining the apex and the centre of the base, the figure is known as a right pyramid. Fig. 16.17 shows a right pyramid having perpendicular height H and base area A.

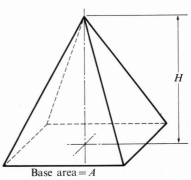

Base area $= A$

Fig. 16.17

$$\text{Volume} = \frac{AH}{3}.$$

$$\frac{\text{Surface}}{\text{area}} = \frac{\text{area of}}{\text{base}} + \frac{\text{sum of areas of}}{\text{sloping sides}}.$$

16.5. VOLUME, DENSITY AND MASS

The density of a body is defined as the mass per unit volume, for example, the number of kilograms per cubic metre (kg/m^3) or grams per cubic centimetre (g/cm^3).

$$\text{Density } (\rho) = \frac{\text{mass } (m)}{\text{volume } (V)}.$$

Thus, mass = volume × density,
or, in symbols, $m = V\rho$.

The relative density of a substance may be defined as the ratio:

$$\frac{\text{density of the substance}}{\text{density of pure water at } 4\,°\text{C}}$$

or

$$\frac{\text{mass of the substance}}{\text{mass of an equal volume of water}}.$$

TABLE 16.1: The following table shows typical values for the densities and relative densities of some common substances. These values may be affected by factors such as purity, temperature change, etc.

Note that the relative density is numerically equal to the density in grams per cubic centimetre.

The figures for the gases are at standard temperature and pressure (i.e. 0 °C, 101 325 Pa).

Substance	Density, ρ		Relative density, d
	kg/m³	g/cm³	
Aluminium	2720	2.72	2.72
Acetylene	1.17	0.001 17	0.001 17
Copper	8790	8.79	8.79
Iron (cast)	7200	7.2	7.2
Oxygen	1.43	0.001 43	0.001 43
Petrol	720	0.72	0.72
Water (pure)	1000	1.00	1.00
Zinc	7120	7.12	7.12

EXAMPLE 16.2. A bar of brass is 304 mm long and has a section of 25 mm × 6 mm. Calculate the mass of the bar given that the density of the brass is 8480 kg/m³.

SOLUTION
Volume of bar = length × sectional area,

$$= 304 \text{ mm} \times 25 \text{ mm} \times 6 \text{ mm},$$
$$= 45\,600 \text{ mm}^3.$$

But $1.0 \times 10^9 \text{ mm}^3 = 1.0 \text{ m}^3$.

$$\therefore \text{ volume of bar} = \frac{45\,600}{10^9} \text{ m}^3.$$

Mass of bar = volume × density,

$$= \frac{45\,600}{10^9} \text{ m}^3 \times 8480 \, \frac{\text{kg}}{\text{m}^3},$$
$$= 0.3867 \text{ kg}.$$

16.6. VOLUMES, MASSES, AND SURFACE AREAS OF SIMILAR SOLID FIGURES

If the linear dimensions of one solid figure are n times the corresponding linear dimensions of another solid figure, the figures are said to be similar.

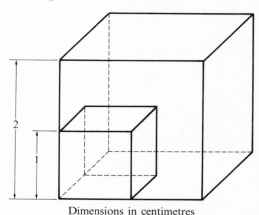

Dimensions in centimetres

Fig. 16.18

Consider Fig. 16.18 which shows one square prism, having 1 cm sides, in a corner of a second square prism, having 2 cm sides.

$$\frac{\text{Length of side of large prism}}{\text{Length of side of small prism}} = \frac{2 \text{ cm}}{1 \text{ cm}} = 2.$$

The length, breadth, and depth of the large prism are respectively twice the length, breadth, and depth of the small prism. The prisms are, therefore, similar.

$$\text{Volume of large prism} = 2 \text{ cm} \times 2 \text{ cm} \times 2 \text{ cm}$$
$$= 8 \text{ cm}^3,$$

and

$$\text{Volume of small prism} = 1 \text{ cm} \times 1 \text{ cm} \times 1 \text{ cm}$$
$$= 1 \text{ cm}^3.$$

$$\therefore \frac{\text{Volume of large prism}}{\text{Volume of small prism}} = \frac{8 \text{ cm}^3}{1 \text{ cm}^3}$$
$$= 8, \text{ which is } 2^3.$$

Thus, the volumes of the similar solid prisms are in the ratio of the cubes (i.e. third powers) of their corresponding linear dimensions.

In the same way, for all solid figures, if a solid A has its linear dimensions n times the corresponding linear dimensions of another solid B, then:

$$\frac{\text{Volume of solid } A}{\text{Volume of solid } B} = n^3.$$

It has been seen (section 16.5) that:

$$\text{mass} = \text{volume} \times \text{density}.$$

Therefore, for a given material, mass is proportional to volume.

In symbols, $m \propto V$.

Thus, for similar solids of the same material,

$$\frac{m_1}{m_2} = \frac{V_1}{V_2}.$$

In words, the ratio of the masses is equal to the ratio of the volumes for similar solids made of the same material.

The surface areas of similar solids are proportional to the squares of their linear dimensions. This is readily understood after a careful study of Fig. 16.18.

$$\frac{\text{Surface area } A_2}{\text{Surface area } A_1} = \left(\frac{\text{Length } L_2}{\text{Length } L_1}\right)^2.$$

EXAMPLE 16.3. A spherical steel ball has a diameter of 24 mm, the density of the steel being 7.82 g/cm³.
(a) Calculate:
   (i) the surface area of the ball,
   (ii) the volume of the ball,
   (iii) the mass of the ball.
(b) Find the corresponding quantities for a spherical steel ball of diameter 6 mm.

SOLUTION
(a) For the 24 mm diameter ball:
   (i) the surface area $= 4\pi R^2$,
$$= 4\pi \times 12^2,$$
$$= 1810 \text{ mm}^2.$$

   (ii) the volume $= \dfrac{4\pi R^3}{3}$,
$$= \frac{4\pi \times 12^3}{3},$$
$$= 7238 \text{ mm}^3.$$

   (iii) the mass $= V\rho$

where
$$V = 7238 \text{ mm}^3$$
$$\rho = 7.82 \text{ g/cm}^3$$
But
$$1.0 \text{ cm}^3 = 1.0 \times 10^3 \text{ mm}^3,$$
so that
$$V = \frac{7238}{1000} = 7.238 \text{ cm}^3.$$
$\therefore$ mass $= 7.238 \text{ cm}^3 \times 7.82 \text{ g/cm}^3$,
$$= 56.6 \text{ g}.$$

(b) For the 6 mm diameter ball:
the ratio of the diameters of the balls is $\frac{6}{24} = \frac{1}{4}$.
For the similar solid figures—
   (i) the surface area $= A_1 \cdot n^2$,
$$= 1810 \times (\tfrac{1}{4})^2,$$
$$= 113.1 \text{ mm}^2.$$

   (ii) the volume $= V_1 \cdot n^3$,
$$= 7238 \times (\tfrac{1}{4})^3,$$
$$= 113.1 \text{ mm}^3.$$

   (iii) the mass $= m_1 \cdot n^3$
$$= 56.6 \times (\tfrac{1}{4})^3,$$
$$= 0.884 \text{ g}.$$

EXERCISES 16

1. A triangular metal plate has edges measuring 30 mm, 40 mm, and 50 mm. What is its perimeter? Calculate the area of one side of the plate.

2. Calculate the area of an equilateral triangle of side 24 mm. Deduce the area of a similar triangle of side 36 mm.

3. Find the cross-sectional area of the beam section shown in Fig. 16.19.

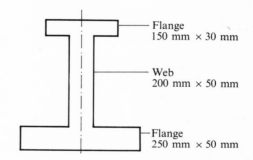

Fig. 16.19

4. A triangular hole is cut in a rectangular plate as shown in Fig. 16.20. For one side of the plate, calculate the area of material remaining.

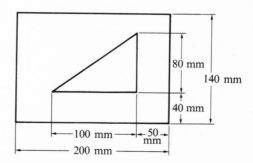

Fig. 16.20

5. A rhombus has sides of length 100 mm, the acute angles of the rhombus each being 30°. Calculate the area of the rhombus.

6. Calculate the angle θ for the template shown in Fig. 16.21. Determine the perimeter of the template, and the area of the surface shown.

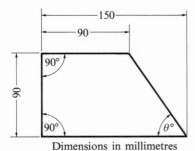

Dimensions in millimetres

Fig. 16.21

7. A steel disc of diameter 140 mm has a hole of diameter 40 mm punched in it as shown in Fig. 16.22. Calculate the circumference of the disc, and the area of one of its sides.

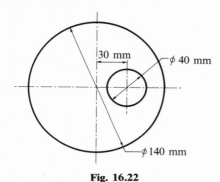

Fig. 16.22

8. Calculate the area of one side of the plate shown in Fig. 16.23.

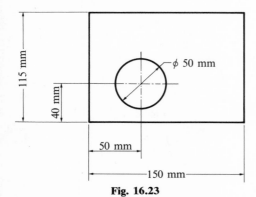

Fig. 16.23

9. For the template shown in Fig. 16.24, calculate:
(a) the radius R,
(b) the perimeter,
(c) the area of one face.

10. PQ is a chord of length 60 mm in a circle of diameter 80 mm. Calculate the area of the minor segment thus formed.

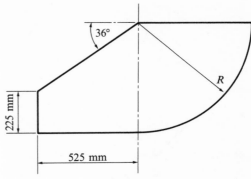

Fig. 16.24

11. Two tangents from a point P meet a circle, centre O, at the points Q and R as shown in Fig. 16.25. If the angle QPR between the tangents is 70°, and QR is 24 mm, calculate:
(a) the radius of the circle,
(b) the length of the minor arc QR,
(c) the area of the minor sector QOR.

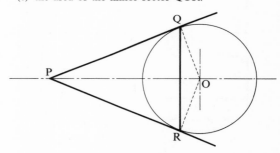

Fig. 16.25

12. A chord 8 cm long subtends an angle of 60° at the centre of a circle. Calculate:
(a) the radius of the circle,
(b) the length of the minor arc,
(c) the area of the minor sector,
(d) the area of the minor segment.

13. The distance across the flats of a regular hexagon is 5.0 mm. Calculate the area of the hexagon, and its length of side. What is the area of a regular hexagon 50 mm across its flats?

14. Find the volume of the right prism shown in Fig. 16.26.

15. A cylindrical oil drum is to have a length of 1.0 metre and a volume of 0.25 m³. Calculate the required diameter, giving the answer in whole millimetres.
  What is the total surface area of the drum? Neglect the thickness of the drum material.

16. A steel roller is shown in Fig. 16.27. Calculate the volume of metal in the roller. What percentage of the original cylinder was removed when the blind hole was bored as shown?

17. A flat 65 mm wide has to be milled along the length of a steel shaft of 100 mm diameter. Calculate the depth of cut.

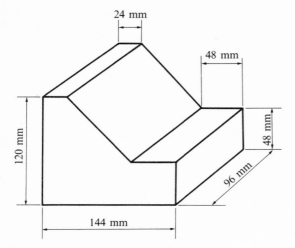

Fig. 16.26

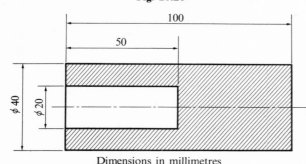

Dimensions in millimetres

Fig. 16.27

If the length of the shaft is 250 mm, and steel has a density of 7800 kg/m³, calculate the cross-sectional area and the mass of the finished shaft.

18. A boiler is to be made in the form of a cylinder with hemispherical ends. Calculate the length of the cylindrical part if its diameter is 3.0 m and the total volume is to be 50 m³.

19. A closed cylindrical fuel oil tank, with plane ends, has a diameter of 12.75 m and a length of 25 m. Calculate its volume, and its external surface area.

20. A right cone has a diameter of base 14 cm and perpendicular height 24 cm. Determine:
(a) its volume,
(b) its curved surface area.

21. A right square pyramid has a base whose edges each measure 20 cm and whose perpendicular height is 30 cm. Calculate the volume and the total surface area of the pyramid.

22. A concrete pyramid has a rectangular base of sides 6.0 m and 4.0 m. Each slant edge is 8.0 m long. Calculate the perpendicular height and volume of the pyramid.

23. (a) The length of a cylindrical storage tank is 1.4 times its

diameter. Construct a formula for the volume V in terms of the diameter d.
(b) Transpose the formula obtained in part (a) to give a formula for d in terms of V.
(c) The tank has a volume of one million litres, where 1000 litres = 1 m³. Calculate, giving the answers in metres to three significant figures,
(i) the diameter, and
(ii) the length.
(U.E.I.)

24. (a) A regular hexagon has a width across flats of W millimetres. With the aid of a labelled diagram, prove that the area A of the hexagon is given by the formula:
$$A = 0.866 \, W^2 \text{ square millimetres.}$$
(b) Brass billets, of diameter 56 mm and length 160 mm, are extruded into hexagonal rods 20 mm across flats. Assuming no reduction in volume in the process, calculate the length of rod obtained when a billet is completely extruded.
(U.E.I.)

25. A storage tank is in the form of a sphere having an inside diameter of 3 metres. Calculate
(a) the volume of the tank, and
(b) the time taken to fill the tank, from empty, if the bore of the supply pipe is 100 mm diameter and liquid is pumped through the pipe at a speed of 1.4 m/s.
(U.E.I.)

26. The dimensions of a certain rivet are shown in Fig. 16.28, all dimensions being in millimetres. Calculate the mass of 1000 similar rivets given that the density of the rivet material is 7800 kg/m³.
(U.E.I.)

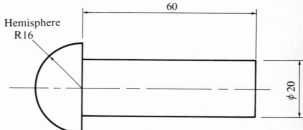

Fig. 16.28

27. A storage tank is made in the form of a cylinder with a hemispherical top, as shown in Fig. 16.29. Neglecting the thickness of the plates, and assuming butt joints, calculate:
(a) the total capacity of the tank, and
(b) its internal surface area.
(U.E.I.)

28. A cylindrical steel pipe, open at both ends, has a length L, an external radius R and uniform wall thickness t, all dimensions being in millimetres. Show that the volume of metal in the pipe is given by the formula
$$V = \pi t L (2R - t) \text{ cubic millimetres.}$$
If a 1 metre length of the pipe has a mass of 7.8 kg and a wall thickness of 7 mm, calculate the external radius given that the density of the steel is 7800 kg/m³.
(U.E.I.)

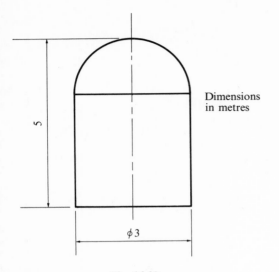

Dimensions
in metres

5

$\phi\,3$

Fig. 16.29

29. (a) Fig. 16.30 below shows a blank for a square-headed
bolt. The blanks are to be made by cutting from rod of
diameter 14 mm to lengths of L mm and forging the
heads. Assuming that the total volume does not
change in the process, calculate the length L. (Take π
as $\frac{22}{7}$.)

(b) If a one metre length of rod of diameter 14 mm has a
mass of 1.2 kg, calculate the mass of rod required for
1000 blanks. (It may be assumed that no material is
scrapped in the cutting-off process.)

(C.G.L.I.)

30. Aluminium-alloy strip of width 90 mm and thickness 2 mm
is being fed through a press. At every stroke, five discs of
diameter 28 mm are punched from the material in alternate rows of three and two. For every five discs a length of
52 mm of strip is fed through.

(a) Taking π as $\frac{22}{7}$, calculate the percentage of material
that is left as scrap.

(b) Taking the density of the material as 2.8 g/cm³, calculate the mass of strip required, in kilograms, per
thousand discs. (You would be well advised to make
use of centimetres in this calculation.)

(C.G.L.I.)

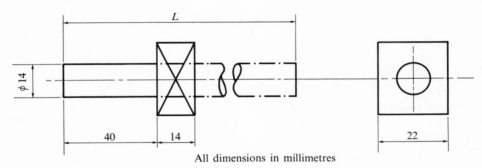

L

$\phi\,14$

40   14

22

All dimensions in millimetres

Fig. 16.30

ANSWERS TO EXERCISES 16

1. 120 mm, 600 mm².

2. 249.4 mm², 561.2 mm².

3. 27 000 mm².

4. 24 000 mm².

5. 5000 mm².

6. 56.31°, 438.2 mm, 10 800 mm².

7. 439.8 mm, 14 137 mm².

8. 15 286.5 mm².

9. (a) 606.4 mm,   (b) 2958 mm,   (c) 507 050 mm².

10. 563.1 mm².

11. (a) 14.65 mm,   (b) 28.12 mm,   (c) 206 mm².

12. (a) 8 cm,   (b) 8.38 cm,   (c) 33.51 cm²,   (d) 5.8 cm².

13. 21.65 mm², 2.887 mm, 2165 mm².

14. 1 078 272 mm³.

15. 565 mm, 4.56 m².

16. 109 956 mm³, 12.5%.

17. 12 mm, 7325 mm², 14.3 kg.

18. 5.06 m.

19. 3192 m³, 1257 m².

20. (a) 1232 cm³,   (b) 550 cm².

21. 4000 cm³, 1665 cm².

22. 7.14 m, 57.1 m³.

23. (a) $V = 1.1d^3$,   (b) $d = \sqrt[3]{(V/1.1)}$,   (c) 9.69 m, 13.6 m.

24. (b) 1137.6 mm.

25. (a) 14.14 m³,   (b) 1285 s.

26. 213.9 kg.

27. (a) 31.82 m³,   (b) 54.21 m².

28. 26.225 mm.

29. (a) 84 mm,   (b) 100.8 kg.

30. (a) 34.2 %,   (b) 5.24 kg.

17 | Statistics

17.1. NATURE OF STATISTICS

Essentially statistics is the branch of study concerned with the collection and classification of numerical facts. The facts so collected and classified are also themselves referred to as 'statistics'.

Statistics may be divided into two main aspects:

(i) *Descriptive statistics*, dealing with the classification and representation of numerical data in a more readily understandable form;
(ii) *Analytical statistics*, dealing with the use of data in arriving at decisions and often taking action as a result.

17.2. COLLECTION AND CLASSIFICATION OF DATA

In any statistical work, the first step is to collect the required data. This is a very important part of the work as any mistakes or bias introduced during the collection will subsequently be reflected in any conclusions drawn.

In statistics, the characteristic that is being counted or measured is called the *variable*. When a variable can have any value (within practical limits) it is called a *continuous variable*. Examples of such characteristics are length and temperature. A variable having only certain distinct values is called a *discrete variable*, an example being drill sizes.

When data are collected they are divided into classes (or categories, or intervals) and the number of times a given value occurs is known as the *frequency*. The *relative frequency* of a class is the frequency of that class divided by the sum of the frequencies of all the classes. The sum of all the relative frequencies is, therefore, unity (1). If a relative frequency is multiplied by 100 the result is known as the *relative frequency percentage*. The sum of all the relative frequency percentages is 100%. A tabular arrangement of the classes and the frequencies is known as a *frequency distribution*.

17.3. TABULATION OF DATA

After data are collected and classified it is necessary to arrange the figures in an orderly manner so that the important results can be easily seen and, if possible, any relationship between the factors discovered. This is the main purpose of tabulation.

Tables must always be neat and clear with the figures suitably arranged in columns and rows. The following are some general rules for the tabulation of data.

1. Classify the data.
2. Name all columns and rows.
3. State all units of measurement.
4. Define all symbols used.
5. Underline totals and other important results.
6. Quote the source of the data.
7. Title the table.

17.4. DIAGRAMS AND CHARTS

Various types of diagrams and charts are commonly used to illustrate in a simple and effective fashion data, and relationships between data, which might otherwise be more difficult to understand if in, say, tabular form.

Some types of diagrams and charts in everyday use are:

(a) Pictograms.
(b) Bar charts.
(c) Pie diagrams.

17.4.1. Pictograms. A *pictogram*, or *ideograph*, uses pictures to represent data. The best kind of pictogram is that in which exactly the same picture is shown repeatedly. Each picture has the same size and, therefore, indicates the same proportion of the total number of items represented. It is not recommended to attempt to express the degree of accuracy to more than half a unit as it is often difficult to draw accurately fractions of a picture.

The following table gives the annual output over four years of a factory manufacturing thermionic valves for television sets.

Year	1974	1975	1976	1977
No. of valves	30 000	40 000	55 000	70 000

A corresponding pictogram is shown below in Fig. 17.1.

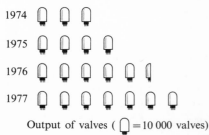

Output of valves (= 10 000 valves)

Fig. 17.1

Another kind of pictogram uses pictures which change in size, the size of the picture indicating the value of the figure being represented, as shown in Fig. 17.2. The relative sizes of the pictures are often difficult to assess, and the method is not recommended.

Output of valves

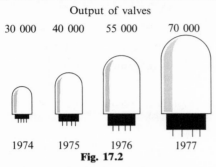

30 000   40 000   55 000   70 000

1974   1975   1976   1977

Fig. 17.2

The main advantages and disadvantages of pictograms are:

1. Easy to understand (if of the type shown in Fig. 17.1).
2. Suitable only in cases requiring simple and less accurate information.
3. Drawing of repeated symbols is often difficult and tedious.

17.4.2. Simple bar charts. Bar charts are similar to graphs. In simple bar charts, bars of equal width are constructed with their height (or length) proportional to the size of the figure represented. A scale is placed at the side of the chart to give some idea of the size of the quantity represented by a bar.

The following table gives the annual profits over six years of an electronics group of companies.

Year	1972	1973	1974	1975	1976	1977
Profit	£3.2m	£4.3m	£6.2m	£9.6m	£19.6m	£32.7m

The corresponding bar chart is shown below in Fig. 17.3, the bars being drawn vertically.

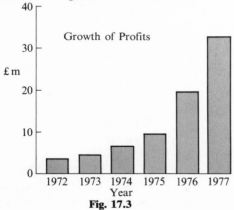

Growth of Profits

£m

1972   1973   1974   1975   1976   1977
Year

Fig. 17.3

It is often convenient to arrange the bars horizontally, particularly when it is required to represent a directional change in conditions. The change is measured from a vertical line where an increase is represented by a bar drawn to the right and a decrease by a bar drawn to the left.

The following table shows the annual profit (and losses) made by five companies A, B, C, D, and E, in an engineering group.

Company	A	B	C	D	E
Profit	£43 000	−£18 000	£34 000	£66 000	−£12 000

The corresponding bar chart is shown in Fig. 17.4 below, the bars being drawn horizontally.

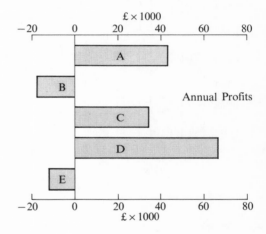

£ × 1000

Annual Profits

£ × 1000

Fig. 17.4

The main advantages and disadvantages of bar charts are:

1. Easy to construct.
2. Fairly accurate.
3. Can be used to indicate sizes of component figures.
4. Component bar charts (e.g. percentage bar charts—see section 17.4.3) restricted to three or four component figures only, otherwise they lose their effectiveness.

17.4.3. Percentage bar charts. Percentage bar charts are basically the same as simple bar charts except that the bars are divided into component parts, the individual component height (or length) representing the percentage each component forms of the overall total. A series of such bars will be of the same total height (or length), i.e. 100%.

132 Statistics

The following table shows imports as a percentage of UK car sales over five years.

Year	1972	1973	1974	1975	1976
Imports	23%	27%	28%	33%	38%

A corresponding percentage bar chart is shown in Fig. 17.5.

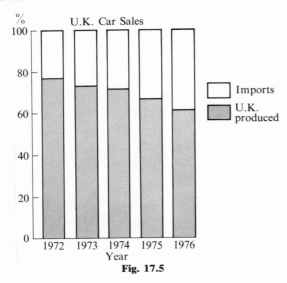

Fig. 17.5

17.4.4. Pie diagrams. A pie diagram is a circle divided by radial lines into sectors so that the area (and hence the angle and the length of arc) of each sector is proportional to the size of the quantity represented. It provides a convenient method of showing the relative sizes of component quantities.

To construct a pie diagram, the angle of a sector is calculated using:

$$\text{angle} = \frac{\text{component size}}{\text{total size}} \times 360°$$

The main advantages and disadvantages of pie diagrams are:

1. show the relative proportions of the figures that go to make up the overall total;
2. fairly easy to construct but require calculation of the sector angles;
3. effectiveness tends to diminish above seven or eight component figures;
4. values of items cannot be read off from the diagram but must be given.

EXAMPLE 17.1. Zinc is used in the following ways for every 1 tonne (1000 kg) produced:

Galvanizing	400 kg
Brass products	300 kg
Die castings	150 kg
Rolled zinc	120 kg
Other uses	30 kg

Construct a pie diagram to represent these values.

SOLUTION

It is first necessary to calculate the angles of the sectors representing each of the uses. The total mass of the zinc is 1000 kg.

Galvanizing: 400 kg,

$$\text{angle of sector} = \frac{400 \text{ kg}}{1000 \text{ kg}} \times 360° = 144°.$$

Brass products: 300 kg,

$$\text{angle of sector} = \frac{300 \text{ kg}}{1000 \text{ kg}} \times 360° = 108°.$$

Die castings: 150 kg,

$$\text{angle of sector} = \frac{150 \text{ kg}}{1000 \text{ kg}} \times 360° = 54°.$$

Rolled zinc: 120 kg,

$$\text{angle of sector} = \frac{120 \text{ kg}}{1000 \text{ kg}} \times 360° = 43.2°, \text{ say } 43°.$$

Other uses: 30 kg,

$$\text{angle of sector} = \frac{30 \text{ kg}}{1000 \text{ kg}} \times 360° = 10.8°, \text{ say } 11°.$$

The pie diagram is now drawn as shown in Fig. 17.6.

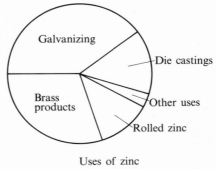

Uses of zinc
Fig. 17.6

17.5. FREQUENCY DISTRIBUTIONS

When a variable is classified, a tabular arrangement of the classes and the frequencies is known as a frequency distribution. The interval used for the classification is known as the *class-interval* and the number of times a value occurs in the class interval is known as the *class-frequency*. The class-intervals may be equal (if possible this should be so in order that the class-frequencies can be readily compared) or unequal.

17.5.1. Tally diagrams. Suppose that 50 steel rollers were taken at random for inspection and the measured diameters, in millimetres, recorded as shown in Table 17.1.

TABLE 17.1

20.01	19.99	20.00	20.01	19.98
20.02	20.00	20.03	20.00	20.02
20.00	20.01	20.00	19.99	20.03
19.99	20.00	20.01	20.03	20.00
20.00	19.99	20.00	20.02	20.01
19.99	20.00	20.02	19.99	20.00
20.03	20.01	19.99	19.98	19.99
19.98	19.99	20.02	20.01	20.03
20.01	20.02	20.00	20.00	19.99
20.00	19.99	19.98	19.99	20.02

The figures presented in this way are practically meaningless and are better rearranged into a frequency distribution. To do this a *tally diagram* is used, the construction of which is as described below.

TABLE 17.2

CLASS Measured diameter (mm)	TALLY MARKS No. of rollers	FREQUENCY
19.98	||||	4
19.99	⫻⫻ ⫻⫻ ||	12
20.00	⫻⫻ ⫻⫻ ||||	14
20.01	⫻⫻ |||	8
20.02	⫻⫻ ||	7
20.03	⫻⫻	5
		Total 50

TABLE 17.3

CLASS-INTERVAL Measured diameter (mm)	TALLY MARKS No. of rollers	FREQUENCY
19.98—under 20.00	⫻⫻ ⫻⫻ ⫻⫻ |	16
20.00—under 20.02	⫻⫻ ⫻⫻ ⫻⫻ ⫻⫻ | ⫻⫻ ||	22
20.02—under 20.04	⫻⫻ ⫻⫻ ⫻⫻ ||	12
		Total 50

(i) Pick out the lowest and highest of the measured values (19.98 and 20.03 in Table 17.1) and decide upon and list the classes.

With small totals, the classes may be the various measured sizes as shown in column 1 of Table 17.2. With large totals, class-intervals may be used as shown in column 1 of Table 17.3.

(ii) Take each of the measured values and place a tally mark (\|) against the appropriate class. Every fifth tally mark is made diagonally (/) across the previous four in order to aid the totalling.

(iii) Total the tally marks in each class.

(iv) Total all the tally marks as a check against the original measured total.

The frequency distribution is now complete and the measured figures are presented in a much more meaningful way.

17.5.2. Histograms. A histogram is similar to a vertical bar chart but with this important difference—it is the *area* of a rectangle, not its height (or length), which represents the frequency.

The construction of a histogram is as outlined below:

(i) Make the horizontal axis with a continuous scale (just like with ordinary graphs) extending from the lowest to the highest values in the frequency distribution.

(ii) For each class-interval erect a vertical rectangle such that its area is proportional to the frequency in the class.

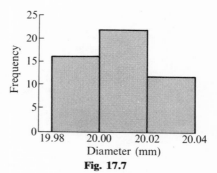

Fig. 17.7

From Fig. 17.7, which is a histogram of the data from Table 17.3, it will be seen that there are no gaps between the rectangles of a histogram. Also, for equal class-intervals the heights of the rectangles are, like the areas, proportional to the class-frequencies.

EXERCISES 17

1. List the advantages and disadvantages of pictograms, bar charts, and pie diagrams.

2. Define the following terms: (a) frequency, (b) relative frequency percentage, (c) histogram.

3. Quantities in the following proportions are to be represented in a pie diagram. Construct the pie diagram and

indicate the angles of the sectors.
(a) 1, 2, 4, 5.
(b) 3, 5, 6, 7, 9.
(c) 10 %, 15 %, 20 %, 25 %, 30 %.
(d) 12½ %, 22½ %, 25 %, 40 %.

4. The monthly expenditure of a small engineering company was made up as follows:

Materials   17½ %
Energy   5 %
Wages and salaries 55 %
Maintenance   7½ %
Depreciation   10 %
Other expenses   5 %

Illustrate the data on a pie diagram and state the angle used for each sector.

5. Fig. 17.8 shows how a total of 10 000 tonnes of steel tubes are produced from six plants *A*, *B*, *C*, *D*, *E*, and *F*. Calculate the sector angle *θ* for plant *E* and determine the output from each individual plant.

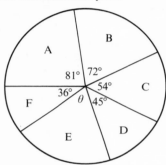

Fig. 17.8

6. The uses of tin are outlined by Fig. 17.9. Represent the same data by a 100 % bar chart. Compare and contrast the two diagrams.

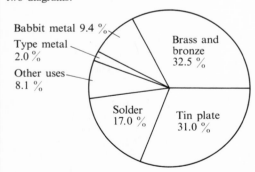

Fig. 17.9

7. The 'lives' of 50 of the same type of electric lamp (in hours) are given in the following table:

```
695  676  697  722  694  716  697  710  692  671
730  710  660  717  689  694  703  656  689  715
717  696  700  738  692  701  726  696  698  699
662  696  684  705  681  682  695  680  724  699
682  702  676  714  721  690  732  707  708  663
```

By grouping these values with a class-interval of 10 hours, make a tally diagram and form a frequency distribution. Construct a histogram.

8. The following table shows the growth in exports for a certain group of engineering companies. Draw a bar chart to illustrate the data.

Year	1972	1973	1974	1975	1976	1977
Growth of Exports (in £ million)	9.5	10.6	18.7	28.4	49.1	75.2

9. Exports of North Sea Oil from the United Kingdom in 1976 were as follows:

Country	Quantity (tonnes)
Sweden	700 000
U.S.A.	658 000
West Germany	562 000
France	550 000
Holland	280 000
Norway	104 000
Belgium	71 000
Portugal	56 000

Illustrate this data diagrammatically.

10. The time required to produce a certain component was made up as follows:

Operation	Time required (in minutes)
1. Preparation of machine and workpiece	10
2. Machining components	25
3. Gauging completed components	3
4. Cleaning components etc.	12

Express each operation time as a percentage of the total time and construct a percentage bar chart showing the composition of the whole operation.

11. The life in hours of 100 electric light bulbs tested to destruction is given in the table below. Construct a histogram to illustrate the data.

Life (h)	Frequency
1500—1599	8
1600—1699	10
1700—1799	12
1800—1899	24
1900—1999	30
2000—2099	10
2100—2199	6

12. Construct a histogram to illustrate the following wage structure of a small engineering company.

Wage per week(£)	50–55	55–60	60–70	70–80	over 80
No. of employees	8	14	30	28	16

13. The masses of fifty forgings, in kilograms, are as follows:

66 56 58 71 78 63 69 73 76 78 64 67 75 82 60 62
56 70 74 63 67 72 80 85 75 70 67 66 51 73 69 65
54 65 87 64 62 68 73 65 60 61 70 63 70 66 83 53
67 62

Draw a tally chart and a frequency table for the groups 50–54, 55–59, 60–64, etc. Construct a histogram from this data.

ANSWERS TO EXERCISES 17

1. See section 17.4.

2. See sections 17.2 and 17.5.2.

3. (a) 30°, 60°, 120°, 150°.
   (b) 36°, 60°, 72°, 84°, 108°.
   (c) 36°, 54°, 72°, 90°, 108°.
   (d) 45°, 81°, 90°, 144°.

4. 63°, 18°, 198°, 27°, 36°, 18°.

5. 72°, 2250 t, 2000 t, 1500 t, 1250 t, 2000 t, 1000 t.

6. See sections 17.4.3 and 17.4.4.

7. See section 17.5.

8. See section 17.4.2.

9. See section 17.4.2.

10. See section 17.4.3.

11. See section 17.5.2.

12. See section 17.5.2.

13. See section 17.5.1 and 17.5.2.